Excel® VBA Programming

5th Edition

by Michael Alexander and John Walkenbach

for dummies®

A Wiley Brand

Excel® VBA Programming For Dummies®, 5th Edition

Published by: **John Wiley & Sons, Inc.,** 111 River Street, Hoboken, NJ 07030-5774, www.wiley.com

Copyright © 2019 by John Wiley & Sons, Inc., Hoboken, New Jersey

Published simultaneously in Canada

For general information on our other products and services, please contact our Customer Care Department within the U.S. at 877-762-2974, outside the U.S. at 317-572-3993, or fax 317-572-4002. For technical support, please visit https://hub.wiley.com/community/support/dummies.

Wiley publishes in a variety of print and electronic formats and by print-on-demand. Some material included with standard print versions of this book may not be included in e-books or in print-on-demand. If this book refers to media such as a CD or DVD that is not included in the version you purchased, you may download this material at http://booksupport.wiley.com. For more information about Wiley products, visit www.wiley.com.

Library of Congress Control Number: 2018957226

ISBN 978-1-119-51817-4 (pbk); ISBN 978-1-119-51823-5 (ebk); ISBN 978-1-119-51824-2 (ebk)

Manufactured in the United States of America

G10004942_100218

Contents at a Glance

Table of Contents

Introduction

Greetings, prospective Excel programmer. . .

You no doubt have your reasons for picking up a book on VBA programming. Maybe you got a new job (congratulations). Maybe you're trying to automate some of the repetitive data crunching tasks you have to do. Maybe you're just a nerd at heart. Whatever the reason, thank you for choosing this book.

Inside, you find everything you need to get up and running with VBA fast. Even if you don't have the foggiest idea of what programming is all about, this book can help. Unlike most programming books, this one is filled with information designed to include just what you need to know to quickly ramp your VBA programming skillset.

About This Book

Go to any large bookstore (in-person or online), and you'll find many Excel books. A quick overview can help you decide whether this book is really right for you. This book

>> Is designed for intermediate to advanced Excel users who want to get up to speed with Visual Basic for Applications (VBA) programming.

>> Requires no previous programming experience.

>> Covers the most commonly used commands.

>> Is appropriate for Excel 2013, Excel 2016, or Excel 2019.

>> Just might make you crack a smile occasionally.

If you're using Excel 2003, you need a much older book (and a hug). If you're using Excel 2007 or 2010, this book *might* be okay, but some things have changed. You'd probably be better off with the previous edition.

Oh, yeah — this is *not* an introductory Excel book. If you're looking for a general-purpose Excel book, check out either of the following books, which are both published by Wiley:

>> *Excel 2019 For Dummies,* by Greg Harvey

>> *Excel 2019 Bible,* by Michael Alexander and Dick Kusleika

These books are also available in editions for earlier versions of Excel.

Notice that the title of this book isn't "*The Complete Guide to Excel VBA Programming For Dummies.*" This book doesn't cover all aspects of Excel programming — but then again, you probably don't want to know *everything* about this topic.

If you consume this book and find that you're hungry for a more comprehensive Excel programming book, you might try *Microsoft Excel 2019 Power Programming with VBA,* also published by Wiley. And yes, editions for older versions of Excel are also available.

Obligatory Typographical Conventions Section

All computer books have a section like this. (I think some federal law requires it.) Read it or skip it.

Sometimes, I refer to key combinations — which means you hold down one key while you press another. For example, Ctrl+Z means you hold down the Ctrl key while you press Z.

For menu commands, I use a distinctive character to separate items on the Ribbon or menu. For example, you use the following command to create a named range in a worksheet:

Formulas ➪ Defined Names ➪ Define Name

Formulas is the tab at the top of the Ribbon, Defined Names is the Ribbon group, and Define Name is the actual command.

The Visual Basic Editor still uses old-fashioned menus and toolbars. So Tools ➪ Options means choose the Tools menu and then choose the Options menu item.

Excel programming involves developing *code* — that is, the instructions Excel follows. All code in this book appears in a monospace font, like this:

```
Range("A1:A12").Select
```

Some long lines of code don't fit between the margins in this book. In such cases, I use the standard VBA line-continuation character sequence: a space followed by an underscore character. Here's an example:

```
Selection.PasteSpecial Paste:=xlValues, _
Operation:=xlNone, SkipBlanks:=False, _
Transpose:=False
```

When you enter this code, you can type it as written or place it on a single line (omitting the space and underscore combination).

Check Your Security Settings

It's a cruel world out there. It seems that some scam artist is always trying to take advantage of you or cause some type of problem. The world of computing is equally cruel. You probably know about computer viruses, which can cause some nasty things to happen to your system. But did you know that computer viruses can also reside in an Excel file? It's true. In fact, it's relatively easy to write a computer virus by using VBA. An unknowing user can open an Excel file and spread the virus to other Excel workbooks and to other systems.

Over the years, Microsoft has become increasingly concerned about security issues. This is a good thing, but it also means that Excel users need to understand how things work. You can check Excel's security settings by choosing File ⇨ Options ⇨ Trust Center ⇨ Trust Center Settings. There is a plethora of options in there, and people have been known to open that dialog box and never be heard from again.

If you click the Macro Settings tab (on the left side of the Trust Center dialog box), your options are as follows:

- **Disable all macros without notification.** Macros will not work, regardless of what you do.

- **Disable all macros with notification.** When you open a workbook with macros, you see the Message Bar open with an option you can click to enable macros, or (if the Visual Basic Editor window is open) you get a message asking if you want to enable macros.

>> **Disable all macros except digitally signed macros.** Only macros with a digital signature are allowed to run (but even for those signatures you haven't marked as trusted, you still get the security warning).

>> **Enable all macros.** All macros run with no warnings. This option is not recommended because potentially dangerous code can be executed.

Consider this scenario: You spend a week writing a killer VBA program that will revolutionize your company. You test it thoroughly and then send it to your boss. He calls you into his office and claims that your macro doesn't do anything at all. What's going on? Chances are, your boss's security setting doesn't allow macros to run. Or maybe he chose to go along with Microsoft's default suggestion and disable the macros when he opened the file.

Bottom line? Just because an Excel workbook contains a macro no guarantee that the macro will ever be executed. It all depends on the security setting and whether the user chooses to enable or disable macros for that file.

To work with this book, you need to enable macros for the files you work with. My advice is to use the second security level. Then, when you open a file that you've created, you can simply enable the macros. If you open a file from someone you don't know, you should disable the macros and check the VBA code to ensure that it doesn't contain anything destructive or malicious. Usually, it's pretty easy to identify suspicious VBA code.

Another option is to designate a trusted folder. Choose File ⇨ Options ⇨ Trust Center ⇨ Trust Center Settings. Select the Trusted Locations option and then designate a particular folder as a trusted location. Store your trusted workbooks there, and Excel won't bug you about enabling macros. For example, if you download the sample files for this book, you can put them in a trusted location.

Foolish Assumptions

People who write books usually have a target reader in mind. The following points more or less describe the hypothetical target reader for this book:

>> You have access to a PC at work — and probably at home. And those computers are connected to the Internet.

>> You're running Excel 2013, Excel 2016, or Excel 2019.

>> You've been using computers for several years.

>> You use Excel frequently in your work, and you consider yourself to [be] knowledgeable about Excel than the average bear.

>> You need to make Excel do some things that you currently can't ma[ke]

>> You have little or no programming experience.

>> You understand that the Help system in Excel can actually be useful. Face it — this book doesn't cover everything. If you get on good speaking terms with the Help system, you'll be able to fill in some of the missing pieces.

>> You need to accomplish some work, and you have a low tolerance for thick, boring computer books.

Icons Used in This Book

TIP

Don't skip information marked with this icon. It identifies a shortcut that can save you lots of time (and maybe even allow you to leave the office at a reasonable hour).

This icon is also used to let you know that the code being discussed is available on the web. Download it to eliminate lots of typing.

REMEMBER

This icon tells you when you need to store information in the deep recesses of your brain for later use.

TECHNICAL STUFF

This icon flags material that you might consider technical. You may find it interesting, but you can safely skip it if you're in a hurry.

WARNING

Read anything marked with this icon. Otherwise, you may lose your data, blow up your computer, cause a nuclear meltdown — or maybe even ruin your whole day.

Sample Files Online

This book has its very own website where you can download the example files. To get these files, point your web browser to

```
www.dummies.com/go/vbaprogfd5e
```

Please note that this URL is case-sensitive and uses all lowercase letters. If you don't type it exactly, it won't work.

Having the sample files will save you a lot of typing. Better yet, you can play around with them and experiment with various changes. In fact, experimentation is the best way to master VBA.

Where to Go from Here

This book contains everything you need to learn VBA programming at a mid-advanced level. The book starts off with the basics of recording macros and builds, chapter by chapter.

If you're completely new to Excel macros, start with Part 1 to get a refresher on the fundamentals of recording macros. If you have experience recording macros, but want to better understand the VBA behind them, go to Part 2. There, you gain a concise understanding of how VBA works, along with the basic foundation you need to implement your own code.

Finally, if you're familiar with programming concepts and just want to get a quick runthrough of some of the more advanced techniques like creating your custom functions and add-ins, feel free to jump to Part 4.There's also the cheat sheet filled with handy shortcuts. Go to dummies.com and search for "Excel VBA programming cheat sheet" to find it.

1
Getting Started with Excel VBA Programming

IN THIS CHAPTER

» **Getting a conceptual overview of VBA**

» **Finding out what you can do with VBA**

» **Discovering the advantages and disadvantages of using VBA**

» **Getting the lowdown on what VBA is**

» **Staying Excel compatible**

Chapter **1**

What Is VBA?

f you're eager to jump into VBA programming, hold your horses. This chapter is completely devoid of any hands-on training material. It does, however, contain some essential background information that assists you in becoming an Excel programmer. In other words, this chapter paves the way for everything else that follows and gives you a feel for how Excel programming fits into the overall scheme of the universe. It's not as boring as you might think, so please try to resist the urge to jump to Chapter 2.

Okay, So What Is VBA?

VBA, which stands for *Visual Basic for Applications,* is a programming language developed by Microsoft — you know, the company that tries to get you to buy a new version of Windows every few years. Excel, along with the other members of Microsoft Office, includes the VBA language (at no extra charge). In a nutshell, VBA is the tool that people use to develop programs that control Excel.

Imagine an intelligent robot that knows all about Excel. This robot can read instructions, and it can also operate Excel very fast and accurately. When you want the robot to do something in Excel, you write a set of robot instructions by using special codes. Then you tell the robot to follow your instructions while you sit back and drink a glass of lemonade. That's kind of what VBA is all about — a code language for robots. Note, however, that Excel does not come with a robot or lemonade.

A FEW WORDS ABOUT TERMINOLOGY

Excel programming terminology can be a bit confusing. For example, VBA is a programming language, but it also serves as a macro language. In this context, a macro is a set of instructions Excel performs to imitate keystrokes and mouse actions. What do you call something written in VBA and executed in Excel? Is it a *macro,* or is it a *program*? Excel's Help system often refers to VBA procedures as *macros,* so that terminology is used in this book. But you can also call this stuff a *program*.

You'll see the term *automate* throughout this book. This term means that a series of steps are completed automatically. For example, if you write a macro that adds color to some cells, prints the worksheet, and then removes the color, you have *automated* those three steps.

By the way, *macro* doesn't stand for **M**essy **A**nd **C**onfusing **R**epeated **O**peration. Rather, it comes from the Greek *makros,* which means large — which also describes your paycheck after you become an expert macro programmer.

What Can You Do with VBA?

You're probably aware that people use Excel for thousands of different tasks. Here are just a few examples:

» Analyzing scientific data

» Budgeting and forecasting

» Creating invoices and other forms

» Developing charts from data

» Keeping lists of things such as customers' names, students' grades, or holiday gift ideas (a nice fruitcake would be lovely)

» Yadda, yadda, yadda

The list could go on and on, but you get the idea. The point is simply that Excel is used for a wide variety of tasks, and everyone reading this book has different needs and expectations regarding Excel. One thing virtually every reader has in common is the *need to automate some aspect of Excel*. That, dear reader, is what VBA is all about.

For example, you might create a VBA program to import some numbers and then format and print your month-end sales report. After developing and testing the program, you can execute the macro with a single command, causing Excel to automatically perform many time-consuming procedures. Rather than struggle through a tedious sequence of commands, you can click a button and then hop on over to Facebook and kill some time while your macro does the work.

The following sections briefly describe some common uses for VBA macros. One or two of these may push your button.

Inserting a bunch of text

If you often need to enter your company name, address, and phone number in your worksheets, you can create a macro to do the typing for you. You can extend this concept as far as you like. For example, you might develop a macro that automatically enters a list of all salespeople who work for your company.

Automating a task you perform frequently

Assume you're a sales manager and you need to prepare a month-end sales report to keep your boss happy. If the task is straightforward, you can develop a VBA program to do it for you. Your boss will be impressed by the consistently high quality of your reports, and you'll be promoted to a new job for which you are highly unqualified.

Automating repetitive operations

If you need to perform the same action on, say, 12 different Excel workbooks, you can record a macro while you perform the task on the first workbook and then let the macro repeat your action on the other workbooks. The nice thing about this is that Excel never complains about being bored. Excel's macro recorder is similar to recording live action on a video recorder. But it doesn't require a camera, and the battery never needs to be recharged.

Creating a custom command

Do you often issue the same sequence of Excel commands? If so, save yourself a few seconds by developing a macro that combines these commands into a single custom command, which you can execute with a single keystroke or button click. You probably won't save *that* much time, but you'll probably be more accurate. And the guy in the next cubicle will be really impressed.

Creating a custom button

You can customize your Quick Access toolbar with your own buttons that execute the macros you write. Office workers tend to be very impressed by buttons that perform magic. And if you *really* want to impress your fellow employees, you can even add new buttons to the Ribbon.

Developing new worksheet functions

Although Excel includes hundreds of built-in functions (such as SUM and AVERAGE), you can create *custom* worksheet functions that can greatly simplify your formulas. You'll be surprised by how easy this is. (You can explore how to do this in Chapter 20.) Even better, the Insert Function dialog box displays your custom functions, making them appear built-in. Very snazzy stuff.

Creating custom add-ins for Excel

You're probably familiar with some of the add-ins that ship with Excel. For example, the Analysis ToolPak is a popular add-in. You can use VBA to develop your own special-purpose add-ins.

Advantages and Disadvantages of VBA

This section outlines the good things about VBA — and also its darker side.

VBA advantages

You can automate almost anything you do in Excel. To do so, you write instructions that Excel carries out. Automating a task by using VBA offers several advantages:

>> Excel always executes the task in exactly the same way. (In most cases, consistency is a good thing.)

>> Excel performs the task much faster than you can do it manually. (Unless, of course, you're Clark Kent.)

>> If you're a good macro programmer, Excel always performs the task without errors (which probably can't be said about you, no matter how careful you are).

» If you set up things properly, someone who doesn't know anything about Excel can perform the task by running the macro.

» You can do things in Excel that are otherwise impossible — which can make you a very popular person around the office.

» For long, time-consuming tasks, you don't have to sit in front of your computer and get bored. Excel does the work while you hang out at the water cooler.

VBA disadvantages

It's only fair to give equal time to the disadvantages (or *potential* disadvantages) of VBA:

» You have to know how to write programs in VBA (but that's why you bought this book, right?). Fortunately, it's not as difficult as you might expect.

» Other people who need to use your VBA programs must have their own copies of Excel. It would be nice if you could press a button that transforms your Excel/VBA application into a stand-alone program, but that isn't possible. (And probably never will be.)

» Sometimes, things go wrong. In other words, you can't blindly assume that your VBA program will always work correctly under all circumstances. Welcome to the world of debugging and, if others are using your macros, technical support.

» VBA is a moving target. As you know, Microsoft is continually upgrading Excel. Even though Microsoft puts great effort into compatibility between versions, you may discover that the VBA code you've written doesn't work properly with older versions or with a future version of Excel.

VBA in a Nutshell

Just to let you know what you're in for, here's a quick-and-dirty summary of what VBA is all about.

» **You perform actions in VBA by writing (or recording) code in a VBA module.** You view and edit VBA modules by using the Visual Basic Editor (VBE).

» **A VBA module consists of Sub procedures.** A Sub procedure has nothing to do with underwater vessels or tasty sandwiches. Rather, it's a chunk of computer code that performs some action on or with objects (discussed in a moment). The following example shows a simple Sub procedure called AddEmUp. This amazing program, when executed, displays the result of 1 plus 1:

```
Sub AddEmUp( )
    Sum = 1 + 1
    MsgBox "The answer is " & Sum
End Sub
```

A Sub procedure that doesn't perform properly is said to be substandard.

» **A VBA module can also have Function procedures.** A Function procedure returns a single value. You can call it from another VBA procedure or even use it as a function in a worksheet formula. An example of a Function procedure (named AddTwo) follows. This Function accepts two numbers (called arguments) and returns the sum of those values:

```
Function AddTwo(arg1, arg2)
    AddTwo = arg1 + arg2
End Function
```

A Function procedure that doesn't work correctly is said to be dysfunctional.

» **VBA manipulates objects.** Excel provides dozens and dozens of objects that you can manipulate. Examples of objects include a workbook, a worksheet, a cell range, a chart, and a shape. You have many more objects at your disposal, and you can manipulate them by using VBA code.

» **Objects are arranged in a hierarchy.** Objects can act as *containers* for other objects. At the top of the object hierarchy is Excel. Excel itself is an object called Application. The Application object contains other objects, such as Workbook objects and Add-In objects. The Workbook object can contain other objects, such as Worksheet objects and Chart objects. A Worksheet object can contain objects such as Range objects and PivotTable objects. The term *object model* refers to the arrangement of these objects. (Object-model mavens can find out more in Chapter 4.)

» **Objects of the same type form a collection.** For example, the Worksheets collection consists of all the worksheets in a particular workbook. The Charts collection consists of all Chart objects in a workbook. Collections are themselves objects.

» **You refer to an object by specifying its position in the object hierarchy, using a dot (aka a period) as a separator.** For example, you can refer to the workbook Book1.xlsx as

```
Application.Workbooks("Book1.xlsx")
```

This refers to the workbook Book1.xlsx in the Workbooks collection. The Workbooks collection is contained in the Application object (that is, Excel). Extending this to another level, you can refer to Sheet1 in Book1.xlsx as

```
Application.Workbooks("Book1.xlsx").Worksheets("Sheet1")
```

You can take this to still another level and refer to a specific cell (in this case, cell A1):

```
Application.Workbooks("Book1.xlsx").Worksheets("Sheet1").
    Range("A1")
```

» **If you omit specific references, Excel uses the *active* objects.** If Book1.xlsx is the active workbook, you can simplify the preceding reference as follows:

```
Worksheets("Sheet1").Range("A1")
```

If you know that Sheet1 is the active sheet, you can simplify the reference even more:

```
Range("A1")
```

» **Objects have properties.** You can think of a property as a *setting* for an object. For example, a Range object has such properties as Value and Address. A Chart object has such properties as HasTitle and Type. You can use VBA to determine object properties and also to change properties.

» **You refer to a property of an object by combining the object name with the property name, separated by a dot.** For example, you can refer to the Value property in cell A1 on Sheet1 as follows:

```
Worksheets("Sheet1").Range("A1").Value
```

» **You can assign values to variables.** A *variable* is a named element that stores information. You can use variables in your VBA code to store such things as values, text, and property settings. To assign the value in cell A1 on Sheet1 to a variable called *Interest,* use the following VBA statement:

```
Interest = Worksheets("Sheet1").Range("A1").Value
```

>> **Objects have methods.** A *method* is an action Excel performs with an object. For example, one of the methods for a Range object is ClearContents. This aptly named method clears the contents of the range.

>> **You specify a method by combining the object with the method, separated by a dot.** For example, the following statement clears the contents of cell A1:

```
Worksheets("Sheet1").Range("A1").ClearContents
```

>> **VBA includes all the constructs of modern programming languages, including variables, arrays, and looping.** In other words, if you're willing to spend a little time learning the ropes, you can write code that does some incredible things.

Believe it or not, the preceding list pretty much describes VBA in a nutshell. Now you just have to find out the details. That's why this book has more pages.

Excel Compatibility

REMEMBER

This book is written for the desktop versions of Excel 2016 and Excel 2019. If you don't have one of those versions, you run the risk of getting confused in a few places.

If you plan to distribute your Excel/VBA files to other users, it's vitally important that you understand which versions of Excel they use. People using older versions won't be able to take advantage of features introduced in later versions. For example, if you write VBA code that references cell XFD1048576 (the last cell in a workbook), those who use a version prior to Excel 2007 will get an error because those pre-Excel 2007 worksheets had only 65,536 rows and 255 columns (the last cell is IV65536).

Excel 2010 and later also have some new objects, methods, and properties. If you use these in your code, users with an older version of Excel will get an error when they run your macro — and you'll get the blame.

IN THIS CHAPTER

» Developing a useful VBA macro: A hands-on, step-by-step example

» Recording your actions by using Excel's macro recorder

» Examining and testing recorded code

» Changing a recorded macro

» Dealing with macro security issues

Chapter **2**

Jumping Right In

The best way to get into a cold body of water is to jump right in — no sense prolonging the agony. By wading through this chapter, you can get your feet wet immediately but avoid getting in over your head.

By the time you reach the end of this chapter, you may start feeling better about this Excel programming business, and you'll be glad you took the plunge. This chapter provides a step-by-step demonstration of how to develop a simple but useful VBA macro.

First Things First

Before you can call yourself an Excel programmer, you must go through the initiation rites. That means you need to make a small change so Excel will display a new tab at the top of the screen: Developer. Getting Excel to display the Developer tab is easy (and you only have to do it one time). Just follow these steps:

1. **Right-click any part of the Ribbon and choose Customize the Ribbon from the shortcut menu.**

2. **In the Customize Ribbon tab of the Excel Options dialog box, locate Developer in the box on the right.**

3. Put a check mark next to Developer.

4. Click OK.

You're back to Excel with a brand-new tab: Developer.

When you click the Developer tab, the Ribbon displays information that is of interest to programmers (that's you!). Figure 2-1 shows how the Ribbon looks when the Developer tab is selected in Excel 2019.

FIGURE 2-1: The Developer tab is normally hidden, but it's easy to unhide.

What You'll Be Doing

In this chapter, you create your first macro. The macro that you're about to create does this:

» Types your name in a cell

» Enters the current date and time in the cell below

» Formats both cells to display bold

» Changes the font size of both cells to 16 point

This macro won't be winning any prizes in the Annual VBA Programmer's Competition, but everyone must start somewhere. The macro accomplishes all these steps in a single action. As described in the following sections, you start by recording your actions as you go through these steps. Then you test the macro to see whether it works. Finally, you edit the macro to add some finishing touches. Ready?

Taking the First Steps

This section describes the steps you take prior to recording the macro. In other words, you need to make a few preparations before the fun begins:

1. **Start Excel, if it's not already running.**

2. **If necessary, create a new, empty workbook.**

 Pressing Ctrl+N is a quick favorite way to do that.

3. **Click the Developer tab, and take a look at the Use Relative References button in the Code group.**

 If the color of that button is different from the other buttons, you're in good shape. If the Use Relative References button is the same color as the other buttons, you need to click it to enable this option.

You explore the Relative References button in Chapter 6. For now, just make sure that the option is turned on. When it's turned on, the Use Relative References button will be a different color.

Recording the Macro

Here comes the hands-on part. Follow these instructions carefully:

1. **Select a cell.**

 Any cell will do.

2. **Choose Developer ➪ Code ➪ Record Macro or click the macro recording button on the status bar.**

 The Record Macro dialog box appears, as shown in Figure 2-2.

3. **Enter a name for the macro.**

 Excel provides a default name (something like *Macro1*), but it's better to use a more descriptive name. *NameAndTime* (with no spaces) is a good name for this macro.

4. **Click the Shortcut Key box, and enter Shift+N (for an uppercase N) as the shortcut key.**

 Specifying a shortcut key is optional. If you do specify one, you can execute the macro by pressing a key combination — in this case, Ctrl+Shift+N. Be aware that if you assign a common shortcut key (for instance Ctrl+C), you lose the normal functionality for that shortcut key; Excel will trigger your macro instead.

5. **Make sure the Store Macro In setting is This Workbook.**

6. **You can enter some text in the Description box, if you like.**

 This step is optional. Some people like to describe what the macro does (or is *supposed* to do).

7. **Click OK.**

The Record Macro dialog box closes, and Excel's macro recorder is turned on. From this point, Excel monitors everything you do and converts it to VBA code.

8. **Type your name in the active cell.**

9. **Move the cell pointer to the cell below and enter this formula:**

```
=NOW( )
```

The formula displays the current date and time.

10. **Select the formula cell, and press Ctrl+C to copy that cell to the Clipboard.**

11. **Choose Home ➪ Clipboard ➪ Paste ➪ Values (V).**

This command converts the formula to its value.

12. **With the date cell selected, press Shift+up arrow to select that cell and the one above it (which contains your name).**

13. **Use the controls in the Home ➪ Font group to change the formatting to Bold and make the font size 16 point.**

14. **Choose Developer ➪ Code ➪ Stop Recording.**

The macro recorder is turned off.

FIGURE 2-2:
The Record Macro dialog box appears when you're about to record a macro.

Congratulations! You just created your first Excel VBA macro. You may want to phone your mother and tell her the good news.

Testing the Macro

Now you can try this macro and see whether it works properly. To test your macro, move to an empty cell and press Ctrl+Shift+N (or whatever shortcut you assigned).

In a flash, Excel executes the macro. Your name and the current date and time are displayed in large, bold letters.

TIP

Another way to execute the macro is to choose Developer➪Code➪Macros (or press Alt+F8) to display the Macros dialog box. Select the macro from the list (in this case, NameAndTime), and click Run. Make sure you select the cell that will hold your name before executing the macro.

Examining the Macro

You've recorded a macro, and you've tested it. If you're a curious type, you're probably wondering what this macro looks like. And you might even wonder where it's stored.

Remember when you started recording the macro? You indicated that Excel should store the macro in This Workbook. The macro is stored in the workbook, but you need to activate the Visual Basic Editor (VBE, for short) to see it.

Follow these steps to see the macro:

1. **Choose Developer ➪ Code ➪ Visual Basic (or press Alt+F11).**

The Visual Basic Editor program window appears, as shown in Figure 2-3. This window is highly customizable, so your VBE window may look a bit different. The VBE window contains several other windows and is probably very intimidating. Don't fret; you'll get used to it.

2. **In the VBE window, locate the window called Project.**

The Project window (also known as the Project Explorer window) contains a list of all workbooks and add-ins that are currently open. Each project is arranged as a *tree* and can be expanded (to show more information) or contracted (to show less information).

TIP

The VBE uses quite a few different windows, any of which can be open or closed. If a window isn't immediately visible in the VBE, you can choose an option from the View menu to display the window. For instance, if the Project window is not visible, you can choose View ➪ Project Explorer (or press Ctrl+R)

to display it. You can display any other VBE window in a similar manner. The components of the VBE are covered in Chapter 3.

3. Select the project that corresponds to the workbook in which you recorded the macro.

If you haven't saved the workbook, the project is probably called VBAProject (Book1).

4. Click the plus sign (+) to the left of the folder named Modules.

The tree expands to show Module1, which is the only module in the project.

5. Double-click Module1.

The VBA code in that module is displayed in a Code window (see Figure 2-3). Your screen may not look exactly the same as Figure 2-3. The code that's recorded depends on the specific actions you made while recording the macro.

```
(General)                                                              NameAndTime

Sub NameAndTime()
'
' NameAndTime Macro
'
' Keyboard Shortcut: Ctrl+Shift+N
'
    ActiveCell.FormulaR1C1 = "Mike"
    Range("B3").Select
    ActiveCell.FormulaR1C1 = "=NOW()"
    Range("B3").Select
    Selection.Copy
    Selection.PasteSpecial Paste:=xlPasteValues, Operation:=xlNone, SkipBlanks _
        :=False, Transpose:=False
    Range("B2:B3").Select
    Range("B3").Activate
    Selection.Font.Bold = True
    With Selection.Font
        .Name = "Calibri"
        .Size = 16
        .Strikethrough = False
        .Superscript = False
        .Subscript = False
        .OutlineFont = False
        .Shadow = False
        .Underline = xlUnderlineStyleNone
        .ThemeColor = xlThemeColorLight1
        .TintAndShade = 0
        .ThemeFont = xlThemeFontMinor
    End With
End Sub
```

FIGURE 2-3:
The VBE displays
the VBA code in
Module1 of
Book1.

At this point, the macro probably looks like Greek to you. Don't worry. Travel a few chapters down the road, and all will be as clear as the view from Olympus.

The NameAndTime macro consists of several statements. Excel executes the statements one by one, from top to bottom. A statement that's preceded by an apostrophe (') is a comment. Comments are included only for your information and are ignored by Excel. In other words, Excel skips right over comments.

The first VBA statement (which begins with the word *Sub*) identifies the macro as a Sub procedure and gives its name; you provided this name before you started recording the macro. If you read through the code, you may be able to make sense of some of it. You see your name, the formula you entered, and lots of additional code that changes the font. The Sub procedure ends with the End Sub statement.

Modifying the Macro

As you might expect, you not only view your macro in the VBE, but can also change it. Even though you probably have no idea what you're doing at this point, these changes are easy to make:

>> Change the name that's entered in the active cell. If you have a dog, use your dog's name.

>> Change the font name or size.

>> See if you can figure out the appropriate location for this new statement that makes the cells italic:

```
Selection.Font.Italic = True
```

TIP

Working in a VBA code module is much like working in a word-processing document (except there's no word wrap, and you can't format the text). On second thought, it's more like working in Windows Notepad. You can press Enter to start a new line, and the familiar editing keys work as expected.

After you've made your changes, jump back to Excel and try the revised macro to see how it works. Just as you can press Alt+F11 in Excel to display the VBE, you can press Alt+F11 in the VBE to switch back to Excel.

Saving Workbooks That Contain Macros

If you store one or more macros in a workbook, the file must be saved as a *macro-enabled* file type. In other words, the file must be saved with an XLSM extension rather than the normal XLSX extension.

For example, when you save the workbook that contains your NameAndTime macro, the file format in the Save As dialog box defaults to XLSX (a format that cannot contain macros). Unless you change the file format to XLSM, Excel displays the warning shown in Figure 2-4. You need to click No and then choose Excel Macro-Enabled Workbook (*.xlsm) from the Save As Type drop-down list.

FIGURE 2-4:
If your workbook contains macros, and you attempt to save it in a macro-free file format, Excel warns you.

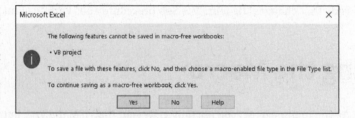

Understanding Macro Security

Macro security is a key feature in Excel. The reason is that VBA is a powerful language — so powerful that it's possible to create a macro that can do serious damage to your computer. A macro can delete files, send information to other computers, and even destroy Windows so that you can't even start your system.

The macro security features introduced in Excel 2007 were created to help prevent these types of problems.

Figure 2-5 shows the Macro Settings section of the Trust Center dialog box. To display this dialog box, choose Developer ➪ Code ➪ Macro Security.

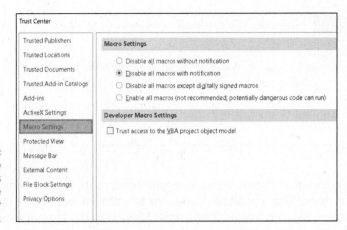

FIGURE 2-5:
The Macro
Settings
section of the
Trust Center
dialog box.

By default, Excel uses the Disable All Macros with Notification option. With this setting in effect, if you open a workbook that contains macros (and the file is not digitally "signed" or stored in a trusted location), Excel displays a warning like the one in Figure 2-6. If you are certain that the workbook comes from a trusted source, click Enable Macros, and the macros will be enabled.

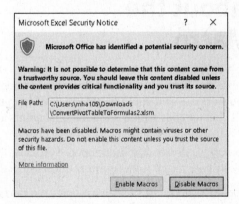

FIGURE 2-6:
Excel's warning
that the file to be
opened contains
macros.

REMEMBER

You see the pop-up box in Figure 2-6 only when the VBE is open. Otherwise, Excel displays an eye-catching Security Warning above the Formula bar, as shown in Figure 2-7. If you know the workbook is safe, click the Enable Content button to enable the macros. To use the workbook without macros, click the X to dismiss the warning.

Excel remembers when you've designated a workbook to be safe. So the next time you open it, you won't see the Security Warning.

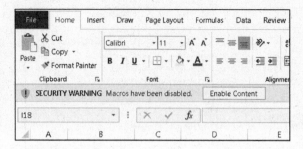

Perhaps the best way to handle macro security is to designate one or more folders as *trusted locations*. All the workbooks in a trusted location are opened without a macro warning. You designate trusted folders in the Trusted Locations section of the Trust Center dialog box.

If you want to find out what the other macro security settings imply, press F1 while the Macro Settings section of the Trust Center dialog box is in view. You get a Help screen that describes the security settings.

Revealing More about the NameAndTime Macro

By the time you finish this book, you should completely understand how the NameAndTime macro works — and you'll be able to develop more sophisticated macros. For now, this chapter ends with a few additional points about the macro:

» For this macro to work, its workbook must be open. If you close the workbook, the macro isn't available so it can't work (and its shortcut keys have no effect).

» As long as the workbook containing the macro is open, you can run the macro while any workbook is active. In other words, the macro's own workbook doesn't have to be active.

» The macro isn't "pro-quality" code. It will overwrite existing text with no warning — and its effects can't be undone.

» Before you started recording the macro, you assigned it a new shortcut key. This is just one of several ways to execute the macro. (You discover other ways in Chapter 5.)

» You can create this macro manually rather than record it. To do so, you need a good understanding of VBA. (Be patient; you'll get there.)

» You can store this macro in your Personal Macro Workbook. If you do so, the macro is available automatically whenever you start Excel. (See Chapter 6 for details about your Personal Macro Workbook.)

» You can also convert the workbook to an add-in file. (More about this in Chapter 21.)

Congratulations. You've been initiated into the world of Excel programming. (Sorry, there's no secret handshake or decoder ring.)

2

How VBA Works with Excel

Chapter **3**

Working in the Visual Basic Editor

As a more experienced-than-average Excel user, you probably know a good deal about workbooks, formulas, charts, and other Excel goodies. Now it's time to expand your horizons and explore an entirely new aspect of Excel: the Visual Basic Editor. In this chapter, you find out how to work with the Visual Basic Editor, and you get down to the nitty-gritty of writing some VBA code.

What Is the Visual Basic Editor?

The Visual Basic Editor (often refered to as the VBE) is a separate application where you write and edit your VBA macros. Beginning with Excel 2013, every workbook displays in a separate window. However, there is only one VBE window, and it works with all open Excel windows.

REMEMBER

You can't run the VBE separately; Excel must be running for the VBE to run.

Activating the VBE

The quickest way to activate the VBE is to press Alt+F11 when Excel is active. To return to Excel, press Alt+F11 again. Or you can just click the Close button on the VBE's title bar. When the VBE window closes, Excel is activated.

You can also activate the VBE by choosing Developer ⇨ Code ⇨ Visual Basic. If you don't have a Developer tab at the top of your Excel window, refer to Chapter 2, where you learn how to get that handy Developer tab to show up.

Understanding VBE components

TIP

Figure 3-1 shows the VBE program, with some of the key parts identified.

Toolbar Project window Code window Menu bar

FIGURE 3-1:
The VBE is your customizable friend.

Properties window Immediate window

Chances are that your VBE program window won't look exactly like what you see in Figure 3-1. The VBE contains several windows, and it's highly customizable. You can hide windows, rearrange windows, dock windows, and so on.

Menu bar

The VBE menu bar works just like every other menu bar you've encountered. It contains commands that you use to do things with the various components in the VBE. You also find that many of the menu commands have shortcut keys associated with them.

TIP

The VBE also features shortcut menus. You can right-click virtually anything in the VBE and get a shortcut menu of common commands.

Toolbar

The Standard toolbar, which is directly below the menu bar by default (refer to Figure 3-1), is one of the four VBE toolbars available. You can customize the toolbars, move them around, display other toolbars, and so on. If you're so inclined, choose View⇔Toolbars to work with the VBE toolbars. Most people just leave them as they are.

Project window

The Project window displays a tree diagram that shows every workbook currently open in Excel (including add-ins and hidden workbooks). Double-click items to expand or contract them within the outline. See the upcoming "Working with the Project Window" section for more detail.

If the Project window is not visible, press Ctrl+R or choose View⇔Project Explorer. To hide the Project window, click the Close button on its title bar. Or right-click anywhere in the Project window and choose Hide from the shortcut menu.

Code window

A Code window is where you put your VBA code. Every object in a project has an associated Code window. To view an object's Code window, double-click the object in the Project window. For example, to view the Code window for the Sheet1 object in Book1, double-click Sheet1 in the VBAProject for Book1. Unless you've added some VBA code, the Code window is empty.

You find out more about Code windows later in this chapter's "Working with a Code Window" section.

Immediate window

The Immediate window may or may not be visible. If it isn't visible, press Ctrl+G or choose View⇔Immediate Window. To close the Immediate window, click the Close button on its title bar (or right-click anywhere in the Immediate window and choose Hide from the shortcut menu).

The Immediate window is most useful for executing VBA statements directly and for debugging your code. If you're just starting out with VBA, this window won't be all that useful, so feel free to hide it and free some screen space for other things.

Chapter 13 covers the Immediate window in detail. It may just become your good friend!

Working with the Project Window

When you're working in the VBE, each Excel workbook and add-in that's open is a project. You can think of a *project* as a collection of objects arranged as an outline. You can expand a project by clicking the plus sign (+) at the left of the project's name in the Project window. Collapse a project by clicking the minus sign (−) to the left of a project's name. Or you can double-click the items to expand them.

REMEMBER

If a project is password-protected, you're prompted for the password when you double-click a project name. If you don't know the password, you can't expand the project — which means that you can't view or modify any part of the project.

Figure 3-2 shows a Project window with four projects listed: an add-in named pup7.xlam, an unsaved workbook named Book1, a workbook named investments. xlsm, and the Personal Macro Workbook (which is always named PERSONAL. XLSB). Of the four, only the investments.xlsm project is expanded to show all of its objects.

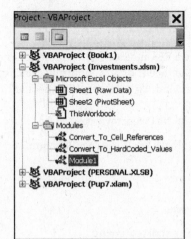

FIGURE 3-2:
This Project
window lists four
projects. One of
them is expanded
to show its
objects.

Every project expands to show at least one *node* called Microsoft Excel Objects. This node expands to show an item for each sheet in the workbook (each sheet is considered an object) and another object called ThisWorkbook (which represents the Workbook object). If the project has any VBA modules, the project listing also shows a Modules node. And as you find out in Part 4, a project may also contain a node called Forms, which contains UserForm objects (which hold custom dialog boxes).

The concept of objects may be a bit fuzzy for you. But don't worry. Things become much clearer in subsequent chapters. Don't be too concerned if you don't understand what's going on at this point.

Adding a new VBA module

Follow these steps to add a new VBA module to a project:

1. **In the VBE, select the project's name in the Project window.**

2. **Choose Insert ⇨ Module.**

Or

1. **Right-click the project's name.**

2. **Choose Insert ⇨ Module from the shortcut menu.**

TIP

When you record a macro, Excel automatically inserts a VBA module to hold the recorded code. Which workbook holds the module for the recorded macro depends on where you chose to store the recorded macro, just before you started recording.

Removing a VBA module

Sometimes, you need to remove a VBA module from a project. For example, it may contain code that you no longer need, or it's empty because you inserted the module and then changed your mind. To remove a VBA module from a project:

1. Select the module's name in the Project window.

2. Choose File ⇨ Remove *xxx*, where *xxx* is the module name.

Or

1. Right-click the module's name.

2. Choose Remove *xxx* from the shortcut menu.

> Excel, always trying to keep you from doing something you'll regret, asks whether you want to export the code in the module before you delete it. Almost always, you don't. (If you *do* want to export the module, see the next section.)

You can remove VBA modules, but there is no way to remove the other code modules — those for the Sheet objects or ThisWorkbook.

Exporting and importing objects

Every object in a VBA project can be saved to a separate file. Saving an individual object in a project is known as *exporting*. It stands to reason that you can also *import* objects into a project. Exporting and importing objects might be useful if you want to use a particular object (such as a VBA module or a UserForm) in a different project. Or maybe you want to send a co-worker a copy of a VBA module, which she can then import into her project.

Follow these steps to export an object:

1. Select an object in the Project window.

2. Choose File ⇨ Export File or press Ctrl+E.

> You get a dialog box that asks for a filename. Note that the object remains in the project; only a copy of it is exported. Excel provides the file extension for you, and the extension depends on what type of object you're exporting. In all cases, the result is a text file. If you're so inclined, you can open it with a text editor and take a look.

Importing a file to a project goes like this:

1. **Select the project's name in the Explorer window.**

2. **Choose File ⟹ Import File or press Ctrl+M.**

 You get a dialog box that asks for a file.

3. **Locate the file, and click Open.**

You should import VBA object files only if you know who it came from. Otherwise, you could be introducing macros that perform malicious actions.

REMEMBER

Working with a Code Window

As you become proficient with VBA, you spend lots of time working in Code windows. Macros that you record are stored in a module, and you can type VBA code directly in a VBA module.

REMEMBER

Minimizing and maximizing windows

If you have several projects open, the VBE may have lots of Code windows at any given time. Figure 3-3 shows an example.

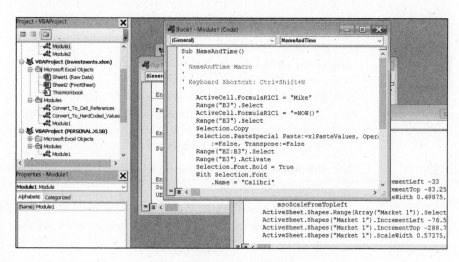

FIGURE 3-3: Code window overload isn't a pretty sight.

Code windows are much like workbook windows in Excel. You can minimize them, maximize them, resize them, hide them, rearrange them, and so on. Most people find it much easier to maximize the Code window that they're working on. Doing so lets you see more code and keeps you from getting distracted.

To maximize a Code window, click the Maximize button on its title bar (right next to the X). Or just double-click its title bar to maximize it. To restore a Code window to its original size, click the Restore button. When a window is maximized, its title bar isn't visible, so you'll find the Restore button below the VBE title bar.

Sometimes, you may want to have two or more Code windows visible. For example, you may want to compare the code in two modules or copy code from one module to another. You can arrange the windows manually or choose Window⇨Tile Horizontally or Window⇨Tile Vertically to arrange them automatically.

You can quickly switch among Code windows by pressing Ctrl+F6. If you repeat that key combination, you keep cycling through all the open Code windows. Pressing Ctrl+Shift+F6 cycles through the windows in reverse order.

TIP

Minimizing a Code window gets it out of the way. You can also click the window's Close button (which displays X) on a Code window's title bar to close the window. (Closing a window just hides it; you won't lose anything.) To open it again, just double-click the appropriate object in the Project window. By the way, working with these Code windows *sounds* more difficult than it really is.

Creating a module

In general, a VBA module can hold three types of code:

>> **Declarations:** One or more information statements that you provide to VBA. For example, you can declare the data type for variables you plan to use or set some other module-wide options. Declarations are basically housekeeping statements. They aren't actually executed.

>> **Sub procedures:** A set of programming instructions that, when executed, performs some action.

>> **Function procedures:** A set of programming instructions that returns a single value (similar in concept to a worksheet function, such as SUM).

A single VBA module can store any number of Sub procedures, Function procedures, and declarations. Well, there *is* a limit — about 64,000 characters per module. It's unlikely you'll even get close to reaching the 64,000-character limit. But if you did, the solution is simple: Just insert a new module.

How you organize a VBA module is completely up to you. Some people prefer to keep all their VBA code for an application in a single VBA module; others like to split the code into several modules. It's a personal choice, just like arranging furniture.

Getting VBA code into a module

An empty VBA module is like the fake food you see in the windows of some Chinese restaurants; it looks good but it doesn't really do much for you. Before you can do anything meaningful, you must have some VBA code in the VBA module. You can get VBA code into a VBA module in three ways:

» Enter the code directly.

» Use the Excel macro recorder to record your actions and convert those actions to VBA code (see Chapter 6).

» Copy the code from one module and paste it into another.

Entering code directly

Sometimes, the best route is the most direct one. Entering code directly involves . . . well, entering the code directly. In other words, you type the code by using your keyboard. Entering and editing text in a VBA module works as you might expect. You can select, copy, cut, paste, and do other things to the text.

Use the Tab key to indent some of the lines to make your code easier to read. Indenting isn't necessary, but it's a good habit to acquire. As you study the code in this book, you'll understand why indenting code lines is helpful.

TECHNICAL STUFF

PAUSE FOR A TERMINOLOGY BREAK

Throughout this book, you'll see the terms *Sub procedure, routine, program, procedure,* and *macro.* These terms are a bit confusing. Programming folks usually use the word *procedure* to describe an automated task. Technically, a procedure can be a Sub procedure or a Function procedure — both of which are sometimes called *routines* — or even *programs.* All these terms are used interchangeably. As detailed in later chapters, however, there is an important difference between Sub and Function procedures. For now, don't worry about the terminology. Just try to understand the concepts.

REMEMBER

A single line of VBA code can be as long as you need it to be. However, you may want to use the line-continuation characters to break up lengthy lines of code. To continue a single line of code (also known as a *statement*) from one line to the next, end the first line with a space followed by an underscore (_). Then continue the statement on the next line. And don't forget the space. An underscore character that's not preceded by a space won't do the job.

Here's an example of a single statement split into three lines:

```
Selection.Sort Key1:=Range("A1"), _
    Order1:=xlAscending, Header:=xlGuess, _
    Orientation:=xlTopToBottom
```

This statement would perform exactly the same way if it were entered in a single line (with no line-continuation characters). Notice that the second and third lines of this statement are indented. Indenting is optional, but it helps clarify the fact that these lines are not separate statements.

TIP

The white-coated engineers who designed the VBE anticipated that people like us would be making mistakes. Therefore, the VBE has multiple levels of undo and redo. If you deleted a statement that you shouldn't have, click the Undo button on the toolbar (or press Ctrl+Z) until the statement shows up again. After undoing, you can click the Redo button to perform the changes you've undone. Are you ready to enter some real-live code? Try the following steps:

1. **Create a new workbook in Excel.**

2. **Press Alt+F11 to activate the VBE.**

3. **Click the new workbook's name in the Project window.**

4. **Choose Insert ⇨ Module to insert a VBA module into the project.**

5. **Type the following code in the module:**

```
Sub GuessName()
    Msg = "Is your name " & Application.UserName & "?"
    Ans = MsgBox(Msg, vbYesNo)
    If Ans = vbNo Then MsgBox "Oh, never mind."
    If Ans = vbYes Then MsgBox "I must be psychic!"
End Sub
```

6. **Position the cursor anywhere within the text you typed and press F5 to execute the procedure.**

F5 is a shortcut for Run⇨Run Sub/UserForm. If you entered the code correctly, Excel executes the procedure, and you can respond to the simple dialog box shown in Figure 3-4. The text in the dialog box will be different from the text shown in the figure.

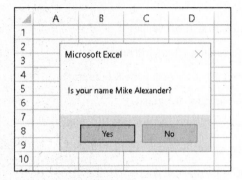

FIGURE 3-4:
The GuessName procedure displays this dialog box.

When you enter the code listed in Step 5, you might notice that the VBE makes some adjustments to the text you enter. For example, after you type the Sub statement, the VBE automatically inserts the End Sub statement. And if you omit the space before or after an equal sign, the VBE inserts the space for you. Also, the VBE changes the color and capitalization of some text. This is all perfectly normal. It's just the VBE's way of keeping things neat and readable.

COMPILE ERROR?

There's a chance that the GuessName macro won't work. When you try to run it, Excel may complain and pop up an error message: `Compile Error: Variable Not Defined`. Don't worry; there's an easy fix for that.

If you get that error, look at the top of your module, and you'll see this text: `Option Explicit`. Just delete that line, and the macro should work. That line, when present at the top of a module, means that you must "declare" all your variables. (See Chapter 7 for more about variables). If that line was added, it means that your VBE is set up to add the line automatically. For now, don't worry about it. Just delete the line and forget about the rude interruption.

If you followed the previous steps, you just wrote a VBA Sub procedure, also known as a *macro*. When you press F5, Excel executes the code and follows the instructions. In other words, Excel evaluates each statement and does what you told it to do. (Don't let this newfound power go to your head.) You can execute this macro any number of times — although it tends to lose its appeal after a few dozen times.

For the record, this simple macro uses the following concepts, all of which are covered later in this book:

» Defining a Sub procedure (the first line)

» Assigning values to variables (Msg and Ans)

» *Concatenating* (joining) a string (using the & operator)

» Using a built-in VBA function (MsgBox)

» Using built-in VBA constants (vbYesNo, vbNo, and vbYes)

» Using an If-Then construct (twice)

» Ending a Sub procedure (the last line)

Not bad for a beginner, eh?

Using the macro recorder

Another way you can get code into a VBA module is by recording your actions, using the Excel macro recorder. If you worked through the hands-on exercise in Chapter 2, you already have some experience with this technique.

By the way, there is absolutely no way you can record the GuessName procedure shown in the preceding section. You can record only things that you can do directly in Excel. Displaying a message box is not in Excel's normal repertoire. (It's a VBA thing.) The macro recorder is useful, but in many cases, you'll probably need to enter at least some code manually.

Here's a step-by-step example that shows how to record a macro that inserts a new worksheet and hides all but the first ten rows and all but the first ten columns. If you want to try this example, start with a new, blank workbook and follow these steps:

1. **Activate a worksheet in the workbook.**

Any worksheet will do.

2. **Click the Developer tab, and make sure that Use Relative References is *not* highlighted.**

This macro is recorded using Absolute References.

3. **Choose Developer ⇨ Code ⇨ Record Macro, or click the icon next to the Ready indicator on the left end of the status bar.**

Excel displays its Record Macro dialog box.

4. **In the Record Macro dialog box, name the macro TenByTen, specify that you want the macro stored in This Workbook, and press Shift+T for the shortcut key.**

The macro can be executed when you press Ctrl+Shift+T.

5. **Click OK to start recording.**

Excel automatically inserts a new VBA module into the project that corresponds to the active workbook. From this point on, Excel converts your actions to VBA code. While you're recording, the icon in the status bar turns into a small square. This is a reminder that the macro recorder is running. You can also click that icon to stop the macro recorder.

6. **Click the New Sheet icon to the right of the last sheet tab.**

Excel inserts a new worksheet.

7. **Select the entire Column K (the 11th column) and press Ctrl+Shift+right arrow; then right-click any selected column and choose Hide from the shortcut menu.**

Excel hides all of the selected columns.

8. **Select the entire Row 11 and press Ctrl+Shift+down arrow; then right-click any selected row and choose Hide from the shortcut menu.**

Excel hides all of the selected columns.

9. **Select cell A1.**

10. **Choose Developer ⇨ Code ⇨ Stop Recording, or click the Stop Recording button on the status bar (the small square).**

Excel stops recording your actions.

To view this newly recorded macro, press Alt+F11 to activate the VBE. Locate the workbook's name in the Project window. You see that the project has a new module listed. The name of the module depends on whether you had any other modules in the workbook when you started recording the macro. If you didn't, the module is named Module1. You can double-click the module to view the Code window for the module.

Here's the code generated by your actions:

```vba
Sub TenByTen()
'
' TenByTen Macro
'
' Keyboard Shortcut: Ctrl+Shift+T
'
    Sheets.Add After:=ActiveSheet
    Columns("K:K").Select
    Range(Selection, Selection.End(xlToRight)).Select
    Selection.EntireColumn.Hidden = True
    Rows("11:11").Select
    Range(Selection, Selection.End(xlDown)).Select
    Selection.EntireRow.Hidden = True
    Range("A1").Select
End Sub
```

To try this macro, activate any worksheet and press the shortcut key that you assigned in Step 4: Ctrl+Shift+T.

If you didn't assign a shortcut key to the macro, don't worry. Here's how to display a list of all macros available and run the one you want:

1. **Choose Developer ⇨ Code ⇨ Macros.**

Keyboard fans can press Alt+F8. Either of these methods displays a dialog box that lists all the available macros.

2. **Select the macro in the list (in this case, TenByTen).**

3. **Click the Run button.**

Excel executes the macro, and you get a new worksheet with ten visible rows and ten visible columns.

You can execute any number of commands and perform any number of actions while the macro recorder is running. Excel dutifully translates your mouse actions and keystrokes to VBA code.

And, of course, you can also edit the macro after you record it. To test your new skills, try editing the macro so that it inserts a worksheet with nine visible rows and columns — perfect for a Sudoku puzzle.

Copying VBA code

The final method for getting code into a VBA module is to copy it from another module or from some other place (such as a website). For example, a Sub or Function procedure that you write for one project might also be useful in another project. Instead of wasting time reentering the code, you can activate the module and use the normal Clipboard copy-and-paste procedures. (You're probably rather fond of the keyboard shortcuts Ctrl+C to copy and Ctrl+V to paste.) After pasting the code into a VBA module, you can modify the code if necessary.

By the way, you'll find lots of VBA code examples on the web. If you'd like to try them, select the code in your browser and press Ctrl+C to copy it. Then activate a module and press Ctrl+V to paste it.

When you copy code from a website, it sometimes requires some fixing. For example, quote characters may be "smart quotes" and they must be converted to simple quote characters. And sometimes, long lines wrap around. Erroneous statements are easy to spot in the VBE because they appear in red.

Customizing the VBA Environment

If you're serious about becoming an Excel programmer, you'll spend a lot of time with VBA modules on your screen. To help make things as comfortable as possible (no, please keep your shoes on), the VBE provides quite a few customization options.

When the VBE is active, choose Tools ⇨ Options. You'll see a dialog box with four tabs: Editor, Editor Format, General, and Docking. Some of the most useful options are discussed in the sections that follow.

Using the Editor tab

Figure 3-5 shows the options you can access by clicking the Editor tab of the Options dialog box. Use the options in the Editor tab to control how certain things work in the VBE.

Auto Syntax Check option

The Auto Syntax Check setting determines whether the VBE pops up a dialog box if it discovers a syntax error while you're entering your VBA code. The dialog box tells roughly what the problem is. If you don't choose this setting, the VBE flags syntax errors by displaying them in a different color from the rest of the code, and you don't have to deal with any dialog boxes popping up on your screen.

FIGURE 3-5:
The Editor tab of the Options dialog box.

Require Variable Declaration option

If the Require Variable Declaration option is set, VBE inserts the following statement at the beginning of each new VBA module you insert:

```
Option Explicit
```

Changing this setting affects only new modules, not existing modules. If this statement appears in your module, you must explicitly define each variable you use. Chapter 7 goes into the details why you should develop this habit.

Auto List Members option

If the Auto List Members option is set, the VBE provides some help when you're entering your VBA code. It displays a list that would logically complete the statement you're typing. This bit of magic is sometimes called *IntelliSense*.

This is one of the best features of the VBE. Figure 3-6 shows an example (which will make lots more sense when you start writing VBA code).

Auto Quick Info option

If the Auto Quick Info option is set, the VBE displays information about functions and their arguments as you type. This can be very helpful. Figure 3-7 shows this feature in action, telling you about the arguments for the MsgBox function.

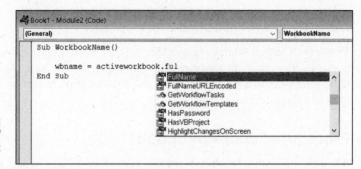

FIGURE 3-6:
An example of
Auto List
Members.

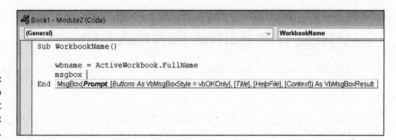

FIGURE 3-7:
Auto Quick Info
offers help about
the MsgBox
function.

Auto Data Tips option

If the Auto Data Tips option is set, the VBE displays the value of the variable over which your cursor is placed when you're debugging code. When you enter the wonderful world of debugging, as described in Chapter 13, you'll appreciate this option.

Auto Indent setting

The Auto Indent setting determines whether the VBE automatically indents each new line of code the same as the previous line.

TIP

Use the Tab key to indent your code, not the space bar. Also, you can press Shift+Tab to "unindent" a line of code. If you want to indent more than just one line, select all the lines you want to indent. Then press the Tab key.

TIP

The VBE's Edit toolbar (which is hidden by default) contains two useful buttons: Indent and Outdent. These buttons let you quickly indent or "unindent" a block of code. Select the code and click one of these buttons to change the block's indenting.

Drag-and-Drop Text Editing option

The Drag-and-Drop Text Editing option, when enabled, lets you copy and move text by dragging and dropping with your mouse.

Default to Full Module View option

The Default to Full Module View option sets the default state for new modules. (It doesn't affect existing modules.) If this option is set, procedures in the Code window appear as a single scrollable list. If this option is turned off, you can see only one procedure at a time.

Procedure Separator option

When the Procedure Separator option is turned on, separator bars appear between procedures in a Code window.

Using the Editor Format tab

Figure 3-8 shows the Editor Format tab of the Options dialog box. With this tab, you can customize the way the VBE looks.

FIGURE 3-8: Change the VBE's looks with the Editor Format tab.

Code Colors option

The Code Colors option lets you set the text color and background color displayed for various elements of VBA code. This is largely a matter of personal preference.

Font option

The Font option lets you select the font that's used in your VBA modules. For best results, stick with a fixed-width font such as Courier New. In a *fixed-width font*, all characters are exactly the same width. This makes your code more readable

because the characters are nicely aligned vertically, and you can easily distinguish multiple spaces (which is sometimes useful).

Size setting

The Size setting specifies the point size of the font in the VBA modules. This setting is a matter of personal preference determined by your video display resolution and how many carrots you've been eating.

Margin Indicator Bar option

This option controls the display of the vertical margin indicator bar in your modules. You should keep this turned on; otherwise, you won't be able to see the helpful graphical indicators when you're debugging your code.

Using the General tab

Figure 3-9 shows the options available on the General tab of the Options dialog box. In almost every case, the default settings are just fine.

FIGURE 3-9: The General tab of the Options dialog box.

The most important setting is Error Trapping. It's considered a best practice to use the Break on Unhandled Errors setting (which is the default). If you use a different setting, your error-handling code won't work. You can read more about this in Chapter 12.

If you're really interested in these options, click the Help button for details.

Using the Docking tab

Figure 3-10 shows the Docking tab. These options determine how the various windows in the VBE behave. When a window is *docked*, it's fixed in place along one of the edges of the VBE program window. This makes it much easier to identify and locate a particular window. If you turn off all docking, you have a big, confusing mess of windows. Generally, the default settings work fine.

FIGURE 3-10:
The Docking tab
of the Options
dialog box.

REMEMBER

Sometimes the VBE seems to have a mind of its own when you're trying to dock a window. If docking doesn't seem to work correctly, just stick with it, and you'll get the hang of things.

» Finding out about the Excel object hierarchy

» Understanding object collections

» Referring to specific objects in your VBA code

» Accessing or changing an object's properties

» Performing actions with an object's methods

Chapter **4**

Introducing the Excel Object Model

Everyone is familiar with the word *object.* Well, folks, forget the definition you think you know. In the world of programming, the word *object* has a different meaning. You often see it used as part of the expression *object-oriented programming,* or *OOP* for short. OOP is based on the idea that software deals with distinct objects that have attributes (or properties) and can be manipulated. These objects are not material things. Rather, they exist in the form of bits and bytes.

In this chapter, you'll be introduced to the Excel object model, which is a hierarchy of objects contained in Excel. By the time you finish this chapter, you'll have a pretty good feel for what OOP is all about — and why you need to understand this concept to become a VBA programmer. After all, Excel programming really boils down to manipulating the objects that make up Excel. It's as simple as that.

Excel Is an Object?

You've used Excel for quite a while, but you probably never thought of it as an object. The more you work with VBA, the more you view Excel in those terms. You'll understand that Excel is an object and that it contains other objects. Those objects, in turn, contain still more objects. In other words, VBA programming involves working with an object hierarchy.

At the top of this hierarchy is the Application object — in this case, Excel itself (the mother of all objects).

Climbing Down the Object Hierarchy

The Application object contains other objects. The following are some of the more useful objects contained in the Excel application:

>> Addin

>> Window

>> Workbook

>> WorksheetFunction

Each object contained in the Application object can contain other objects. For example, the following are some objects that can be contained in a Workbook object:

>> Chart (which is a chart sheet)

>> Name

>> VBProject

>> Window

>> Worksheet

In turn, each of these objects can contain still other objects. Consider a Worksheet object, which is contained in a Workbook object, which is contained in the Application object. Some of the objects that can be contained in a Worksheet object are

>> Comment

>> Hyperlink

- **»** Name
- **»** PageSetup
- **»** PivotTable
- **»** Range

Put another way, if you want to do something with a range on a particular worksheet, you may find it helpful to visualize that range in the following manner:

Range ⇨ contained in Worksheet ⇨ contained in Workbook ⇨ contained in Excel

Is this beginning to make sense?

REMEMBER

When you start digging around, you'll find that Excel has more objects than you can shake a stick at. Even power users can get overwhelmed. The good news is that you'll never have to actually deal with most of these objects. When you're working on a problem, you can just focus on a few relevant objects — which you can often discover by recording a macro.

Wrapping Your Mind around Collections

Collections are another key concept in VBA programming. A *collection* is a group of objects of the same type. And to add to the confusion, a collection is itself an object.

Here are a few examples of commonly used collections:

- **»** **Workbooks:** A collection of all currently open Workbook objects
- **»** **Worksheets:** A collection of all Worksheet objects contained in a particular Workbook object
- **»** **Charts:** A collection of all Chart objects (chart sheets) contained in a particular Workbook object
- **»** **Sheets:** A collection of all sheets (regardless of their type) contained in a particular Workbook object

You may notice that collection names are all plural, which makes sense.

"What are collections for?" you may rightfully ask. Well, for example, they're very useful when you want to work with not just one worksheet, but with a couple of them or all of them. As you'll see, your VBA code can loop through all members of a collection and do something to each one.

Referring to Objects

Referring to an object is important because you must identify the object that you want to work with. After all, VBA can't read your mind — yet.

You can work with an entire collection of objects in one fell swoop. More often, however, you need to work with a specific object in a collection (such as a particular worksheet in a workbook). To reference a single object from a collection, you put the object's name or index number in parentheses after the name of the collection, like this:

```
Worksheets("Sheet1")
```

Notice that the sheet's name is in quotation marks. If you omit the quotation marks, Excel won't be able to identify the object (and will assume that it's a variable name).

If you want to work with the first worksheet in the collection, you can also use the following reference:

```
Worksheets(1)
```

REMEMBER

In this case, the number is *not* in quotation marks. Bottom line? If you refer to an object by using its name, use quotation marks. If you refer to an object by using its index number, use a plain number without quotation marks.

What about chart sheets? A chart sheet contains a single chart. It has a sheet tab, but it's not a worksheet. Well, as it turns out, the object model has a collection called Charts. This collection contains all the chart sheet objects in a workbook (and does not include charts embedded in a worksheet). And just to keep things logical, there's another collection called Sheets. The Sheets collection contains all sheets (worksheets and chart sheets) in a workbook. The Sheets collection is handy if you want to work with all sheets in a workbook and don't care if they are worksheets or chart sheets.

So, a single worksheet named Sheet1 is a member of two collections: the Worksheets collection and the Sheets collection. You can refer to it in either of two ways:

```
Worksheets("Sheet1")
Sheets("Sheet1")
```

Navigating through the hierarchy

If you want to work with Excel objects, they are all under the Application object. So start by typing **Application**.

Every other object in Excel's object model is under the Application object. You get to these objects by moving down the hierarchy and connecting each object on your way with the dot (.) operator. To get to the Workbook object named Book1.xlsx, start with the Application object and navigate down to the Workbooks collection object:

```
Application.Workbooks("Book1.xlsx")
```

To navigate to a specific worksheet, add a dot operator and access the Worksheets collection object:

```
Application.Workbooks("Book1.xlsx").Worksheets(1)
```

Not far enough yet? If you really want to get the value from cell A1 on the first Worksheet of the Workbook named Book1.xlsx, you need to navigate one more level to the Range object:

```
Application.Workbooks("Book1.xlsx").Worksheets(1).Range("A1").
  Value
```

When you refer to a Range object in this way, it's called a *fully qualified reference*. You've told Excel exactly which range you want, on which worksheet and in which workbook, and have left nothing to the imagination. Imagination is good in people but not so good in computer programs.

By the way, workbook names also have a dot to separate the filename from the extension (for example, Book1.xlsx). That's just a coincidence. The dot in a filename has nothing at all to do with the dot operator referred to a few paragraphs ago.

Simplifying object references

If you were required to fully qualify every object reference you make, your code would get quite long, and it might be more difficult to read. Fortunately, Excel provides some shortcuts that can improve the readability (and save you some typing). For starters, the Application object is always assumed. There are only a few cases when it makes sense to type it. Omitting the Application object reference shortens the example from the previous section to

```
Workbooks("Book1.xlsx").Worksheets(1).Range("A1").Value
```

That's a pretty good improvement. But wait, there's more. If you're sure that Book1.xlsx is the active workbook, you can omit that reference, too. Now you're down to

```
Worksheets(1).Range("A1").Value
```

Now you're getting somewhere. Have you guessed the next shortcut? That's right. If you know the first worksheet is the currently active worksheet, Excel assumes that reference and allows you to just type

```
Range("A1").Value
```

REMEMBER

Contrary to what some people may think, Excel does not have a Cell object. A *cell* is simply a Range object that consists of just one element.

The shortcuts described here are great, but they can also be dangerous. What if you only *think* Book1.xlsx is the active workbook? You could get an error, or worse, you could get the wrong value and not even realize it's wrong. For that reason, it's often best to fully qualify your object references.

Chapter 14 discusses the With–End With structure, which helps you fully qualify your references but also helps to make the code more readable and cuts down on the typing. The best of both worlds!

Diving into Object Properties and Methods

Although knowing how to refer to objects is important, you can't do anything useful by simply referring to an object (as in the examples in the preceding sections). To accomplish anything meaningful, you must do one of two things:

» Read or modify an object's *properties*.

» Specify a *method* of action to be used with an object.

ANOTHER SLANT ON MCOBJECTS, MCPROPERTIES, AND MCMETHODS

Here's an analogy, comparing Excel to a fast-food chain, that may help you understand the relationships among objects, properties, and methods in VBA.

The basic unit of Excel is a Workbook object. In a fast-food chain, the basic unit is an individual restaurant. With Excel, you can add a workbook and close a workbook, and all the open workbooks are known as Workbooks (a collection of Workbook objects). Similarly, the management of a fast-food chain can add a restaurant and close a restaurant, and all the restaurants in the chain can be viewed as the Restaurants collection (a collection of Restaurant objects).

An Excel workbook is an object, but it also contains other objects such as worksheets, chart sheets, VBA modules, and so on. Furthermore, each object in a workbook can contain its own objects. For example, a Worksheet object can contain Range objects, PivotTable objects, Shape objects, and so on.

Continuing with the analogy, a fast-food restaurant (like a workbook) contains objects such as the Kitchen, DiningArea, and Tables (a collection). Furthermore, management can add or remove objects from the Restaurant object. For example, management may add more tables to the Tables collection. Each of these objects can contain other objects. For example, the Kitchen object has a Stove object, VentilationFan object, Chef object, Sink object, and so on.

So far, so good. This analogy seems to work.

Excel's objects have properties. For example, a Range object has properties such as Value and Name, and a Shape object has properties such as Width, Height, and so on. Not surprisingly, objects in a fast-food restaurant also have properties. The Stove object, for example, has properties such as Temperature and NumberofBurners. The VentilationFan has its own set of properties (TurnedOn, RPM, and so on).

Besides properties, Excel's objects also have methods, which perform an operation on an object. For example, the ClearContents method erases the contents of a Range object. An object in a fast-food restaurant also has methods. You can easily envision a ChangeThermostat method for a Stove object or a SwitchOn method for a VentilationFan object.

(continued)

(continued)

In Excel, methods sometimes change an object's properties. The ClearContents method for a Range changes the Range's Value property. Similarly, the ChangeThermostat method on a Stove object affects its Temperature property. With VBA, you can write procedures to manipulate Excel's objects. In a fast-food restaurant, the management can give orders to manipulate the objects in the restaurants ("Turn the stove on and switch the ventilation fan to high").

The next time you visit your favorite fast-food joint, just say, "Use the Grill method on a Burger object with the Onion property set to False."

Object properties

Every object has properties. You can think of *properties* as attributes that describe the object. An object's properties determine how it looks, how it behaves, and even whether it's visible. Using VBA, you can do two things with an object's properties:

» Examine the current setting for a property.

» Change the property's setting.

For example, a single-cell Range object has a property called Value. The Value property stores the value contained in the cell. You can write VBA code to display the Value property, or you may write VBA code to set the Value property to a specific value. The following macro uses the VBA built-in MsgBox function to bring up a box that displays the value in cell A1 on Sheet1 of the active workbook (see Figure 4-1):

```
Sub ShowValue()
    Contents = Worksheets("Sheet1").Range("A1").Value
    MsgBox Contents
End Sub
```

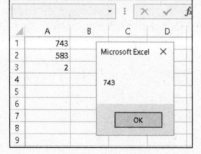

FIGURE 4-1:
This message box displays a Range object's Value property.

By the way, MsgBox is a very useful function. You can use it to display results while Excel executes your VBA code. You find out more about this function in Chapter 15, so be patient (or just flip ahead and read all about it).

The code in the preceding example displays the current setting of a cell's Value property. What if you want to change the setting for that property? The following macro changes the value in cell A1 by changing the cell's Value property:

```
Sub ChangeValue()
    Worksheets("Sheet1").Range("A1").Value = 994.92
End Sub
```

After Excel executes this procedure, cell A1 on Sheet1 of the active workbook contains the value 994.92. If the active workbook doesn't have a sheet named Sheet1, the result of executing that macro is an error message. VBA just follows instructions, and it can't work with a sheet that doesn't exist.

Each object has its own set of properties, although some properties are common to many objects. For example, many (but not all) objects have a Visible property. Most objects also have a Name property.

Some object properties are read-only properties, which means that your code can get the property's value, but it can't change it. For example, the Application object has a property called Version that returns the version number of the Excel that's running. You can't change the Version property index; it's read-only.

REMEMBER

As mentioned earlier in this chapter, a collection is also an object. This means that a collection also has properties. For example, you can determine how many workbooks are open by accessing the Count property of the Workbooks collection. The following VBA procedure displays a message box that tells you how many workbooks are open:

```
Sub CountBooks()
    MsgBox Workbooks.Count
End Sub
```

Object methods

In addition to properties, objects have methods. A *method* is an action you perform with an object. A method can change an object's properties or make the object do something.

This simple example uses the ClearContents method on a Range object to erase the contents of 12 cells on the active sheet:

```
Sub ClearRange()
    Range("A1:A12").ClearContents
End Sub
```

Some methods take one or more arguments. An *argument* is a value that further specifies the action to perform. You place the arguments for a method after the method, separated by a space. Multiple arguments are separated by a comma.

The following example activates Sheet1 (in the active workbook) and then copies the contents of cell A1 to cell B1 by using the Range object's Copy method. In this example, the Copy method has one argument, which is the destination range for the copy operation:

```
Sub CopyOne()
    Worksheets("Sheet1").Activate
    Range("A1").Copy Range("B1")
End Sub
```

Notice that the worksheet reference is omitted when referring to the Range objects. You can do this safely due to the statement to activate Sheet1 (using the Activate method).

Another way to specify an argument for a method is to use the official name of the argument followed by a colon and an equal sign. Using named arguments is optional, but doing so can often make your code easier to understand. The second statement in the CopyOne procedure could be written like this:

```
Range("A1").Copy Destination:=Range("B1")
```

In Figure 4-2, notice the little prompt as the statement is being typed. That prompt shows the official name of the argument.

FIGURE 4-2:
The VBE displays a list of arguments while you type.

Because a collection is also an object, collections have methods. The following macro uses the Add method for the Workbooks collection:

```
Sub AddAWorkbook()
    Workbooks.Add
End Sub
```

As you may expect, this statement creates a new workbook. In other words, it adds a new workbook to the Workbooks collection. After you execute this macro, a fresh workbook is the active workbook.

Object events

This section briefly touches on one more topic that you need to know about: events. Objects respond to various *events* that occur. For example, when you're working in Excel and you activate a different workbook, a Workbook Activate event occurs. You could, for example, have a VBA macro that is designed to execute whenever an Activate event occurs for a particular Workbook object.

Excel supports many events, but not all objects can respond to all events. And some objects don't respond to any events. The only events you can use are those made available by the programmers of Microsoft Excel. The concept of an event becomes clear in Chapter 11 and also in Part 4.

Finding Out More

Consider yourself initiated into the wonderful world of objects, properties, methods, and events. You find out more about these concepts in the chapters that follow. If you just can't get enough, you may also be interested in three other excellent tools:

>> VBA's Help system

>> The Object Browser

>> Auto List Members

Using VBA's Help system

The VBA Help system describes every object, property, and method available to you, and also provides sample code. This is an excellent resource for finding out

about VBA, and it's more comprehensive than any book on the market. But it's also very boring to read.

REMEMBER

If you're using Excel 2013 or later, you must be connected to the Internet to use the VBA Help system (previous versions don't have this requirement). You can, however, download the VBA Help system from Microsoft's website. Do a web search for *download excel vba documentation*, and you'll find it.

If you're working in a VBA module and want information about a particular object, method, or property, move the cursor to the word you're interested in and press F1. In a few seconds, you see the appropriate Help topic displayed in your web browser, complete with cross-references and perhaps even an example or two.

Figure 4-3 shows part of a screen from the VBA Help system — in this case, for a Worksheet object.

Syntax

expression . **Worksheets**

expression A variable that represents an **Application** object.

Remarks

Using this property without an object qualifier returns all the worksheets in the active workbook.

This property doesn't return macro sheets; use the Excel4MacroSheets property or the Excel4IntlMacroSheets property to return those sheets.

Example

This example displays the value in cell A1 on Sheet1 in the active workbook.

```
MsgBox Worksheets("Sheet1").Range("A1").Value
```

FIGURE 4-3:
An example from VBA's Help system.

Using the Object Browser

The VBE includes another tool known as the Object Browser. As the name implies, this tool lets you browse through the objects available to you. To access the Object Browser, press F2 when the VBE is active (or choose View⇨Object Browser). You see a window like the one shown in Figure 4-4.

The drop-down list at the top contains a list of all currently available object libraries. Figure 4-4 shows All Libraries. If you want to browse through Excel's objects, select Excel from the drop-down list.

FIGURE 4-4:
Browsing for objects with the Object Browser.

The second drop-down list is where you enter a search string. For example, if you want to look at all Excel objects that deal with comments, type **comment** in the second field and click the Search button. (It has a pair of binoculars on it.) The Search Results window displays everything in the object library that contains the text *comment.* If you see something that looks like it may be of interest, select it and press F1 for more information online.

Automatically listing properties and methods

Chapter 3 introduces you to a handy feature called Auto List Members. This feature provides a list of properties and methods as you type. Figure 4-5 shows an example for the Workbooks collection.

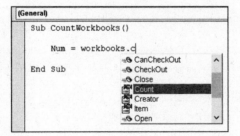

FIGURE 4-5:
The Auto List Members feature helps you identify properties and methods for an object.

After typing the dot after *workbooks*, the VBE volunteers to help by displaying a list of properties and methods for that collection. Typing the letter (like the letter *c*), narrows the list to items that begin with that letter. With each letter you type, the VBE further narrows the list of choices. Highlight the item you need, press Tab, and voilà! You've eliminated some typing — and also ensured that the property or method was spelled correctly.

Chapter **5**

VBA Sub and Function Procedures

n the preceding chapters, you've seen the term *Sub procedures* and *Function procedures*. The differences between the two kinds of procedures are probably still a mystery to you at this point, but fear not. This chapter clears up any confusion you may have about these concepts.

Understanding Subs versus Functions

The VBA code that you write in the Visual Basic Editor is known as a *procedure*. The two most common types of procedures are Sub procedures and Function procedures.

» A *Sub procedure* is a group of VBA statements that performs an action (or a sequence of actions) with Excel.

» A *Function procedure* is a group of VBA statements that performs a calculation and returns a single value (or, sometimes, an array).

Most of the macros you write in VBA are Sub procedures. You can think of a Sub procedure as being like a command: Execute the Sub procedure, and something happens. (Of course, exactly *what* happens depends on the Sub procedure's VBA code.)

A Function is also a procedure, but it's quite different from a Sub. You're already familiar with the concept of a function. Excel includes many worksheet functions that you use every day (well, at least every weekday). Examples include SUM, PMT, and VLOOKUP. You use these worksheet functions in formulas. Each function takes one or more arguments (although a few functions don't use any arguments). The function does some behind-the-scenes calculations using those arguments and then returns a single value. Function procedures that you develop with VBA work the same way.

Looking at Sub procedures

Every Sub procedure starts with the keyword Sub and ends with an End Sub statement. Here's an example:

```
Sub ShowMessage()
    MsgBox "That's all folks!"
End Sub
```

This example shows a procedure named ShowMessage. A set of parentheses follows the procedure's name. In most cases, these parentheses are empty. However, you may pass arguments to Sub procedures from other procedures. If your Sub uses arguments, list them between the parentheses.

REMEMBER

When you record a macro with the Excel macro recorder, the result is always a Sub procedure that takes no arguments.

As you see later in this chapter, Excel provides quite a few ways to execute a VBA Sub procedure.

Looking at Function procedures

Every Function procedure starts with the keyword Function and ends with an End Function statement. Here's a simple example:

```
Function CubeRoot(number)
    CubeRoot = number ^ (1 / 3)
End Function
```

This function, named CubeRoot, takes one argument (a variable named *number*), which is enclosed in parentheses. Functions can have as many as 255 arguments or none at all. When you execute this function, it returns a single value — the cube root of the argument passed to the function.

TIP

VBA allows you to specify what type of information (also known as *data type*) is returned by a Function procedure. For example, a value can be a currency, date, or text string. Chapter 7 contains more information on specifying data types.

You can execute a Function procedure in only two ways: You can execute it from another procedure (a Sub or another Function procedure) or use it in a worksheet formula.

REMEMBER

No matter how hard you try, you can't use the Excel macro recorder to record a Function procedure. You must manually enter every Function procedure that you create.

Naming Subs and Functions

Like humans, pets, and hurricanes, every Sub and Function procedure must have a name. Although it's perfectly acceptable to name your dog Hairball Harris, it's usually not a good idea to use such a freewheeling attitude when naming procedures. When naming procedures, you must follow a few rules:

>> You can use letters, numbers, and some punctuation characters, but the first character must be a letter.

>> You can't use any spaces or periods in the name.

>> VBA does not distinguish between uppercase and lowercase letters.

>> You can't use any of the following characters in a procedure name: #, $, %, &, @, ^, *, or !. In other words, your procedure name can't look like comic-strip curse words.

>> If you write a Function procedure for use in a formula, avoid using a name that looks like a cell address (for example, A1 or B52). Actually, Excel allows such function names, but why make things more confusing than they are already?

>> Procedure names can be no longer than 255 characters. (Of course, you would never make a procedure name this long.)

Ideally, a procedure's name describes the routine's purpose. A good practice is to create a name by combining a verb and a noun — for example, ProcessData, PrintReport, Sort_Array, or CheckFilename.

Some programmers prefer using sentencelike names that provide a complete description of the procedure. Some examples include WriteReportToTextFile and Get_Print_Options_and_Print_Report. The use of such lengthy names has pros and cons. On the one hand, such names are descriptive and usually unambiguous. On the other hand, they take longer to type. Everyone develops a naming style, but if your macro isn't just a quick-and-dirty temporary macro, it's a good idea to be descriptive and to avoid meaningless names such as DoIt, Update, Fix, and the ever-popular Macro1.

Executing Sub procedures

Although you may not know much about developing Sub procedures at this point, it's important to know how to execute these procedures. A Sub procedure is worthless unless you know how to execute it.

By the way, *executing* a Sub procedure means the same thing as *running* or *calling* a Sub procedure. You can use whatever terminology you like.

You can execute a VBA Sub in many ways; that's one reason you can do so many useful things with Sub procedures. Here's an exhaustive list of the ways to execute a Sub procedure:

>> Choose Run⇨Run Sub/UserForm (in the VBE). Excel executes the Sub procedure in which the cursor is located. This menu command has two alternatives: the F5 key and the Run Sub/UserForm button on the Standard toolbar in the VBE. These methods don't work if the procedure requires one or more arguments.

>> Use Excel's Macro dialog box. You open this box by choosing Developer⇨ Code⇨Macros or by choosing View⇨Macros⇨Macros. Or bypass the Ribbon and just press Alt+F8. When the Macro dialog box appears, select the Sub procedure you want and click Run. This dialog box lists only the procedures that don't require an argument.

>> Press Ctrl+key (or Ctrl+Shift+key) assigned to the Sub procedure (assuming you assigned one).

>> Click a button or a shape on a worksheet. The button or shape must have a Sub procedure assigned to it — which is very easy to do.

>> From another Sub procedure that you write.

>> Click a button that you've added to the Quick Access toolbar. (See Chapter 19.)

>> From a custom item you've added to the Ribbon. (See Chapter 19.)

>> When an event occurs. As explained later in Chapter 11, these events include opening the workbook, closing the workbook, saving the workbook, making a change to a cell, activating a sheet, and other things.

>> From the Immediate window in the VBE. Just type the name of the Sub procedure and press Enter.

Some of these techniques are covered in the following sections. To follow along, you need to enter a Sub procedure in a VBA module:

1. **Start with a new workbook.**

2. **Press Alt+F11 to activate the VBE.**

3. **Select the workbook in the Project window.**

4. **Choose Insert⇨Module to insert a new module.**

5. **Enter the following in the module:**

```
Sub ShowCubeRoot()
    Num = InputBox("Enter a positive number")
    MsgBox Num ^ (1/3) & " is the cube root."
End Sub
```

This procedure asks the user for a number and then displays that number's cube root in a message box. Figures 5-1 and 5-2 show what happens when you execute this procedure.

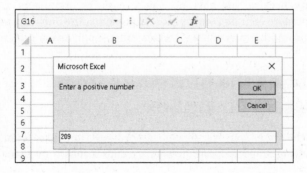

FIGURE 5-1:
Using the built-in VBA InputBox function to get a number.

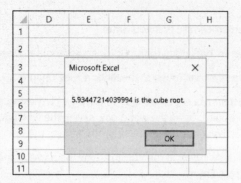

FIGURE 5-2:
Displaying the
cube root of a
number via the
MsgBox function.

By the way, ShowCubeRoot is not an example of a *good* macro. It doesn't check for errors, so it fails easily. Try clicking the Cancel button in the input box or entering a negative number. Either action results in an error message. Chapter 12 describes how to deal with these types of errors.

Executing the Sub procedure directly

One way to execute this procedure is by doing so directly from the VBA module in which you defined it. Follow these steps:

1. Activate the VBE, and select the VBA module that contains the procedure.

2. Move the cursor anywhere in the procedure's code.

3. Press F5 (or choose Run ➪ Run Sub/UserForm).

4. Respond to the input box, and click OK.

The procedure displays the cube root of the number you entered.

REMEMBER

You can't use Run ➪ Run Sub/UserForm to execute a Sub procedure that uses arguments, because you have no way to pass the arguments to the procedure. If the procedure contains one or more arguments, the only way to execute it is to call it from another procedure — which must supply the argument(s).

Executing the procedure from the Macro dialog box

Most of the time, you execute Sub procedures from Excel, not from the VBE. The following steps describe how to execute a macro by using Excel's Macro dialog box:

1. **If you're working in the VBE, activate Excel.**

 Pressing Alt+F11 is the express route.

2. **Choose Developer ⇨ Code ⇨ Macros (or press Alt+F8).**

 Excel displays the dialog box shown in Figure 5-3.

3. **Select the macro.**

4. **Click Run (or double-click the macro's name in the list box).**

FIGURE 5-3:
The Macro dialog box lists all available Sub procedures.

REMEMBER

The Macro dialog box doesn't display Sub procedures that use arguments. That's because there is no way for you to specify the arguments.

Executing a macro by using a shortcut key

Another way to execute a macro is to press its shortcut key. But before you can use this method, you must assign a shortcut key to the macro.

You have the opportunity to assign a shortcut key in the Record Macro dialog box when you begin recording a macro. If you create the procedure without using the macro recorder, you can assign a shortcut key (or change an existing shortcut key) by using the following steps:

1. **Choose Developer ⇨ Code ⇨ Macros.**

2. **Select the Sub procedure name from the list box.**

 In this example, the procedure is named ShowCubeRoot.

3. **Click the Options button.**

Excel displays the Macro Options dialog box shown in Figure 5-4.

4. **Click the Shortcut Key option and enter a letter in the box labeled Ctrl.**

The letter you enter corresponds to the key combination you want to use for executing the macro. For example, if you enter the lowercase letter *c*, you can execute the macro by pressing Ctrl+C. If you enter an uppercase letter, you need to add the Shift key to the key combination. For example, if you enter *C*, you can execute the macro by pressing Ctrl+Shift+C.

5. **Click OK to close the Macro Options dialog box and then click Cancel to close the Macro dialog box.**

FIGURE 5-4:
The Macro Options dialog box lets you set options for your macros.

After you've assigned a shortcut key, you can press that key combination to execute the macro. A shortcut key doesn't work if it's assigned to a macro that uses an argument.

WARNING

The shortcut keys you assign to macros override Excel's built-in shortcut keys. For example, Ctrl+C is the standard shortcut key to copy data. If you assign Ctrl+C to a macro, you can't use Ctrl+C to copy. This is usually not a big deal because Excel almost always provides other ways to execute commands.

Executing the procedure from a button or shape

Sometimes, you might like the idea of assigning the macro to a button (or any other shape) on a worksheet. To assign the macro to a button, follow these steps:

1. **Activate a worksheet.**

2. **Add a button from the Form Controls group.**

To display the Form Controls group, choose Developer⇨Controls⇨Insert (see Figure 5-5).

3. **Click the Button tool in the Form Controls group.**

It's the first button in the first row of controls.

4. **Drag in the worksheet to create the button.**

After you add the button to your worksheet, Excel reads your mind and displays the Assign Macro dialog box shown in Figure 5-6.

5. **Select the macro you want to assign to the button.**

6. **Click OK.**

FIGURE 5-5:
The Ribbon, showing the controls available when you click Insert on the Developer tab.

FIGURE 5-6:
When you add a button to a worksheet, Excel automatically displays the Assign Macro dialog box.

After you've made the assignment, clicking the button executes the macro — just like magic.

When you add a button, note that the drop-down box shows two sets of controls: Form Controls and ActiveX Controls. These two groups of controls look similar, but they are actually very different. In practice, the Form Controls are easier to use.

You can also assign a macro to any other shape or object. For example, assume you'd like to execute a macro when the user clicks a Rectangle object. Follow these steps:

1. **Add the rectangle to the worksheet.**

Insert a rectangle by choosing Insert ➪ Illustrations ➪ Shapes.

2. **Right-click the rectangle.**

3. **Choose Assign Macro from its shortcut menu.**

4. **Select the macro in the Assign Macro dialog box.**

5. **Click OK.**

After you've performed these steps, clicking the rectangle executes the assigned macro.

Executing the procedure from another procedure

You can also execute a procedure from another procedure. Follow these steps if you want to give this a try:

1. **Activate the VBA module that holds the ShowCubeRoot routine.**

2. **Enter this new procedure (either above or below ShowCubeRoot code — it makes no difference):**

```
Sub NewSub()
    Call ShowCubeRoot
End Sub
```

3. **Execute the NewSub macro.**

The easiest way to do this is to move the cursor anywhere within the NewSub code and press F5. Notice that this NewSub procedure simply executes the ShowCubeRoot procedure.

By the way, the keyword Call is optional. The statement can consist of only the Sub procedure's name. However, using the Call keyword makes it perfectly clear that a procedure is being called.

Executing Function procedures

Functions, unlike Sub procedures, can be executed in only two ways:

» By calling the function from another Sub procedure or Function procedure

» By using the function in a worksheet formula

Try this simple function. Enter it in a VBA module:

```
Function CubeRoot(number)
    CubeRoot = number ^ (1 / 3)
End Function
```

This function is pretty wimpy; it merely calculates the cube root of the number passed to it as its argument. It does, however, provide a starting point for understanding functions. It also illustrates an important concept about functions: how to return the value. (You do remember that a function returns a value, right?)

Notice that the single line of code that makes up this Function procedure performs a calculation. The result of the math (number to the power of $\frac{1}{3}$) is assigned to the variable CubeRoot. Not coincidentally, CubeRoot is also the name of the function. To tell the function what value to return, you assign that value to the name of the function.

Calling the function from a Sub procedure

Because you can't execute a function directly, you must call it from another procedure. Enter the following simple procedure in the same VBA module that contains the CubeRoot function:

```
Sub CallerSub()
    Ans = CubeRoot(125)
    MsgBox Ans
End Sub
```

When you execute the CallerSub procedure (using any of the methods described earlier in this chapter), Excel displays a message box that contains the value of the Ans variable, which is 5.

Here's what's going on: The CubeRoot function is executed, and it receives an argument of 125. The calculation is performed by the function's code (using the value passed as an argument), and the function's returned value is assigned to the Ans variable. The MsgBox function then displays the value of the Ans variable.

Try changing the argument that's passed to the CubeRoot function and run the CallerSub macro again. It works just like it should — assuming that you give the function a valid argument (a positive number).

By the way, the CallerSub procedure could be simplified a bit. The Ans variable is not really required unless your code will use that variable later. You could use this single statement to obtain the same result:

```
MsgBox CubeRoot(125)
```

Calling a function from a worksheet formula

Now it's time to call this VBA Function procedure from a worksheet formula. Activate a worksheet in the same workbook that holds the CubeRoot function definition. Then enter the following formula in any cell:

```
=CubeRoot(1728)
```

The cell displays 12, which is indeed the cube root of 1,728.

As you might expect, you can use a cell reference as the argument for the CubeRoot function. For example, if cell A1 contains a value, you can enter **=CubeRoot(A1)**. In this case, the function returns the number obtained by calculating the cube root of the value in A1.

You can use this function any number of times in the worksheet. Like Excel's built-in functions, your custom functions appear in the Insert Function dialog box. Click the Insert Function toolbar button, and choose the User Defined category. As shown in Figure 5-7, the Insert Function dialog box lists your very own function.

If you want the Insert Function dialog box to display a description of the function, follow these steps:

1. **Choose Developer⇨Code⇨Macros.**

Excel displays the Macro dialog box, but CubeRoot doesn't appear in the list. (CubeRoot is a Function procedure, and this list shows only Sub procedures.) Don't fret.

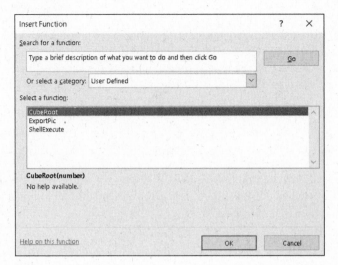

FIGURE 5-7:
The CubeRoot
function appears
in the User
Defined category
of the Insert
Function
dialog box.

2. **Type the word CubeRoot in the Macro Name box.**

3. **Click the Options button.**

4. **Enter a description of the function in the Description box.**

5. **Click OK to close the Macro Options dialog box.**

6. **Close the Macro dialog box by clicking the Cancel button.**

 This descriptive text now appears in the Insert Function dialog box.

Figure 5-8 shows the CubeRoot function being used in worksheet formulas.

FIGURE 5-8:
Using the
CubeRoot
function in
formulas.

By now, things may be starting to come together for you. You've found out lots about Sub and Function procedures. You start creating macros in Chapter 6, which discusses the ins and outs of developing macros by using the Excel macro recorder. And Chapter 20 reveals even more about Function procedures.

Chapter **6**

Using the Excel Macro Recorder

Y ou can use two methods to create an Excel macro:

» Record it by using the Excel macro recorder.

» Write it manually.

This chapter deals specifically with the ins and outs of using the Excel macro recorder. Recording a macro isn't always the best approach, and some macros simply can't be recorded, no matter how hard you try. You'll see, however, that the Excel macro recorder is very useful. Even if your recorded macro isn't quite what you want, the macro recorder can almost always lead you in the right direction.

Recording Basics

You take the following basic steps when recording a macro.

1. **Determine what you want the macro to do.**

2. **Get things set up properly.**

 This step determines how well your macro works.

3. **Determine whether you want cell references in your macro to be relative or absolute.**

4. **Click the Record Macro button on the left side of the status bar (or choose Developer ⇨ Code ⇨ Record Macro).**

 Excel displays its Record Macro dialog box.

5. **Enter a name, shortcut key, macro location, and description.**

 Each of these items — with the exception of the name — is optional.

6. **Click OK in the Record Macro dialog box.**

 Excel automatically inserts a VBA module in the workbook specified in the Store Macro In box. From this point, Excel converts your actions to VBA code. It also displays a square Stop Recording button on your status bar.

7. **Perform the actions you want to record by using the mouse or the keyboard.**

8. **When you finish, click the Stop Recording button on the status bar (or choose Developer ⇨ Code ⇨ Stop Recording).**

 Excel stops recording your actions.

9. **Test the macro to make sure it works correctly.**

10. **(Optional) Clean up the code by removing extraneous statements or add some comments to your code to explain what it does.**

The macro recorder is best suited for simple, straightforward macros. For example, you may want a macro that applies formatting to a selected range of cells or that sets up row and column headings for a new worksheet.

REMEMBER

The macro recorder is for Sub procedures only. You can't use the macro recorder to create Function procedures.

You may also find the macro recorder helpful for developing more complex macros. That is to say, you can record some actions and then copy the recorded code into another, more complex macro. In most cases, you need to edit the recorded code and add some new VBA statements.

The macro recorder *cannot* generate code for any of the following tasks, which are described later in the book:

>> Performing any type of repetitive looping

>> Performing any type of conditional actions (using an If-Then statement)

>> Assigning values to variables

>> Specifying data types

>> Displaying pop-up messages

>> Displaying custom dialog boxes

REMEMBER

The macro recorder's limited capability certainly doesn't diminish its importance. Recording your actions is perhaps the best way to master VBA. When in doubt, try recording. Although the result may not be exactly what you want, viewing the recorded code may reveal some objects, properties, and methods that you weren't aware of and steer you in the right direction.

Preparing to Record

Before you take the big step and turn on the macro recorder, spend a minute or two thinking about what you're going to do. You record a macro so that Excel can automatically repeat the actions you record, so you'll want those actions to be accurate.

REMEMBER

Ultimately, the success of a recorded macro depends on five factors:

>> How the workbook is set up while you record the macro

>> What is selected when you start recording

>> Whether you use absolute or relative recording mode

>> The accuracy of your recorded actions

>> The context in which you play back the recorded macro

The importance of these factors becomes more clear as you go through the recording process.

Relative or Absolute?

When recording your actions, Excel normally records absolute references to cells. (This is the default recording mode.) But quite often, this is the *wrong* recording mode. If you use absolute recording mode, Excel records actual cell references. If you use relative recording, Excel records *relative* references to cells. Keep reading to see the difference.

Recording in absolute mode

Open a new workbook and follow these steps to record a simple macro in absolute mode. This macro simply enters three month names in a worksheet:

1. Make sure that the Developer⇨Code⇨Use Relative References button is *not* highlighted and then choose Developer⇨Code⇨Record Macro.

2. Type Absolute as the name for this macro.

3. Click OK to begin recording.

4. Activate cell B1, and type Jan in that cell.

5. Move to cell C1, and type Feb.

6. Move to cell D1, and type Mar.

7. Click cell B1 to activate it again.

8. Stop the macro recorder.

9. Press Alt+F11 to activate the VBE.

10. Examine the Module1 module.

Excel generates the following code:

```
Sub Absolute()
'
' Absolute Macro
'
    Range("B1").Select
    ActiveCell.FormulaR1C1 = "Jan"
    Range("C1").Select
    ActiveCell.FormulaR1C1 = "Feb"
    Range("D1").Select
```

```
      ActiveCell.FormulaR1C1 = "Mar"
      Range("B1").Select
   End Sub
```

When executed, this macro selects cell B1 and inserts the three month names into the range B1:D1. Then the macro reactivates cell B1.

These same actions occur regardless of which cell is active when you execute the macro. A macro recorded by using absolute references always produces the same results when it's executed. In this case, the macro always enters the names of the first three months in the range B1:D1 on the active worksheet.

Recording in relative mode

In some cases, you want your recorded macro to work with cell locations in a *relative* manner. You may want the macro to start entering the month names in the active cell. In such a case, you need to use relative recording.

You can change the manner in which Excel records your actions by clicking the Use Relative References button in the Code group of the Developer tab. This button is a toggle button. When the button appears highlighted in a different color, the recording mode is relative. When the button appears normally, you're recording in absolute mode.

REMEMBER

You can change the recording method at any time, even in the middle of recording.

To see how relative mode recording works, delete the contents of range B1:D1 and then perform the following steps:

1. **Activate cell B1.**

2. **Choose Developer ⇨ Code ⇨ Record Macro.**

3. **Name this macro Relative.**

4. **Click OK to begin recording.**

5. **Click the Use Relative References button to change the recording mode to relative.**

 When you click this button, it changes to a different color from the rest of the ribbon.

6. **Type Jan in cell B1.**

7. **Move to cell C1, and type Feb.**

8. Move to cell D1, and type Mar.

9. Select cell B1.

10. Stop the macro recorder.

Notice that this procedure differs slightly from the previous example. In this example, you activate the beginning cell *before* you start recording. This is an important step when you record macros that use the active cell as a base.

This macro always starts entering text in the active cell. Try it. Move the cell pointer to any cell and then execute the Relative macro. The month names are always entered beginning at the active cell.

With the recording mode set to relative, the code that Excel generates is quite different from the code generated in absolute mode:

```
Sub Relative()
'
' Relative Macro
'
    ActiveCell.FormulaR1C1 = "Jan"
    ActiveCell.Offset(0, 1).Range("A1").Select
    ActiveCell.FormulaR1C1 = "Feb"
    ActiveCell.Offset(0, 1).Range("A1").Select
    ActiveCell.FormulaR1C1 = "Mar"
    ActiveCell.Offset(0, -2).Range("A1").Select
End Sub
```

To test this macro, activate any cell except B1. The month names are entered in three cells, beginning with the cell that you activated.

TECHNICAL STUFF

Notice that the code generated by the macro recorder refers to cell A1. This may seem strange because you never used cell A1 during the recording of the macro. This is simply a byproduct of the way the macro recorder works. (This is discussed in more detail in Chapter 8, where you explore the Offset property.)

What Gets Recorded?

When you turn on the macro recorder, Excel converts your mouse and keyboard actions to valid VBA code. The best way to understand the process is to watch the macro recorder in action. (See Figure 6-1.)

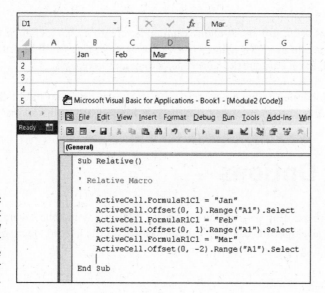

FIGURE 6-1:
A convenient window arrangement for watching the macro recorder do its thing.

Follow these steps:

1. **Start with a blank workbook.**

2. **Make sure that the Excel window is not maximized.**

3. **Press Alt+F11 to activate the VBE (and make sure that *this* program window is not maximized).**

4. **Resize and arrange the Excel window and the VBE window so that both are visible.**

 For best results, position the Excel window above the VBE window and minimize any other applications that are running.

5. **Activate Excel, and choose Developer ⇨ Code ⇨ Record Macro.**

6. **Click OK to start the macro recorder.**

 Excel inserts a new module (named Module1) and starts recording in that module.

7. **Activate the VBE program window.**

8. **In the Project Explorer window, double-click Module1 to display that module in the Code window.**

Jump back to Excel and play around for a while. Choose various Excel commands and watch the code being generated in the VBE window. Select cells, enter data,

format cells, use the Ribbon commands, create a chart, change column widths, manipulate graphics objects, and so on — go crazy! You'll be enlightened as you watch Excel spit out the VBA code before your very eyes.

TIP

If you happen to have a system with dual monitors, you might find it helpful to keep Excel on one monitor and the VBE window on the other one.

Recording Options

When recording your actions to create VBA code, you have several options. Recall that Developer ⇨ Code ⇨ Record Macro displays the Record Macro dialog box before recording begins, as shown in Figure 6-2.

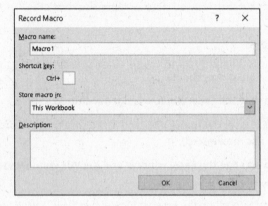

FIGURE 6-2:
The Record
Macro dialog
box provides
several options.

The Record Macro dialog box allows you to specify a few aspects of your macro. The following sections dive into these options.

Macro name

You can enter a name for the Sub procedure that you're recording. By default, Excel uses the names Macro1, Macro2, and so on for each macro you record. Don't worry if you don't give your macro a friendly name in Record Macro dialog box. You can always give it a more descriptive name later by editing the recorded code in the VBE.

Shortcut key

The Shortcut key option allows you to execute the macro by pressing a shortcut key combination. For example, if you enter **w** (lowercase), you can execute the macro by pressing Ctrl+W. If you enter **W** (uppercase), the macro comes alive when you press Ctrl+Shift+W.

REMEMBER

You can add or change a shortcut key at any time, so there's no real reason to set this option when recording a macro. For instructions on assigning a shortcut key to an existing macro, see Chapter 5.

Store Macro In option

The Store Macro In option tells Excel where to store the macro that it's recording. By default, Excel puts the recorded macro in a module in the active workbook. If you prefer, you can record it in a new workbook (Excel opens a blank workbook) or in your Personal Macro Workbook.

Your Personal Macro Workbook is a hidden workbook that opens automatically when Excel starts. This is a good place to store macros that you'll use with multiple workbooks. The Personal Macro Workbook is named PERSONAL.XLSB. This file doesn't exist until you specify it as the location for a recorded macro. If you've made any changes to this file, Excel prompts you to save it when you exit.

Description

If you'd like to add some descriptive comments to your macro, enter it in the Description box. You can put anything you like here, or nothing at all.

Is This Thing Efficient?

You might think that recording a macro would generate some award-winning VBA code — better than you could ever write manually. Think again. Because the macro recorder has to be generic enough to record virtually every combination of actions, it often generates extraneous code that works, but is less than efficient.

To demonstrate just how inefficient the macro recorder's code can be, try this:

1. **Turn on the macro recorder.**
2. **Choose Page Layout ⇨ Page Setup ⇨ Orientation ⇨ Landscape.**
3. **Turn off the macro recorder.**

To take a look at the macro, activate the Module1 sheet. This single (very simple) command generates the following code:

```
Sub Macro1()
Application.PrintCommunication = False
    With ActiveSheet.PageSetup
        .PrintTitleRows = ""
        .PrintTitleColumns = ""
    End With
    Application.PrintCommunication = True
    ActiveSheet.PageSetup.PrintArea = ""
    Application.PrintCommunication = False
    With ActiveSheet.PageSetup
        .LeftHeader = ""
        .CenterHeader = ""
        .RightHeader = ""
        .LeftFooter = ""
        .CenterFooter = ""
        .RightFooter = ""
        .LeftMargin = Application.InchesToPoints(0.7)
        .RightMargin = Application.InchesToPoints(0.7)
        .TopMargin = Application.InchesToPoints(0.75)
        .BottomMargin = Application.InchesToPoints(0.75)
        .HeaderMargin = Application.InchesToPoints(0.3)
        .FooterMargin = Application.InchesToPoints(0.3)
        .PrintHeadings = False
        .PrintGridlines = False
        .PrintComments = xlPrintNoComments
        .PrintQuality = 600
        .CenterHorizontally = False
        .CenterVertically = False
        .Orientation = xlLandscape
        .Draft = False
        .PaperSize = xlPaperLetter
        .FirstPageNumber = xlAutomatic
        .Order = xlDownThenOver
        .BlackAndWhite = False
        .Zoom = 100
        .PrintErrors = xlPrintErrorsDisplayed
        .OddAndEvenPagesHeaderFooter = False
        .DifferentFirstPageHeaderFooter = False
        .ScaleWithDocHeaderFooter = True
```

```
        .AlignMarginsHeaderFooter = True
        .EvenPage.LeftHeader.Text = ""
        .EvenPage.CenterHeader.Text = ""
        .EvenPage.RightHeader.Text = ""
        .EvenPage.LeftFooter.Text = ""
        .EvenPage.CenterFooter.Text = ""
        .EvenPage.RightFooter.Text = ""
        .FirstPage.LeftHeader.Text = ""
        .FirstPage.CenterHeader.Text = ""
        .FirstPage.RightHeader.Text = ""
        .FirstPage.LeftFooter.Text = ""
        .FirstPage.CenterFooter.Text = ""
        .FirstPage.RightFooter.Text = ""
    End With
    Application.PrintCommunication = True
End Sub
```

You may be surprised by the amount of code generated by this single command. Although you changed only one print setting, Excel generated code that set many other print-related properties.

This is a good example of macro-recording overkill. If you want a macro that just switches the page setup to landscape mode, you can simplify this macro considerably by deleting the extraneous code. This makes the macro a bit faster and a lot easier to read. Here's how the macro looks after deleting the irrelevant lines:

```
Sub Macro1()
    With ActiveSheet.PageSetup
        .Orientation = xlLandscape
    End With
End Sub
```

The only line necessary is the one that sets the Orientation property. Actually, you can simplify this macro even more because you don't really need the With-End With construct (you find out more about this construct in Chapter 14):

```
Sub Macro1()
    ActiveSheet.PageSetup.Orientation = xlLandscape
End Sub
```

In this case, the macro changes the Orientation property of the PageSetup object on the active sheet. All other properties are unchanged. By the way, xlLandscape

is a built-in constant that makes your code easier to read. This constant has a value of 2, so the following statement works exactly the same (but isn't as easy to read):

```
ActiveSheet.PageSetup.Orientation = 2
```

Stay tuned for the built-in constants explanations in Chapter 7.

Rather than record this macro, you can enter it directly in a VBA module. To do so, you have to know which objects, properties, and methods to use. Although the recorded macro isn't all that great, by recording it, you realize that the PageSetup object is contained in a Worksheet object and that the PageSetup object has an Orientation property. Armed with this knowledge and a quick trip to the Help system (and probably some experimentation), you can write the macro manually.

This chapter nearly sums it up when it comes to using the macro recorder. The only thing missing is experience. Eventually, you discover which recorded statements you can safely delete. Better yet, you discover how to modify a recorded macro to make it more useful.

3

Programming Concepts

Discover the essential elements of Excel programming: variables, constants, data types, operators, arrays, and so on.

Get acquainted with Range objects; you'll be glad you did.

Find out why VBA functions (and also Excel worksheet functions) are important.

Discover the essence of programming: decision-making and looping.

See how to run code automatically when certain things occur.

Find out about the different types of errors and why error handling is important.

Know what to do when good code does bad things: Get initiated into the bug extermination club.

» Using variables and constants

» Telling VBA what type of data you're using

» Getting familiar with arrays

» Knowing why you may need to use labels in your procedures

Chapter **7**

Essential VBA Language Elements

B ecause VBA is a real, live programming language, it uses many elements common to all programming languages. In this chapter, you're introduced to several of these elements: comments, variables, constants, data types, arrays, and a few other goodies. If you've programmed with other languages, some of this material will be familiar. If you're a programming newbie, it's time to roll up your sleeves and get busy.

Using Comments in Your VBA Code

A *comment* is the simplest type of VBA statement. Because VBA ignores these statements, they can consist of anything you want. You can insert a comment to remind yourself why you did something or to clarify some particularly elegant code you wrote.

TIP

Use comments liberally and extensively to describe what the code does (which isn't always obvious from reading the code itself). Often, code that makes perfect sense today mystifies you tomorrow. Been there. Done that.

You begin a comment with an apostrophe ('). VBA ignores any text that follows an apostrophe in a line of code. You can use a complete line for your comment or insert your comment at the end of a line of code. The following example shows a VBA procedure with four comments:

```vba
Sub FormatCells()
'    Exit if a range is not selected
    If TypeName(Selection) <> "Range" Then
        MsgBox "Select a range."
        Exit Sub
    End If
'    Format the cells
    With Selection
        .HorizontalAlignment = xlRight
        .WrapText = False ' no wrap
        .MergeCells = False ' no merged cells
    End With
End Sub
```

REMEMBER

The "apostrophe indicates a comment" rule has one exception: VBA doesn't interpret an apostrophe inside a set of quotation marks as a comment indicator. For example, the following statement doesn't contain a comment, even though it has an apostrophe:

```vba
Msg = "Can't continue"
```

When you're writing code, you may want to test a procedure by *excluding* a particular statement or group of statements. You *could* delete the statements and then retype them later. But that's a waste of time. A better solution is to simply turn those statements into comments by inserting apostrophes. VBA ignores statements beginning with apostrophes when executing a routine. To reactivate those "commented" statements, just remove the apostrophes.

TIP

Here's a quick way to convert a block of statements to comments. In the VBE, choose View⇨Toolbars⇨Edit to display the Edit toolbar. To convert a block of statements to comments, select the statements and click the Comment Block button. To remove the apostrophes, select the statements and click the Uncomment Block button.

Everyone develops his or her own style of commenting. To be useful, however, comments should convey information that's not immediately obvious from reading the code.

The following tips can help you make effective use of comments:

>> Identify yourself as the author. This can be useful when you get promoted and the person who takes over your job has some questions.

>> Briefly describe the purpose of each Sub or Function procedure you write.

>> Use comments to keep track of changes you make to a procedure.

>> Use a comment to indicate that you're using a function or a construct in an unusual or nonstandard manner.

>> Use comments to describe the variables you use, especially if you don't use meaningful variable names.

>> Use a comment to describe any workarounds you develop to overcome bugs in Excel.

>> Write comments as you develop code instead of saving the task for a final step.

>> Depending on your work environment, consider adding a joke or two as a comment. The person who takes over your job when you get promoted might appreciate the humor.

Using Variables, Constants, and Data Types

VBA's main purpose is to manipulate data. VBA stores the data in your computer's memory, and the data may or may not end up on disk. Some data, such as worksheet ranges, resides in objects. Other data is stored in variables that you create.

Understanding variables

A *variable* is simply a named storage location in your computer's memory that's used by a program. You have lots of flexibility in naming your variables, so make the variable names as descriptive as possible. You assign a value to a variable by using the equal-sign operator. (More about this later in the "Using Assignment Statements" section.)

Here are some examples of variables being assigned values. Note that the last example uses two variables.

```
x = 1
InterestRate = 0.075
LoanPayoffAmount = 243089
DataEntered = False
x = x + 1
UserName = "Bob Johnson"
Date_Started = #3/14/2019#
MyNum = YourNum * 1.25
```

VBA enforces a few rules regarding variable names:

>> You can use letters, numbers, and some punctuation characters, but the first character must be a letter.

>> VBA doesn't distinguish between uppercase and lowercase letters.

>> You can't use any spaces, periods, or mathematical operators in a variable name.

>> You can't use the following characters in a variable name: #, $, %, &, or !.

>> Variable names can be no longer than 255 characters. But nobody even gets close to that limit.

To make variable names more readable, programmers often use mixed case (for example, InterestRate) or the underscore character (interest_rate).

VBA has many reserved words that you can't use for variable names or procedure names. These include words such as Sub, Dim, With, End, Next, and For. If you attempt to use one of these words as a variable, you may get a compile error (which means your code won't run). So if an assignment statement produces an error message, double-check to make sure that the variable name isn't a reserved word. An easy way to do that is to select the variable name and press F1. If your variable name is a reserved word, it will have an entry in the Help system.

VBA does allow you to create variables with names that match names in Excel's object model, such as Workbook and Range. But obviously, using names like that just increases the possibility of getting confused. Here's a perfectly valid (but very confusing) macro that declares Range as a variable name and works with a cell named Range in a worksheet named Range:

```
Sub RangeConfusion()
    Dim Range As Double
    Range = Sheets("Range").Range("Range").Value
    MsgBox Range
End Sub
```

So resist the urge to use a variable named Workbook or Range, and use something like MyWorkbook or MyRange instead.

What are VBA's data types?

When discussing programming languages, the term *data type* refers to the manner in which a program stores data in memory — for example, as integers, real numbers, or strings. Although VBA can take care of these details automatically, it does so at a cost. (There's no free lunch.) Letting VBA handle your data typing results in slower execution and inefficient memory use. For small applications, this usually doesn't present much of a problem. But for large or complex applications, which may be slow or need to conserve every last byte of memory, you need to be on familiar terms with data types.

VBA automatically handles all the data details, which makes life easier for programmers. Not all programming languages provide this luxury. For example, some languages are *strictly typed,* which means the programmer must explicitly define the data type for every variable used.

VBA doesn't require that you declare the variables that you use, but it's definitely a good practice. You see why later in this chapter.

VBA has a variety of built-in data types. Table 7-1 lists the most common types of data that VBA can handle.

In general, choose the data type that uses the smallest number of bytes but can still handle all the data you want to store in the variable.

TECHNICAL STUFF

An exception to the "smallest number of bytes" rule is Long. Most VBA programmers use Long instead of Integer because doing so offers a slight performance increase. But for small procedures, you would never notice any difference between Integer and Long data types.

TABLE 7-1 ## VBA's Built-In Data Types

Data Type	Bytes Used	Range of Values
Byte	1	0 to 255
Boolean	2	True or False
Integer	2	–32,768 to 32,767
Long	4	–2,147,483,648 to 2,147,483,647
Single	4	–3.40E38 to –1.40E-45 for negative values; 1.40E-45 to 3.40E38 for positive values
Double	8	–1.79E308 to –4.94E-324 for negative values; 4.94E-324 to 1.79E308 for positive values
Currency	8	–922,337,203,685,477 to 922,337,203,685,477
Date	8	1/1/0100 to 12/31/9999
Object	4	Any object reference
String	1 per character	Varies
Variant	Varies	Varies

Declaring and scoping variables

If you read the preceding sections, you know a bit about variables and data types. In this section, you discover how to declare a variable as a certain data type.

If you don't declare the data type for a variable you use in a VBA routine, VBA uses the default data type: Variant. Data stored as a variant acts like a chameleon; it changes type depending on what you do with it. For example, if a variable is a Variant data type and contains a text string that looks like a number (such as "143"), you can use this variable for string manipulations as well as numeric calculations. VBA automatically handles the conversion. Letting VBA handle data types may seem like an easy way out — but remember that you sacrifice speed and increase memory used.

Before you use variables in a procedure, it's an excellent practice to *declare* your variables — that is, tell VBA each variable's data type. Declaring your variables makes your macro run faster and use memory more efficiently. The default data type, Variant, causes VBA to repeatedly perform time-consuming checks and

reserve more memory than necessary. If VBA knows a variable's data type, it doesn't have to investigate and can reserve just enough memory to store the data.

To force yourself to declare all the variables you use, include these two words as the first statement in your VBA module:

```
Option Explicit
```

When this statement is present, you won't be able to run your code if it contains any undeclared variables.

REMEMBER

You need to use Option Explicit only once: at the beginning of your module, before the declaration of any procedures in the module. Keep in mind that the Option Explicit statement applies only to the module in which it resides. If you have more than one VBA module in a project, you need an Option Explicit statement for each module.

Suppose that you use an undeclared variable (that is, a Variant) named Current-Rate. At some point in your routine, you insert the following statement:

```
CurentRate = .075
```

The variable name is misspelled (missing an r) and can be very difficult to spot. If you don't notice it, Excel interprets it as a *different* variable, and it will probably cause your routine to give incorrect results. If you use Option Explicit at the beginning of your module (forcing you to declare the CurrentRate variable), Excel generates an error if it encounters a misspelled variation of that variable.

TIP

To ensure that the Option Explicit statement is inserted automatically whenever you insert a new VBA module, turn on the Require Variable Definition option. You find it on the Editor tab of the Options dialog box (in the VBE, choose Tools⇔Options).

TIP

Declaring your variables also allows you to take advantage of a shortcut that can save some typing. Just type the first two or three characters of the variable name and then press Ctrl+space bar. The VBE either completes the entry for you or — if the choice is ambiguous — shows you a list of matching words to choose among. In fact, this slick trick works with reserved words and functions, too. Figure 7-1 shows an example of how this works.

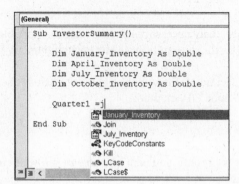

FIGURE 7-1:
Pressing
Ctrl+space bar
displays a list of
variable names,
reserved words,
and functions.

You now know the advantages of declaring variables, but *how* do you do it? The most common way is to use a Dim statement. Here are some examples of variables being declared:

```
Dim YourName As String
Dim January_Inventory As Double
Dim AmountDue As Double
Dim RowNumber As Long
Dim X
```

The first four variables are declared as a specific data type. The last variable, X, is not declared as a specific data type, so it's treated as a Variant (it can be anything).

Besides Dim, VBA has three keywords that are used to declare variables:

>> Static

>> Public

>> Private

The Dim, Static, Public, and Private keywords later are discussed later, but first, two other topics are relevant here: a variable's scope and a variable's life.

A workbook can have any number of VBA modules, and a VBA module can have any number of Sub and Function procedures. A variable's *scope* determines which modules and procedures can use the variable. Table 7-2 has the details.

Confused? Keep turning the pages; some examples make this stuff crystal clear.

TABLE 7-2 **Variable's Scope**

Scope	How the Variable Is Declared
Procedure only	By using a Dim or a Static statement in the procedure that uses the variable
Module only	By using a Dim or a Private statement before the first Sub or Function statement in the module
All procedures in all modules	By using a Public statement before the first Sub or Function statement in a module

Procedure-only variables

The lowest level of scope for a variable is at the procedure level. (A *procedure* is either a Sub or a Function procedure.) Variables declared with this scope can be used only in the procedure in which they're declared. When the procedure ends, the variable no longer exists, and Excel frees up its memory. If you execute the procedure again, the variable comes back to life, but its previous value is lost.

The most common way to declare a procedure-only variable is with a Dim statement. Dim doesn't refer to the mental capacity of the VBA designers. Rather, it's an old programming term that's short for *dimension*, which simply means you're setting aside memory for a particular variable. You usually place Dim statements immediately after the Sub or Function statement and before the procedure's code.

The following example shows some procedure-only variables declared by using Dim statements:

```
Sub MySub()
    Dim x As Integer
    Dim First As Long
    Dim InterestRate As Single
    Dim TodaysDate As Date
    Dim UserName As String
    Dim MyValue
    '  ...    [The procedure's code goes here] ...
End Sub
```

Notice that the last Dim statement in the preceding example doesn't declare a data type for the MyValue variable; it declares only the variable itself. The effect is that the variable MyValue is a Variant data type.

WARNING

Unlike some languages, VBA doesn't allow you to declare a group of variables to be a particular data type by separating the variables with commas. For example, though valid, the following statement does *not* declare all the variables as Integers:

```
Dim i, j, k As Integer
```

In this example, only k is declared to be an Integer; the other variables default to the Variant data type.

If you declare a variable with procedure-only scope, other procedures in the same module can use the same variable name, but each instance of the variable is unique to its own procedure. In general, variables declared at the procedure level are the most efficient because VBA frees up the memory they use when the procedure ends.

Module-only variables

Sometimes, you want a variable to be available to all procedures in a module. If so, just declare the variable (using Dim or Private) *before* the module's first Sub or Function statement — outside any procedures. You do this in the Declarations section, at the beginning of your module. (This is also where the Option Explicit statement is located.)

Figure 7-2 shows how you know when you're working with the Declarations section. Use the drop-down menu on the right, and go directly to the Declarations section. Do not pass Go, and do not collect $200.

FIGURE 7-2:
Each VBA module has a Declarations section, which appears before any Sub or Function procedures.

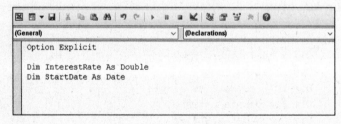

Suppose that you want to declare the CurrentValue variable so that it's available to all the procedures in your module. All you need to do is use the Dim statement in the Declarations section:

```
Dim CurrentValue As Double
```

With this declaration in place — and in the proper place — the CurrentValue variable can be used from any other procedure within the module, and it retains its value from one procedure to another.

Public variables

If you need to make a variable available to all the procedures in all your VBA modules in a workbook, declare the variable at the module level (in the Declarations section) by using the Public keyword. Here's an example:

```
Public CurrentRate As Long
```

The Public keyword makes the CurrentRate variable available to any procedure in the workbook — even those in other VBA modules. You must insert this statement before the first Sub or Function statement in a module.

TECHNICAL STUFF

If you'd like a variable to be available to modules in other workbooks, you must declare the variable as Public and establish a reference to the workbook that contains the variable declaration. Set up a reference by choosing Tools ⇨ References in the VBE. In practice, sharing a variable across workbooks is hardly ever done. But it's nice to know that it can be done, in case it ever comes up as a *Jeopardy!* question.

Static variables

Normally, when a procedure ends, all the procedure's variables are reset. *Static variables* are special cases because they retain their value even when the procedure ends. You declare a static variable at the procedure level. A static variable may be useful if you need to track the number of times you execute a procedure. You can declare a static variable and increment it each time you run the procedure.

As shown in the following example, you declare static variables by using the Static keyword:

```
Sub MySub()
    Static Counter As Integer
    Dim Msg As String
    Counter = Counter + 1
    Msg = "Number of executions: " & Counter
    MsgBox Msg
End Sub
```

The code keeps track of the number of times the procedure was executed and displays the number in a message box. The value of the Counter variable isn't reset when the procedure ends, but it's reset when you close and reopen the workbook.

Even though the value of a variable declared as Static is retained after a variable ends, that variable is unavailable to other procedures. In the preceding MySub procedure example, the Counter variable and its value are available only within the MySub procedure. In other words, it's a procedure-level variable.

Life of variables

Nothing lives forever, including variables. The scope of a variable not only determines where that variable may be used, but also affects the circumstances under which the variable is removed from memory.

You can purge all variables from memory by using three methods:

» Click the Reset toolbar button (the little blue square button on the Standard toolbar in the VBE).

» Click End when a runtime error message dialog box shows up.

» Include an End statement anywhere in your code. This is not the same as an End Sub or End Function statement.

Otherwise, only procedure-level variables will be removed from memory when the macro code has completed running. Static variables, module-level variables, and global (public) variables all retain their values in between runs of your code.

If you use module-level or global-level variables, make sure they have the values you expect them to have. You never know whether one of the situations just mentioned may have caused your variables to lose their content!

Working with constants

A variable's value may (and usually does) change while your procedure is executing. That's why they call it a *variable*. Sometimes, you need to refer to a value or string that never changes. In such a case, you need a *constant* — a named element whose value doesn't change.

As shown in the following examples, you declare constants by using the Const statement. The declaration statement also gives the constant its value:

```
Const NumQuarters As Integer = 4
Const Rate = .0725, Period = 12
Const ModName As String = "Budget Macros"
Public Const AppName As String = "Budget Application"
```

Using constants in place of hard-coded values or strings is an excellent programming practice. For example, if your procedure needs to refer to a specific value (such as an interest rate) several times, it's better to declare the value as a constant and refer to its name rather than the value. This makes your code more readable and easier to change. And if the interest rate changes, you have to change only one statement rather than several.

Like variables, constants have a scope. Keep these points in mind:

» To make a constant available within only a single procedure, declare the constant after the procedure's Sub or Function statement.

» To make a constant available to all procedures in a module, declare the constant in the Declarations section for the module.

» To make a constant available to all modules in the workbook, use the Public keyword and declare the constant in the Declarations section of any module.

Unlike a variable, the value of a constant doesn't vary. If you attempt to change the value of a constant in a VBA routine, you get an error. This isn't too surprising because the value of a constant must remain constant. If you need to change the value of a constant while your code is running, what you really need is a variable.

Premade constants

Excel and VBA contain many predefined constants, which you can use without the need to declare them yourself. The macro recorder usually uses constants rather than actual values. In general, you don't need to know the value of these constants to use them. The following simple procedure uses a built-in constant (xlCalculation Manual) to change the Calculation property of the Application object (in other words, to change the Excel recalculation mode to manual):

```
Sub CalcManual()
    Application.Calculation = xlCalculationManual
End Sub
```

If you look in Excel's Help system for calculation modes, you'll find this:

Name	Value	Description
xlCalculationAutomatic	–4105	Excel controls recalculation.
xlCalculationManual	–4135	Calculation is done when the user requests it.
xlCalculationSemiautomatic	2	Excel controls recalculation but ignores changes in tables.

So the actual value of the built-in xlCalculationManual constant is −4135. Obviously, it's easier to use the constant's name than try to remember such an odd value. As you can see, many of the built-in constants are just arbitrary numbers that have special meaning to VBA.

TIP

To find the actual value of a built-in constant, use the Immediate window in the VBE and execute a VBA statement such as the following:

```
? xlCalculationAutomatic
```

If the Immediate window isn't visible, press Ctrl+G. The question mark is a short-cut for typing **Print**.

Working with strings

Excel can work with both numbers and text, so it should come as no surprise that VBA has this same power. Text is often referred to as a *string*. You can work with two types of strings in VBA:

» **Fixed-length strings** are declared with a specified number of characters. The maximum length is 65,526 characters. That's a lot of characters! As a point of reference, this chapter contains about half that many characters.

» **Variable-length strings** theoretically can hold as many as two billion characters. If you type 5 characters per second, it would take you about 760 days to bang out 2 billion characters — assuming you don't take any breaks to eat or sleep.

When declaring a string variable with a Dim statement, you can specify the maximum length if you know it (it's a fixed-length string) or let VBA handle it dynamically (it's a variable-length string). The following example declares the MyString variable as a string with a maximum length of 50 characters. (Use an asterisk to specify the number of characters, up to the 65,526-character limit.) YourString is also declared as a string, but its length is unspecified:

```
Dim MyString As String * 50
Dim YourString As String
```

WARNING

When declaring a fixed-length string that exceeds 999, don't use a comma in the number that specifies the string size. In fact, never use commas when entering a numeric value in VBA. VBA doesn't like that.

Working with dates

Another data type you may find useful is Date. You can use a string variable to store dates, but then you can't perform date calculations. Using the Date data type gives your routines greater flexibility. For example, you might need to calculate the number of days between two dates. This would be impossible (or at least extremely challenging) if you used strings to hold your dates.

A variable defined as a Date can hold dates ranging from January 1, 0100, to December 31, 9999. That's a span of nearly 10,000 years and more than enough for even the most aggressive financial forecast. You can also use the Date data type to work with time data. (VBA lacks a Time data type.)

These examples declare variables and constants as a Date data type:

```
Dim Today As Date
Dim StartTime As Date
Const FirstDay As Date = #1/1/2019#
Const Noon = #12:00:00#
```

In VBA, place dates and times between two hash marks, as shown in the preceding examples.

REMEMBER

Date variables display dates according to your system's short date format, and they display times according to your system's time format (either 12- or 24-hour formatting). The Windows Registry stores these settings, and you can modify them via the Regional and Language Settings dialog box in the Windows Control Panel. Therefore, the VBA-displayed date or time format may vary, depending on the settings for the system on which the application is running.

When writing VBA code, however, you must use one of the U.S. date formats (such as mm/dd/yyyy). So the following statement assigns a day in October (not November) to the MyDate variable (even if your system is set to use dd/mm/yyyy for dates):

```
MyDate = #10/11/2019#
```

When you display the variable (with the MsgBox function, for example), VBA shows MyDate using your system settings. So if your system uses the dd/mm/yyyy date format, MyDate is displayed as 11/10/2019.

Using Assignment Statements

An *assignment statement* is a VBA statement that assigns the result of an expression to a variable or an object. Excel's Help system defines the term expression as

> . . . a combination of keywords, operators, variables, and constants that yields a string, number, or object. An expression can be used to perform a calculation, manipulate characters, or test data.

Much of your work in VBA involves developing (and debugging) expressions. If you know how to create formulas in Excel, you'll have no trouble creating expressions. With a worksheet formula, Excel displays the result in a cell. A VBA expression, on the other hand, can be assigned to a variable.

Assignment statement examples

In the assignment statement examples that follow, the expressions are to the right of the equal sign:

```
x = 1
x = x + 1
x = (y * 2) / (z * 2)
HouseCost = 375000
FileOpen = True
Range("TheYear").Value = 2019
```

TIP

Expressions can be as complex as you need them to be; use the line continuation character (a space followed by an underscore) to make lengthy expressions easier to read.

Often, expressions use functions: VBA's built-in functions, Excel's worksheet functions, or functions that you develop with VBA. Functions are discussed in Chapter 9.

About that equal sign

As you can see in the preceding example, VBA uses the equal sign as its assignment operator. You're probably accustomed to using an equal sign as a mathematical symbol for equality. Therefore, an assignment statement like the following may cause you to raise your eyebrows:

```
z = z + 1
```

In what crazy universe is z equal to itself plus 1? Answer: No known universe. In this case, the assignment statement (when executed) increases the value of z by 1. So if z is 12, executing the statement makes z equal to 13. Just remember that an assignment uses the equal sign as an operator, not a symbol of equality.

Smooth operators

Operators play major roles in VBA. Besides the equal-sign operator (discussed in the previous section), VBA provides several operators. Table 7-3 lists these operators. These should be familiar to you because they're the same operators used in worksheet formulas (except for the Mod operator).

TABLE 7-3

VBA's Operators

Function	Operator Symbol
Addition	+
Multiplication	*
Division	/
Subtraction	–
Exponentiation	^
String concatenation	&
Integer division (the result is always an integer)	\
Modulo arithmetic (returns the remainder of a division operation)	Mod

When you're writing an Excel formula, you do modulo arithmetic by using the MOD function. For example, the following formula returns 2 (the remainder when you divide 12 by 5):

```
=MOD(12,5)
```

In VBA, the Mod operator is used like this (and z has a value of 2):

```
z = 12 Mod 5
```

TECHNICAL
STUFF

The term *concatenation* is programmer speak for "join together." Thus, if you concatenate strings, you're combining strings to make a new and improved string.

As shown in Table 7-4, VBA also provides a full set of logical operators.

TABLE 7-4

VBA's Logical Operators

Operator	What It Does
Not	Performs a logical negation on an expression
And	Performs a logical conjunction on two expressions
Or	Performs a logical disjunction on two expressions
Xor	Performs a logical exclusion on two expressions
Eqv	Performs a logical equivalence on two expressions
Imp	Performs a logical implication on two expressions

The precedence order for operators in VBA is exactly the same as in Excel formulas. Exponentiation has the highest precedence. Multiplication and division come next, followed by addition and subtraction. You can use parentheses to change the natural precedence order, making whatever's sandwiched in parentheses come before any operator. Take a look at this code:

```
x = 3
y = 2
z = x + 5 * y
```

When the preceding code is executed, what's the value of z? If you answered 13, you get a gold star that proves you understand the concept of operator precedence. If you answered 16, read this: The multiplication operation (5 * y) is performed first, and that result is added to x.

If you have trouble remembering the correct operator precedence, add parenthesis around the parts that get calculated first. For example, the previous assignment statement looks like this with parethesis:

```
z = x + (5 * y)
```

TIP

Don't be shy about using parentheses even when they aren't required — especially if doing so makes your code easier to understand. VBA doesn't care if you use extra parentheses.

Working with Arrays

Like most programming languages, VBA supports arrays. An *array* is a group of variables that share a name. You refer to a specific variable in the array by using the array name and an index number in parentheses. For example, you can define an array of 12 string variables to hold the names of the months of the year. If you name the array *MonthNames*, you can refer to the first element of the array as MonthNames (1), the second element as MonthNames (2), and so on.

Declaring arrays

Before you can use an array, you *must* declare it. No exceptions. Unlike with normal variables, VBA is very strict about this rule. You declare an array with a Dim statement, just as you declare a regular variable. However, you also need to specify the number of elements in the array. You do this by specifying the first index number, the keyword To, and the last index number — all inside parentheses. The following example shows how to declare an array of 100 integers:

```
Dim MyArray(1 To 100) As Integer
```

When you declare an array, you can choose to specify only the upper index. If you omit the lower index, VBA assumes that it's 0. Therefore, both of the following statements declare the same 101-element array:

```
Dim MyArray (0 To 100) As Integer
Dim MyArray (100) As Integer
```

TIP

If you want VBA to assume that 1 (rather than 0) is the lower index for your arrays, include the following statement in the Declarations section at the top of your module:

```
Option Base 1
```

This statement forces VBA to use 1 as the first index number for arrays that declare only the upper index. If this statement is present, the following statements are identical, both declaring a 100-element array:

```
Dim MyArray (1 To 100) As Integer
Dim MyArray (100) As Integer
```

Multidimensional arrays

The arrays created in the previous examples are all one-dimensional arrays. Think of one-dimensional arrays as a single line of values. Arrays you create in VBA can have as many as 60 dimensions — although you rarely need more than two or three dimensions in an array. The following example declares an 81-integer array with two dimensions:

```
Dim MyArray (1 To 9, 1 To 9) As Integer
```

You can think of this array as occupying a 9 x 9 matrix — perfect for storing all numbers in a Sudoku puzzle.

To refer to a specific element in this array, you need to specify two index numbers (similar to its "row" and its "column" in the matrix). The following example shows how you can assign a value to an element in this array:

```
MyArray (3, 4)= 125
```

This statement assigns a value to a single element in the array. If you're thinking of the array in terms of a 9 x 9 matrix, this assigns 125 to the element located in the third row and fourth column of the matrix.

Here's how to declare a three-dimensional array, with 1,000 elements:

```
Dim My3DArray (1 To 10, 1 To 10, 1 To 10) As Integer
```

You can think of a three-dimensional array as a cube. Visualizing an array of more than three dimensions is more difficult.

Dynamic arrays

You can also create *dynamic* arrays. A dynamic array doesn't have a preset number of elements. Declare a dynamic array with an empty set of parentheses:

```
Dim MyArray () As Integer
```

Before you can use this array, you must use the ReDim statement to tell VBA how many elements the array has. Usually, the number of elements in the array is determined while your code is running. You can use the ReDim statement any number of times, changing the array's size as often as needed. The following example demonstrates how to change the number of elements in a dynamic array.

It assumes that the NumElements variable contains a value, which your code calculated.

```
ReDim MyArray (1 To NumElements)
```

WARNING

When you redimension an array by using ReDim, you wipe out any values currently stored in the array elements. You can avoid destroying the old values by using the Preserve keyword. The following example shows how you can preserve an array's values when you redimension the array:

```
ReDim Preserve MyArray (1 To NumElements)
```

If MyArray currently has ten elements, and you execute the preceding statement with NumElements equaling 12, the first ten elements remain intact, and the array has room for two additional elements (up to the number contained in the variable NumElements). If NumElements equals 7 however, the first seven elements are retained but the remaining three elements meet their demise.

The topic of arrays comes up again in Chapter 10, when you explore the concept of looping.

Using Labels

In early versions of BASIC, every line of code required a line number. For example, if you had written a BASIC program in the '70s (dressed, of course, in your bell bottoms), it may have looked something like this:

```
010: LET X=5
020: LET Y=3
030: LET Z=X*Y
040: PRINT Z
050: END
```

REMEMBER

VBA permits the use of such line numbers, and it even permits text labels. You don't typically use a label for each line, but you may occasionally need to use a label. For example, insert a label if you use a GoTo statement (discussed in Chapter 10). A label must begin with the first nonblank character in a line and end with a colon.

Chapter **8**

Working with Range Objects

This chapter digs a bit deeper into Excel's dungeons and takes a closer look at Range objects. Excel is all about cells, and the Range object is a container for cells. Why do you need to know so much about Range objects? Because much of the programming work you do in Excel focuses on Range objects.

A Quick Review

A *Range object* represents a range contained in a Worksheet object. Range objects, like all other objects, have properties (which you can examine and sometimes change) and methods (which perform actions on the object).

A Range object can be as small as a single cell (for example, B4) or as large as every one of the 17,179,869,184 cells in a worksheet (A1:XFD1048576).

When you refer to a Range object, the address is always surrounded by double quotes, like this:

```
Range("A1:C5")
```

If the range consists of one cell, you still need the quotes:

```
Range("K9")
```

If the range happens to have a name (created with Formulas⇨Defined Names⇨Define Name), you can refer to the range by its name (which is also in quotes):

```
Range("PriceList")
```

WARNING

Unless you tell Excel otherwise by qualifying the range reference, it assumes that you're referring to a range on the active worksheet. If anything other than a worksheet is active (such as a chart sheet), the range reference fails, and your macro displays an error message and grinds to a screeching halt.

As shown in the following example, you can refer to a range outside the active sheet by qualifying the range reference with a worksheet name from the active workbook:

```
Worksheets("Sheet1").Range("A1:C5")
```

If you need to refer to a range in a different workbook (that is, any workbook other than the active workbook), you can use a statement like this:

```
Workbooks("Budget.xlsx").Worksheets("Sheet1").Range("A1:C5")
```

A Range object can consist of one or more entire rows or columns. You can refer to an entire row (in this case, row 3) by using syntax like this:

```
Range("3:3")
```

You can refer to an entire column (the fourth column in this example) like this:

```
Range("D:D")
```

In Excel, you select noncontiguous ranges by holding down Ctrl while selecting various ranges with your mouse. Figure 8-1 shows a noncontiguous range selection. You shouldn't be surprised that VBA also allows you to work with noncontiguous ranges. The following expression refers to a two-area noncontiguous range. Notice that a comma separates the two areas.

```
Range("A1:B8,D9:G16")
```

FIGURE 8-1:
A noncontiguous
range selection.

WARNING

Be aware that some methods and properties cause havoc with noncontiguous ranges. You may have to process each area separately by using a loop.

Other Ways to Refer to a Range

The more you work with VBA, the more you realize that it's a fairly well-conceived language and is usually quite logical (despite what you may be thinking right now). Often, VBA provides multiple ways to perform an action. You can choose the most appropriate solution for your problem. This section discusses some of the other ways to refer to a range.

REMEMBER

This chapter barely scratches the surface for the Range object's properties and methods. As you work with VBA, you'll probably need to access other properties and methods. The Help system is the best place to find out about them, but it's also a good idea to record your actions and examine the code Excel generates. You're probably getting tired of hearing that advice by now, but it really is good advice.

The Cells property

Rather than use the VBA Range keyword, you can refer to a range via the Cells property.

TECHNICAL
STUFF

Although Cells may seem like an object (or a collection), it's really not. Rather, Cells is a property that VBA evaluates. VBA then returns an object (more specifically, a Range object). If this seems strange, don't worry. Even Microsoft appears to be confused about this issue. In some earlier versions of Excel, the Cells property was known as the Cells method. Regardless of what it is, just understand that Cells is a handy way to refer to a range.

The Cells property takes two arguments: a row number and a column number. Both of these arguments are numbers, even though you usually refer to columns by using letters. For example, the following expression refers to cell C2 on Sheet2:

```
Worksheets("Sheet2").Cells(2, 3)
```

You can also use the Cells property to refer to a multicell range. The following example demonstrates the syntax you use:

```
Range(Cells(1, 1), Cells(10, 8))
```

This expression refers to an 80-cell range that extends from cell A1 (row 1, column 1) to cell H10 (row 10, column 8).

The following statements both produce the same result; they enter a value of 99 into a 10-by-8 range of cells. More specifically, these statements set the Value property of the Range object:

```
Range("A1:H10").Value = 99
Range(Cells(1, 1), Cells(10, 8)).Value = 99
```

TIP

The advantage of using the Cells property to refer to ranges becomes apparent when you use variables rather than actual numbers as the Cells arguments. And things really start to click when you understand looping, which is in Chapter 10.

The Offset property

The Offset property provides another handy means for referring to ranges. This property, which operates on a Range object and returns another Range object, allows you to refer to a cell that is a particular number of rows and columns away from another cell.

Like the Cells property, the Offset property takes two arguments. The first argument represents the number of rows to offset; the second represents the number of columns to offset.

The following expression refers to a cell one row below cell A1 and two columns to the right of cell A1. In other words, this refers to the cell commonly known as C2:

```
Range("A1").Offset(1, 2)
```

The Offset property can also use negative arguments. A *negative* row offset refers to a row above the range. A negative column offset refers to a column to the left of the range. The following example refers to cell A1:

```
Range("C2").Offset(-1, -2)
```

And as you may expect, you can use 0 as one or both of the arguments for Offset. The following expression refers to cell A1:

```
Range("A1").Offset(0, 0)
```

Here's a statement that inserts the time of day into the cell to the right of the active cell:

```
ActiveCell.Offset(0,1) = Time
```

When you record a macro in relative mode, Excel uses the Offset property quite a bit. Refer to Chapter 6 for an example.

TIP

The Offset property is most useful when you use variables rather than actual values for the arguments. Chapter 10 includes examples that demonstrate this.

Some Useful Range Object Properties

A Range object has dozens of properties. You can write VBA programs nonstop for the next 12 months and never use them all. This section briefly describes some of the most commonly used Range properties. For complete details, consult the Help system in the VBE.

REMEMBER

Some Range properties are *read-only* properties, which means that your code can look at their values but can't change them ("Look, but don't touch"). For example, every Range object has an Address property, which holds the range's address. You can access this read-only property, but you can't change it — which makes perfect sense when you think about it.

By the way, the examples that follow are typically statements rather than complete procedures. If you'd like to try any of these (and you should), create a Sub procedure to do so. Also, many of these statements work properly only if a worksheet is the active sheet.

The Value property

The Value property represents the value contained in a cell. It's a read-write property, so your VBA code can either read or change the value.

The following statement displays a message box that shows the value in cell A1 on Sheet1:

```
MsgBox Worksheets("Sheet1").Range("A1").Value
```

It stands to reason that you can read the Value property only for a single-cell Range object. For example, the following statement generates an error:

```
MsgBox Worksheets("Sheet1").Range("A1:C3").Value
```

You can, however, change the Value property for a range of any size. The following statement enters the number 123 into each cell in a range:

```
Worksheets("Sheet1").Range("A1:C3").Value = 123
```

TIP

Value is the default property for a Range object. In other words, if you omit a property for a Range, Excel uses its Value property. The following statements both enter a value of 75 into cell A1 of the active worksheet:

```
Range("A1").Value = 75
Range("A1") = 75
```

TECHNICAL
STUFF

ASSIGNING THE VALUES IN A MULTICELL RANGE TO A VARIABLE

Even though you can read the Value property only for a single-cell Range object, you can assign the values in a multicell range to a variable, as long as the variable is a variant. That's because a variant can act like an array. Here's an example:

```
Dim x As Variant
x = Range("A1:C3").Value
```

Then you can treat the x variable as though it were an array. This statement, for example, returns the value in cell B1:

```
MsgBox x(1, 2)
```

The Text property

The Text property returns a string that represents the text as it's displayed in a cell — the formatted value. The Text property is read-only. Suppose that cell A1 contains the value 12.3 and is formatted to display two decimals and a dollar sign ($12.30). The following statement displays a message box containing $12.30:

```
MsgBox Worksheets("Sheet1").Range("A1").Text
```

But the next statement displays a message box containing 12.3:

```
MsgBox Worksheets("Sheet1").Range("A1").Value
```

If the cell contains a formula, the Text property returns the result of the formula. If a cell contains text, the Text property and the Value property always return the same thing, because text (unlike a number) can't be formatted to display differently.

The Count property

The Count property returns the number of cells in a range. It counts all cells, not just the nonblank cells. Count is a read-only property, just as you would expect. The following statement accesses a range's Count property and displays the result (9) in a message box:

```
MsgBox Range("A1:C3").Count
```

The Column and Row properties

The Column property returns the column number of a single-cell range. Its sidekick, the Row property, returns the row number of a single-cell range. Both are read-only properties. For example, the following statement displays 6 because cell F3 is in the sixth column:

```
MsgBox Sheets("Sheet1").Range("F3").Column
```

The next expression displays 3 because cell F3 is in the third row:

```
MsgBox Sheets("Sheet1").Range("F3").Row
```

REMEMBER

If the Range object consists of more than one cell, the Column property returns the column number of the first column in the range, and the Row property returns the row number of the first row in the range.

WARNING

Don't confuse the Column and Row properties with the Columns and Rows properties (discussed earlier in this chapter). The Column and Row properties return a single value. The Columns and Rows properties, on the other hand, return a Range object. What a difference an "s" makes.

The Address property

Address, a read-only property, displays the cell address for a Range object as an absolute reference (a dollar sign before the column letter and before the row number). The following statement displays the message box shown in Figure 8-2:

```
MsgBox Range(Cells(1, 1), Cells(5, 5)).Address
```

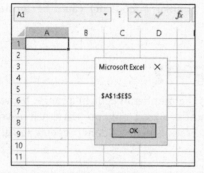

FIGURE 8-2:
This message box
displays the
Address property
of a 5-by-5 range.

The HasFormula property

The HasFormula property (which is read-only) returns True if the single-cell range contains a formula. It returns False if the cell contains something other than a formula (or is empty). If the range consists of more than one cell, VBA returns True only if all cells in the range contain a formula or False if all cells in the range don't have a formula. The property returns Null if the range contains a mixture of formulas and nonformulas. Null is kind of a no-man's land: The answer is neither True nor False, and any cell in the range may or may not have a formula.

WARNING

You need to be careful when you work with properties that can return Null. More specifically, the only data type that can deal with Null is Variant.

For example, assume that cell A1 contains a value and cell A2 contains a formula. The following statements generate an error because the range doesn't consist of all formulas or all nonformulas:

```
Dim FormulaTest As Boolean
FormulaTest = Range("A1:A2").HasFormula
```

The Boolean data type can handle only True or False. Null causes Excel to complain and display an error message. To fix this type of situation, the best thing to do is make sure that the FormulaTest variable is declared as a Variant rather than as a Boolean. The following example uses VBA's handy TypeName function (along with an If-Then-Else construct) to determine the data type of the FormulaTest variable. If the range has a mixture of formulas and nonformulas, the message box displays *Mixed!* Otherwise, it displays *True* or *False*.

```
Sub CheckForFormulas()
    Dim FormulaTest As Variant
    FormulaTest = Range("A1:A2").HasFormula
    If TypeName(FormulaTest) = "Null" Then
        MsgBox "Mixed!"
    Else
        MsgBox FormulaTest
    End If
End Sub
```

See Chapter 10 for more about using the If-Then-Else construct.

The Font property

As noted earlier in this chapter (see "The Cells property"), a property can return an object. The Font property of a Range object is another example of that concept at work. The Font property returns a Font object.

A Font object, as you may expect, has many accessible properties. To change some aspect of a range's font, you must first access the range's Font object and then manipulate the properties of that object. This may be confusing, but perhaps this example will help.

The following statement uses the Font property of the Range object to return a Font object. Then the Bold property of the Font object is set to True. In plain English, this statement makes the cell display in boldface:

```
Range("A1").Font.Bold = True
```

Truth is, you don't really need to know that you're working with a special Font object that's contained in a Range object. As long as you use the proper syntax, it works just fine. Often, recording your actions with the macro recorder tells you everything you need to know about the proper syntax.

See Chapter 6 for more information about recording macros.

The Interior property

Here's yet another example of a property that returns an object. A Range object's Interior property returns an Interior object (strange name, but that's what it's called). This type of object referencing works the same way as the Font property (described in the preceding section).

For example, the following statement changes the Color property of the Interior object contained in the Range object:

```
Range("A1").Interior.Color = 8421504
```

In other words, this statement changes the cell's background to middle gray. What's that? You didn't know that 8421504 is middle gray? For some insights into Excel's wonderful world of color, see the nearby sidebar "A quick-and-dirty color primer."

A QUICK-AND-DIRTY COLOR PRIMER

Before Excel 2007, Microsoft tried to convince us that 56 colors were good enough for a spreadsheet. But things have changed, and we can use more than 16 million colors in a workbook — 16,777,216 colors, to be exact.

Many objects have a Color property, and that property accepts color values that range from 0 to 16777215. Nobody can remember that many color values, so (fortunately) there's an easier way to specify colors: VBA's RGB function. This function takes advantage of the fact that any of these 16 million colors can be represented by various levels of red, green, and blue. The three arguments in the RGB function correspond to the color's red, green, and blue components, and each of these arguments can range from 0 to 255.

Note that $256 \times 256 \times 256 = 16{,}777{,}216$ — which happens to be the number of colors. Don't you just love it when the math works out?

Here's a statement that changes a cell's background color to a random color:

```
Range("A1").Interior.Color = Int(16777216 * Rnd)
```

Following are a few examples that use the RGB function to change a cell's background color:

```
Range("A1").Interior.Color = RGB(0, 0, 0) 'black
Range("A1").Interior.Color = RGB(255, 0, 0) ' pure red
Range("A1").Interior.Color = RGB(0, 0, 255) ' pure blue
Range("A1").Interior.Color = RGB(198, 212, 60) ' ugly green
Range("A1").Interior.Color = RGB(128, 128, 128) ' middle gray
```

What's the exact value of RGB(128, 128, 128)? This statement tells you that it's 8421504:

```
MsgBox RGB(128, 128, 128)
```

If you need to use standard colors, you may prefer to use one of the built-in color constants: vbBlack, vbRed, vbGreen, vbYellow, vbBlue, vbMagenta, vbCyan, or vbWhite. For example, the following statement makes cell A1 yellow:

```
Range("A1").Interior.Color = vbYellow
```

Excel 2007 also introduced *theme colors*. These are the colors that appear when you use color control such as the Fill Color control in the Font group of the Home tab. Try recording a macro while you change colors, and you'll get something like this:

```
Range("A1").Interior.ThemeColor = xlThemeColorAccent4
Range("A1").Interior.TintAndShade = 0.399975585192419
```

Yep, two more color-related properties to deal with. Here, you have a theme color (the basic color, specified as a built-in constant), plus a "tint and shade" value that represents how dark or light the color is. TintAndShade values range from –1.0 to +1.0. Positive values of the TintAndShade property make the color lighter, and negative values make the color darker. When you set a color by using the ThemeColor property, the color changes if you apply a different document theme (by choosing Page Layout ➪ Themes ➪ Themes).

The Formula property

The Formula property represents the formula in a cell. This is a read-write property, so you can access it to either view the formula in a cell or insert a formula into a cell. For example, the following statement enters a SUM formula into cell A13:

```
Range("A13").Formula = "=SUM(A1:A12)"
```

Notice that the formula is a text string and is enclosed in quotation marks. Also notice that the formula begins with an equal sign, as all formulas do.

If the formula itself contains quotation marks, things get a bit tricky. Say that you want to insert this formula by using VBA:

```
=SUM(A1:A12)&" Stores"
```

This formula displays a value followed by the word *Stores*. To make this formula acceptable, you need to replace every quotation mark in the formula with two quotation marks. Otherwise, VBA gets confused and claims that there's a syntax error (because there is!). So here's a statement that enters a formula that contains quotes:

```
Range("A13").Formula = "=SUM(A1:A12)&"" Stores"""
```

By the way, you can access a cell's Formula property even if the cell doesn't have a formula. If a cell has no formula, the Formula property returns the same as its Value property.

If you need to know whether a cell has a formula, use the HasFormula property (discussed earlier in this chapter).

REMEMBER

Be aware that VBA "speaks" U.S. English. This means that to put a formula in a cell, you must use the U.S. syntax. If you use a non-English version of Excel, read up on the FormulaLocal property in the Help system.

The NumberFormat property

The NumberFormat property represents the number format (expressed as a text string) of the Range object. This is a read-write property, so your VBA code can either examine the number format or change it. The following statement changes the number format of column A to a percentage with two decimal places:

```
Columns("A:A").NumberFormat = "0.00%"
```

Follow these steps to see a list of other number formats (better yet, turn on the macro recorder while you do this):

1. **Activate a worksheet.**

2. **Press Ctrl+1 to access the Format Cells dialog box.**

3. **Click the Number tab.**

4. **Select the Custom category to view and apply some additional number format strings.**

Some Useful Range Object Methods

As you know, a VBA method performs an action. A Range object has dozens of methods but, again, you won't need most of these. In this section, you explore some of the most commonly used Range object methods.

The Select method

Use the Select method to select a range of cells. The following statement selects a range in the active worksheet:

```
Range("A1:C12").Select
```

WARNING

Before selecting a range, it's often a good idea to use one additional statement to ensure that the correct worksheet is active. For example, if Sheet1 contains the range you want to select, use the following statements to select the range:

```
Sheets("Sheet1").Activate
Range("A1:C12").Select
```

Contrary to what you may expect, the following statement generates an error if Sheet1 is not already the active sheet. In other words, you must use two statements rather than just one: one to activate the sheet and another to select the range.

```
Sheets("Sheet1").Range("A1:C12").Select
```

TIP

If you use the GoTo method of the Application object to select a range, you can forget about selecting the correct worksheet first. This statement activates Sheet1 and then selects the range:

```
Application.Goto Sheets("Sheet1").Range("A1:C12")
```

The GoTo method is the VBA equivalent of pressing F5 in Excel, which displays the GoTo dialog box.

The Copy and Paste methods

You can perform copy and paste operations in VBA by using the Copy and Paste methods. Note that two different objects come into play. The Copy method is applicable to the Range object, but the Paste method applies to the Worksheet object. It actually makes sense: You copy a range and paste it to a worksheet.

This short macro (courtesy of the macro recorder) copies range A1:A12 and pastes it into the same worksheet, beginning at cell C1:

```
Sub CopyRange()
    Range("A1:A12").Select
    Selection.Copy
    Range("C1").Select
    ActiveSheet.Paste
End Sub
```

TIP

Notice that in the preceding example, the ActiveSheet object is used with the Paste method. This is a special version of the Worksheet object that refers to the currently active worksheet. Also notice that the macro selects the range before copying it. However, you don't have to select a range before doing something with it. In fact, the following procedure accomplishes the same task as the preceding example by using a single statement:

```
Sub CopyRange2()
    Range("A1:A12").Copy Range("C1")
End Sub
```

This procedure takes advantage of the fact that the Copy method can use an argument that corresponds to the destination range for the copy operation. That's something that you can find out by checking with the Help system.

The Clear method

The Clear method deletes the contents of a range, plus all the cell formatting. For example, if you want to zap everything in column D, the following statement does the trick:

```
Columns("D:D").Clear
```

You should be aware of two related methods. The ClearContents method deletes the contents of the range but leaves the formatting intact. The ClearFormats method deletes the formatting in the range but not the cell contents.

The Delete method

Clearing a range differs from deleting a range. When you *delete* a range, Excel shifts the remaining cells around to fill up the range you deleted.

The following example uses the Delete method to delete row 6:

```
Rows("6:6").Delete
```

When you delete a range that's not a complete row or column, Excel needs to know how to shift the cells. (To see how this works, experiment with Home ⇨ Cells ⇨ Delete ⇨ Delete Cells in Excel.)

The following statement deletes a range and then fills the resulting gap by shifting the other cells to the left:

```
Range("C6:C10").Delete xlToLeft
```

The Delete method uses an argument that indicates how Excel should shift the remaining cells. In this case, the built-in constant (xlToLeft) is used for the argument.

» Using the VBA built-in functions

» Using Excel worksheet functions in your VBA code

» Writing custom functions

Chapter **9**

Using VBA and Worksheet Functions

There are three flavors of functions: those built into VBA (vanilla), those built into Excel (strawberry), and other functions written in VBA (chocolate). Previous chapters mention how you can use functions in your VBA expressions, and this chapter provides a full explanation. Functions can make your VBA code perform some powerful feats, with little or no programming effort required. If you like that idea, this chapter's for you.

What Is a Function?

Except for a few people who think Excel is a word processor, all Excel users incorporate worksheet functions in their formulas. The most common worksheet function is the SUM function, and you have more than 500 others at your disposal.

A *function* essentially performs a calculation and returns a single value. The SUM function, of course, returns the sum of a range of values. The same holds true for functions used in your VBA expressions: Each function does its thing and returns a single value.

The functions you use in VBA can come from three sources:

>> Built-in functions provided by VBA

>> Worksheet functions provided by Excel

>> Custom functions that you (or someone else) write, using VBA

The rest of this chapter clarifies the differences.

Using Built-In VBA Functions

VBA provides numerous built-in functions. Some of these functions take arguments, and some do not.

VBA function examples

This section presents a few examples of using VBA functions in code. In many of these examples, the MsgBox function displays a value in a message box. Yes, MsgBox is a VBA function — a rather unusual one, but a function nonetheless. This useful function displays a message in a dialog box and also returns a value. For more details about the MsgBox function, see Chapter 15.

TIP

A workbook that contains all the examples is available at this book's website.

Displaying the system date or time

The first example uses VBA's Date function to display the current system date in a message box:

```
Sub ShowDate()
    MsgBox "Today is: " & Date
End Sub
```

Notice that the Date function doesn't use an argument. Unlike worksheet functions, a VBA function with no argument doesn't require an empty set of parentheses. In fact, if you type an empty set of parentheses, the VBE promptly removes them.

To get the system time, use the Time function. And if you want it all, use the Now function to return both the date and the time.

Finding a string length

The following procedure uses the VBA Len function, which returns the length of a text string. The Len function takes one argument: the string. When you execute this procedure, the message box displays your name, and the number of characters in your name (see Figure 9-1).

```
Sub GetLength()
    Dim MyName As String
    Dim StringLength As Long
    MyName = Application.UserName
    StringLength = Len(MyName)
    MsgBox MyName & " has " & StringLength & " characters."
End Sub
```

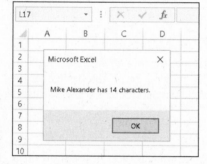

FIGURE 9-1: Calculating the length of your name.

Microsoft Excel

Mike Alexander has 14 characters.

OK

REMEMBER

Excel also has a LEN function, which you can use in your worksheet formulas. The Excel version and the VBA function work the same.

Displaying the name of a month

The following procedure uses the MonthName function, which returns the name of a month. MonthName uses one argument: an integer between 1 and 12.

```
Sub ShowMonthName()
    Dim ThisMonth As Long
    ThisMonth = Month(Date)
    MsgBox MonthName(ThisMonth)
End Sub
```

This procedure uses the Month function to get the current month (as a value), and this value is assigned to the ThisMonth variable. The MonthName function then converts the value to text. So if you run this procedure in April, the message box displays the text April.

Actually, the ThisMonth variable isn't required. You can get the same effect with this expression, which uses three VBA functions:

```
MonthName(Month(Date))
```

Here, the current date is passed as an argument to the Month function, which returns a value that's passed as an argument to the MonthName function.

Determining a file size

The following Sub procedure displays the size, in bytes, of the Excel executable file. It finds this value by using the FileLen function:

```
Sub GetFileSize()
    Dim TheFile As String
    TheFile = "C:\Program Files (x86)\Microsoft Office\root\Office16\EXCEL.EXE"
    MsgBox FileLen(TheFile)
End Sub
```

Notice that this routine *hard-codes* the filename (that is, explicitly states the path). This isn't a good idea. The file may not be on the C drive, or the Excel folder may have a different name. The following statement shows a better approach:

```
TheFile = Application.Path & "\EXCEL.EXE"
```

Path is a property of the Application object. It simply returns the name of the folder in which the application (that is, Excel) is installed (without a trailing backslash).

Identifying the type of a selected object

The following procedure uses the TypeName function, which returns the type of the selection on the worksheet (as a string):

```
Sub ShowSelectionType()
    Dim SelType As String
    SelType = TypeName(Selection)
    MsgBox SelType
End Sub
```

The selection could be a Range, a Picture, a Rectangle, a ChartArea, or any other type of object that can be selected.

TIP

The TypeName function is very versatile. You can also use this function to determine the data type of a variable.

VBA functions that do more than return a value

A few VBA functions go above and beyond the call of duty. Rather than simply return a value, these functions have some useful side effects. Table 9-1 lists them.

TABLE 9-1 **VBA Functions with Useful Side Benefits**

Function	What It Does
MsgBox	Displays a handy dialog box containing a message and buttons. The function returns a code that identifies which button the user clicks. See Chapter 15 for details.
InputBox	Displays a simple dialog box that asks the user for some input. The function returns whatever the user enters in the dialog box. Chapter 15 explores the InputBox function.
Shell	Executes another program. The function returns the *task ID* (a unique identifier) of the other program (or an error if the function can't start the other program).

Discovering VBA functions

How do you find out which functions VBA provides? Good question. The best source is the Excel VBA system. Another way is to type **VBA**, followed by a period. You get a list of items, as shown in Figure 9-2. Those with a green icon are functions. If this feature isn't working, choose VBE's Tools⇨Options, click the Editor tab, and place a check next to Auto List Members.

FIGURE 9-2:
A way to display a list of VBA functions.

There are over 140 different functions available in VBA. Some are so specialized and obscure, you'll never need them. Others, however, are quite useful for many applications. Table 9-2 lists some of the more useful functions.

TABLE 9-2

VBA's Most Useful Built-In Functions

Function	What It Does
Abs	Returns a number's absolute value
Array	Returns a variant containing an array
Choose	Returns a value from a list of items
Chr	Converts an ANSI value to a string
CurDir	Returns the current path
Date	Returns the current system date
DateAdd	Returns a date to which a specified time interval has been added — for example, one month from a particular date
DateDiff	Returns an integer showing the number of specified time intervals between two dates — for example, the number of months between now and your birthday
DatePart	Returns an integer containing the specified part of a given date — for example, a date's day of the year
DateSerial	Converts a date to a serial number
DateValue	Converts a string to a date
Day	Returns the day of the month from a date value
Dir	Returns the name of a file or directory that matches a pattern
Err	Returns the error number of an error condition
Error	Returns the error message that corresponds to an error number
Exp	Returns the base of the natural logarithm (e) raised to a power
FileLen	Returns the number of bytes in a file
Fix	Returns a number's integer portion
Format	Displays an expression in a particular format
GetSetting	Returns a value from the Windows registry
Hour	Returns the hour portion of a time
InputBox	Displays a box to prompt a user for input
InStr	Returns the position of a string within another string (counting from the start)
InStrRev	Returns the position of a string within another string (counting from the end)
Int	Returns the integer portion of a number
IsArray	Returns True if a variable is an array
IsDate	Returns True if an expression is a date

Function	What It Does
IsEmpty	Returns True if a variable has not been initialized
IsError	Returns True if an expression is an error value
IsMissing	Returns True if an optional argument was not passed to a procedure
IsNull	Returns True if an expression contains no valid data
IsNumeric	Returns True if an expression can be evaluated as a number
LBound	Returns the smallest subscript for a dimension of an array
LCase	Returns a string converted to lowercase
Left	Returns a specified number of characters from the left of a string
Len	Returns the number of characters in a string
Mid	Returns a specified number of characters from a string
Minute	Returns the minutes portion of a time value
Month	Returns the month from a date value
MsgBox	Displays a message box and (optionally) returns a value
Now	Returns the current system date and time
Replace	Replaces a substring in a string with another substring
RGB	Returns a numeric RGB value representing a color
Right	Returns a specified number of characters from the right of a string
Rnd	Returns a random number between 0 and 1
Second	Returns the seconds portion of a time value
Shell	Runs an executable program
Space	Returns a string with a specified number of spaces
Split	Splits a string into parts, using a delimiting character
Sqr	Returns a number's square root
String	Returns a repeating character or string
Time	Returns the current system time
Timer	Returns the number of seconds since midnight
TimeSerial	Returns the time for a specified hour, minute, and second
TimeValue	Converts a string to a time serial number

(continued)

TABLE 9-2 *(continued)*

Function	What It Does
Trim	Returns a string without leading or trailing spaces
TypeName	Returns a string that describes a variable's data type
UBound	Returns the largest available subscript for an array's dimension
UCase	Converts a string to uppercase
Val	Returns the numbers contained in a string
Weekday	Returns a number representing a day of the week
Year	Returns the year from a date value

For complete details on a particular function, type the function name in a VBA module, move the cursor anywhere in the text, and press F1.

TIP

Using Worksheet Functions in VBA

Although VBA offers a decent assortment of built-in functions, you might not always find exactly what you need. Fortunately, you can also use most of Excel's worksheet functions in your VBA procedures. The only worksheet functions that you can't use are those that have an equivalent VBA function. For example, you can't use Excel's RAND function (which generates a random number) because VBA has an equivalent function: Rnd.

VBA makes Excel's worksheet functions available through the WorksheetFunction object, which is contained in the Application object. Here's an example of how you can use Excel's SUM function in a VBA statement:

```
Total = Application.WorksheetFunction.SUM(Range("A1:A12"))
```

You can omit either the Application part or the WorksheetFunction part of the expression. In either case, VBA figures out what you're doing. In other words, these three expressions all work exactly the same:

TIP

```
Total = Application.WorksheetFunction.SUM(Range("A1:A12"))
Total = WorksheetFunction.SUM(Range("A1:A12"))
Total = Application.SUM(Range("A1:A12"))
```

Worksheet function examples

Many of Excel's worksheet functions can be used in your VBA expressions. Think of worksheet functions as plug-ins you can use to extend the utility of your own procedures. In this section, you discover how to incorporate Excel worksheet functions into your VBA code.

Finding the maximum value in a range

Here's an example that shows how to use Excel's MAX worksheet function in a VBA procedure. This procedure displays the maximum value in column A of the active worksheet (see Figure 9-3):

```
Sub ShowMax()
    Dim TheMax As Double
    TheMax = WorksheetFunction.MAX(Range("A:A"))
    MsgBox TheMax
End Sub
```

FIGURE 9-3:
Using a worksheet function in your VBA code.

You can use the MIN function to get the smallest value in a range. And as you might expect, you can use other worksheet functions in a similar manner. For example, you can use the LARGE function to determine the kth-largest value in a range. The following expression demonstrates this:

```
SecondHighest = WorksheetFunction.LARGE(Range("A:A"),2)
```

Notice that the LARGE function uses two arguments. The second argument represents the kth part — 2, in this case (the second-largest value).

Calculating a mortgage payment

The next example uses the PMT worksheet function to calculate a mortgage payment. This procedure uses three variables to store the data that's passed to the PMT function as arguments. A message box displays the calculated payment.

```
Sub PmtCalc()
    Dim IntRate As Double
    Dim LoanAmt As Double
    Dim Periods As Long
    IntRate = 0.0625 / 12
    Periods = 30 * 12
    LoanAmt = 150000
    MsgBox WorksheetFunction.PMT(IntRate, Periods, -LoanAmt)
End Sub
```

As the following statement shows, you can also insert the values directly as the function arguments:

```
MsgBox WorksheetFunction.PMT(0.0625 /12, 360, -150000)
```

However, using variables to store the parameters makes the code easier to read and modify, if necessary.

Using a lookup function

The following example uses VBA's InputBox and MsgBox functions, plus Excel's VLOOKUP function. It prompts for a part number and then gets the price from a lookup table. In Figure 9-4, range A1:B13 is named PriceList.

```
Sub GetPrice()
    Dim PartNum As Variant
    Dim Price As Double
    PartNum = InputBox("Enter the Part Number")
    Sheets("Prices").Activate
    Price = WorksheetFunction.VLOOKUP(PartNum, Range("PriceList"), 2, False)
    MsgBox PartNum & " costs " & Price
End Sub
```

You can download this workbook from the book's website.

FIGURE 9-4:
The range, named PriceList, contains prices for parts.

Here's how the GetPrice procedure works:

1. VBA's InputBox function asks the user for a part number.

2. The part number the user enters is assigned to the PartNum variable.

3. The next statement activates the Prices worksheet, just in case it's not already the active sheet.

4. The code uses the VLOOKUP function to find the part number in the table.

Notice that the arguments you use in this statement are the same as those you would use with the function in a worksheet formula. This statement assigns the result of the function to the Price variable.

5. The code displays the price for the part via the MsgBox function.

This procedure doesn't have any error handling, and it fails miserably if you enter a nonexistent part number. (Try it.) If this were an actual application that's used in an actual business, you would want to add some statements that deal with errors more gracefully. Chapter 12 discusses error handling.

Entering worksheet functions

You can't use the Excel Paste Function dialog box to insert a worksheet function into a VBA module. Instead, enter such functions the old-fashioned way: by hand. However, you *can* use the Paste Function dialog box to identify the function you want to use and find out about its arguments.

TIP

You can also take advantage of the VBE's Auto List Members option, which displays a drop-down list of all worksheet functions. Just type **Application.WorksheetFunction**, followed by a period. Then you see a list of the functions you can use, as shown in Figure 9-5. If this feature isn't working, choose the VBE's Tools⇨Options, click the Editor tab, and place a check next to Auto List Members.

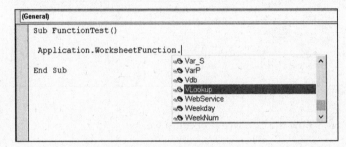

FIGURE 9-5:
Getting a list of worksheet functions that you can use in your VBA code.

More about using worksheet functions

Newcomers to VBA often confuse VBA's built-in functions and Excel's workbook functions. A good rule to remember is that VBA doesn't try to reinvent the wheel. For the most part, VBA doesn't duplicate Excel worksheet functions.

For most worksheet functions that are unavailable as methods of the Worksheet-Function object, you can use an equivalent VBA built-in operator or function. For example, the MOD worksheet function is not available in the WorksheetFunction object because VBA has an equivalent: its built-in Mod operator.

TIP

Bottom line? If you need to use a function, first determine whether VBA has something that meets your needs. If not, check out the worksheet functions. If all else fails, you may be able to write a custom function by using VBA.

Using Custom Functions

After you know how to handle VBA functions and Excel worksheet functions, you can dive into the third category of functions you can use in your VBA procedures: custom functions. A *custom function* (also known as a User Defined Function, or UDF) is one you develop yourself by using (what else?) VBA. To use a custom function, you must define it in the workbook in which you use it — or else define the functions in an add-in (see Chapter 21).

Here's an example of defining a simple Function procedure (MultiplyTwo) and then using it in a VBA Sub procedure (ShowResult):

```
Function MultiplyTwo(num1, num2) As Double
    MultiplyTwo = num1 * num2
End Function

Sub ShowResult()
    Dim n1 As Double, n2 As Double
    Dim Result As Double
    n1 = 123
    n2 = 544
    Result = MultiplyTwo(n1, n2)
    MsgBox Result
End Sub
```

The custom function MultiplyTwo has two arguments. The ShowResult Sub procedure uses this Function procedure by passing two arguments to it (in parentheses). The ShowResult procedure then displays a message box showing the value returned by the MultiplyTwo function.

Of course, most custom functions aren't as trivial as the MultiplyTwo function. But this example should give you an idea of how a Sub procedure can make use of a custom function.

You can also use custom functions in your worksheet formulas. For example, if MultiplyTwo is defined in your workbook, you can write a formula such as this one:

```
=MultiplyTwo(A1,A2)
```

This formula returns the product of the values in cells A1 and A2.

Creating custom worksheet functions is an important (and very useful) topic. So important (and useful) that Chapter 20 includes examples that are actually useful.

Chapter **10**

Controlling Program Flow and Making Decisions

S ome VBA procedures start at the code's beginning and progress line by line to the end, never deviating from this top-to-bottom program flow. Macros that you record always work like this. In many cases, however, you need to control the flow of your code by skipping some statements, executing some statements multiple times, and testing conditions to determine what the procedure does next. Hang on to your hat and enjoy the ride, because you're about to discover the essence of programming.

Going with the Flow, Dude

Some programming newbies can't understand how a dumb computer can make intelligent decisions. The secret is in several programming constructs that most programming languages support. Table 10-1 provides a sneak preview of these constructs. (These are explained later in this chapter.)

TABLE 10-1

Programming Constructs for Making Decisions

Construct	How It Works
GoTo statement	Jumps to a particular statement
If-Then structure	Does something if something else is true
Select Case	Does any of several things, depending on something's value
For-Next loop	Executes a series of statements a specified number of times
Do-While loop	Does something as long as something else remains true
Do-Until loop	Does something until something else becomes true

The GoTo Statement

A GoTo statement offers the most straightforward means for changing a program's flow. The GoTo statement simply transfers program execution to a new statement, which is preceded by a label.

Your VBA procedures can contain as many labels as you like. A *label* is just a text string followed by a colon.

The following procedure shows how a GoTo statement works:

```
Sub CheckUser()
    UserName = InputBox("Enter Your Name: ")
    If UserName <> "Satya Nadella" Then GoTo WrongName
    MsgBox ("Welcome Satya...")
'       ...[More code here] ...
    Exit Sub
WrongName:
    MsgBox "Sorry. Only Satya Nadella can run this."
End Sub
```

The procedure uses the InputBox function to get the user's name. Then a decision is made: If the user enters a name other than Satya Nadella, the program flow jumps to the WrongName label, displays an apologetic message, and the procedure ends. On the other hand, if Mr. Nadella runs this macro and uses his real name, the procedure displays a welcome message and then executes some additional code (not shown in the example).

Notice that the Exit Sub statement ends the procedure before the second MsgBox function has a chance to work. Without that Exit Sub statement, both MsgBox statements would be executed.

WHAT IS STRUCTURED PROGRAMMING? DOES IT MATTER?

If you hang around with programmers, sooner or later you hear the term *structured programming*. This term has been around for decades, and programmers generally agree that structured programs are superior to unstructured programs. So what is structured programming? And can you do that using VBA?

The basic premise of structured programming is that a procedure or code segment should have only one entry point and one exit point. In other words, a block of code should be a stand-alone unit. A program cannot jump into the middle of this unit; neither can it exit at any point except the single exit point. When you write structured code, your program progresses in an orderly manner and is easy to follow — unlike a program that jumps around in a haphazard fashion. This pretty much rules out using the GoTo statement.

In general, a structured program is easier to read and understand. More important, it's also easier to modify when the need arises.

VBA is indeed a structured language. It offers standard structured constructs such as If-Then-Else, For-Next loops, Do-Until loops, Do-While loops, and Select Case structures. Furthermore, it fully supports module code constructions. If you're new to programming, you should try to develop good structure-programming habits early on. End of lecture.

This simple procedure works, but VBA provides several better (and more structured) alternatives than GoTo. In general, you should use GoTo only when you have no other way to perform an action. In real life, the only time you *must* use a GoTo statement is for trapping errors. (You get a detailed review of error handling in Chapter 12.)

By the way, the CheckUser procedure simply demonstrates the GoTo statement. It's not intended to demonstrate an effective security technique!

WARNING

Many hard-core programming types have a deep-seated hatred for GoTo statements because using them tends to result in difficult-to-read (and difficult-to-maintain) "spaghetti code." Therefore, you should never admit that you use GoTo statements when talking with other programmers.

Decisions, Decisions

As in many other aspects of life, effective decision-making is the key to success in writing Excel macros. This section reviews two programming structures that can empower your VBA procedures with some impressive decision-making capabilities: If-Then and Select Case.

The If-Then structure

The If-Then structure is VBA's most important control structure. You'll probably use this command on a daily basis.

Use the If-Then structure when you want to execute one or more statements conditionally. The optional Else clause, if included, lets you execute one or more statements if the condition you're testing is *not* true. Here's the simple CheckUser procedure presented earlier in this chapter, recoded to use the If-Then-Else structure:

```
Sub CheckUser2()
    UserName = InputBox("Enter Your Name: ")
    If UserName = "Satya Nadella" Then
        MsgBox ("Welcome Satya...")
        ...[More code here] ...
    Else
        MsgBox "Sorry. Only Satya Nadella can run this."
    End If
End Sub
```

You would probably agree that this version is much easier to follow.

TIP

A workbook that contains this section's examples can be downloaded from this book's website.

If-Then examples

The following procedure demonstrates the If-Then structure without the optional Else clause:

```
Sub GreetMe()
    If Time < 0.5 Then MsgBox "Good Morning"
End Sub
```

The GreetMe procedure uses VBA's Time function to get the system time. If the current time is less than .5 (in other words, before noon), the procedure displays a friendly greeting. If Time is greater than or equal to .5, the procedure ends, and nothing happens.

To display a different greeting if Time is greater than or equal to .5, you can add another If-Then statement after the first one:

```
Sub GreetMe2()
    If Time < 0.5 Then MsgBox "Good Morning"
    If Time >= 0.5 Then MsgBox "Good Afternoon"
End Sub
```

Notice that the second If-Then statement uses >= (greater than or equal to). This ensures that the entire day is covered. Had it used > (greater than), no message would appear if this procedure were executed at precisely 12:00 noon. That's pretty unlikely, but with an important program like this, you don't want to take any chances.

An If-Then-Else example

Another approach to the preceding problem uses the Else clause. Here's the same procedure recoded to use the If-Then-Else structure:

```
Sub GreetMe3()
    If Time < 0.5 Then MsgBox "Good Morning" Else _
        MsgBox "Good Afternoon"
End Sub
```

Notice the line continuation character (underscore) in the preceding example. The If-Then-Else statement is actually a single statement. VBA provides a slightly different way of coding If-Then-Else constructs that use an End If statement. Therefore, the GreetMe procedure can be rewritten as

```
Sub GreetMe4()
    If Time < 0.5 Then
        MsgBox "Good Morning"
    Else
        MsgBox "Good Afternoon"
    End If
End Sub
```

In fact, you can insert any number of statements under the If part and any number of statements under the Else part. This syntax is easier to read and makes the statements shorter.

What if you need to expand the GreetMe procedure to handle three conditions: morning, afternoon, and evening? You have two options: Use three If-Then statements or use a *nested* If-Then-Else structure. *Nesting* means placing an If-Then-Else structure within another If-Then-Else structure. The first approach, using three If-Then statements, is simpler:

```
Sub GreetMe5()
    Dim Msg As String
    If Time < 0.5 Then Msg = "Morning"
    If Time >= 0.5 And Time < 0.75 Then Msg = "Afternoon"
    If Time >= 0.75 Then Msg = "Evening"
    MsgBox "Good " & Msg
End Sub
```

Now, you can get fancy by using a variable. The Msg variable gets a different text value, depending on the time of day. The MsgBox statement displays the greeting: Good Morning, Good Afternoon, or Good Evening.

The following procedure performs the same action but uses an If-Then-End If structure:

```
Sub GreetMe6()
    Dim Msg As String
    If Time < 0.5 Then
        Msg = "Morning"
    End If
    If Time >= 0.5 And Time < 0.75 Then
        Msg = "Afternoon"
    End If
    If Time >= 0.75 Then
        Msg = "Evening"
    End If
    MsgBox "Good " & Msg
End Sub
```

Using ElseIf

In the previous examples, every statement in the procedure is executed — even in the morning. A slightly more efficient structure would exit the procedure as soon as a condition is found to be true. In the morning, for example, the procedure should display the Good Morning message and then exit — without evaluating the other superfluous conditions.

With a tiny procedure like this, you don't have to worry about execution speed. But for larger applications in which speed is critical, you should know about another syntax for the If-Then structure: ElseIf.

Here's how you can rewrite the GreetMe procedure by using this syntax:

```
Sub GreetMe7()
    Dim Msg As String
    If Time < 0.5 Then
        Msg = "Morning"
    ElseIf Time >= 0.5 And Time < 0.75 Then
        Msg = "Afternoon"
    Else
        Msg = "Evening"
    End If
    MsgBox "Good " & Msg
End Sub
```

When a condition is true, VBA executes the conditional statements, and the If structure ends. In other words, VBA doesn't waste time evaluating the extraneous conditions, which makes this procedure a bit more efficient than the previous examples. The trade-off (there are always trade-offs) is that the code is more difficult to understand. (Of course, you already knew that.)

Another If-Then example

Here's another example that uses the simple form of the If-Then structure. This procedure prompts the user for a quantity and then displays the appropriate discount, based on the quantity the user enters:

```
Sub ShowDiscount()
    Dim Quantity As Long
    Dim Discount As Double
    Quantity = InputBox("Enter Quantity:")
    If Quantity > 0 Then Discount = 0.1
    If Quantity >= 25 Then Discount = 0.15
    If Quantity >= 50 Then Discount = 0.2
    If Quantity >= 75 Then Discount = 0.25
    MsgBox "Discount: " & Discount
End Sub
```

Notice that each If-Then statement in this procedure is executed, and the value for Discount can change as the statements are executed. However, the procedure ultimately displays the correct value for Discount because the If-Then statements are in order of ascending Discount values.

The following procedure performs the same tasks by using the alternative ElseIf syntax. In this case, the procedure ends immediately after executing the statements for a true condition:

```
Sub ShowDiscount2()
    Dim Quantity As Long
    Dim Discount As Double
    Quantity = InputBox("Enter Quantity: ")
    If Quantity > 0 And Quantity < 25 Then
        Discount = 0.1
    ElseIf Quantity >= 25 And Quantity < 50 Then
        Discount = 0.15
    ElseIf Quantity >= 50 And Quantity < 75 Then
        Discount = 0.2
    ElseIf Quantity >= 75 Then
        Discount = 0.25
    End If
    MsgBox "Discount: " & Discount
End Sub
```

As important as the If-Then structure is to VBA, they become cumbersome when a decision involves three or more choices. Fortunately, the Select Case structure, discussed in the next section, offers a simpler and more efficient approach.

The Select Case structure

The Select Case structure is useful for decisions involving three or more options (although it also works with two options, providing an alternative to the If-Then-Else structure).

TIP

The examples in this section are available at this book's website.

A Select Case example

The following example shows how to use the Select Case structure. This also shows another way to code the examples presented in the previous section:

```
Sub ShowDiscount3()
    Dim Quantity As Long
    Dim Discount As Double
    Quantity = InputBox("Enter Quantity: ")
    Select Case Quantity
        Case 0 To 24
            Discount = 0.1
```

```
        Case 25 To 49
            Discount = 0.15
        Case 50 To 74
            Discount = 0.2
        Case Is >= 75
            Discount = 0.25
    End Select
    MsgBox "Discount: " & Discount
End Sub
```

In this example, the Quantity variable is being evaluated. The procedure checks for four different cases (0–24, 25–49, 50–74, and 75 or greater).

Any number of statements can follow each Case statement, and they all are executed if the case is true. If you use only one statement, as in this example, you can put the statement on the same line as the Case keyword, preceded by a colon — the VBA statement separator character. This tends to make your code more compact and a bit clearer. Here's how the procedure looks in this format:

```
Sub ShowDiscount4 ()
    Dim Quantity As Long
    Dim Discount As Double
    Quantity = InputBox("Enter Quantity: ")
    Select Case Quantity
        Case 0 To 24: Discount = 0.1
        Case 25 To 49: Discount = 0.15
        Case 50 To 74: Discount = 0.2
        Case Is >= 75: Discount = 0.25
    End Select
    MsgBox "Discount: " & Discount
End Sub
```

When VBA executes a Select Case structure, the structure is exited as soon as VBA finds a true case and executes the statements for that case.

A nested Select Case example

As demonstrated in the following example, you can nest Select Case structures. This procedure examines the active cell and displays a message describing the cell's contents. Notice that the procedure has three Select Case structures, and each has its own End Select statement:

```
Sub CheckCell()
    Dim Msg As String
    Select Case IsEmpty(ActiveCell)
```

```
        Case True
            Msg = "is blank."
        Case Else
            Select Case ActiveCell.HasFormula
        Case True
            Msg = "has a formula"
        Case Else
            Select Case IsNumeric(ActiveCell)
                Case True
                    Msg = "has a number"
                Case Else
                    Msg = "has text"
            End Select
        End Select
    End Select
    MsgBox "Cell " & ActiveCell.Address & " " & Msg
End Sub
```

The logic goes something like this:

1. Find out whether the cell is empty.

2. If it's not empty, see whether it contains a formula.

3. If there's no formula, find out whether it contains a numeric value or text.

When the procedure ends, the Msg variable contains a string that describes the cell's contents. As shown in Figure 10-1, the MsgBox function displays that message.

You can nest Select Case structures as deeply as you need to, but make sure that each Select Case statement has a corresponding End Select statement.

FIGURE 10-1: A message displayed by the CheckCell procedure.

TIP

If you're still not convinced that indenting code is worth the effort, the previous listing serves as a good example. The indentations really make the nesting levels clear. Take a look at the same procedure without any indentation:

```vba
Sub CheckCell()
Dim Msg As String
Select Case IsEmpty(ActiveCell)
Case True
Msg = "is blank."
Case Else
Select Case ActiveCell.HasFormula
Case True
Msg = "has a formula"
Case Else
Select Case IsNumeric(ActiveCell)
Case True
Msg = "has a number"
Case Else
Msg = "has text"
End Select
End Select
End Select
MsgBox "Cell " & ActiveCell.Address & " " & Msg
End Sub
```

Fairly incomprehensible, eh?

Knocking Your Code for a Loop

The term *looping* refers to repeating a block of VBA statements numerous times. Why use loops? Your code can . . .

>> Loop through a range of cells, working with each cell individually.

>> Loop through all open workbooks (the Workbooks collection) and do something with each one.

>> Loop through all worksheets in a workbook (the Worksheets collection) and do something with each one.

>> Loop through all the elements in an array.

>> Loop through all characters in a cell.

>> Loop through all charts on a worksheet (the ChartObjects collection) and do something with each chart.

VBA supports several types of loops, and the examples that follow demonstrate a few ways that you can use them.

For-Next loops

The examples in this section are all available at this book's website.

The simplest type of loop is a For-Next loop. The looping is controlled by a counter variable, which starts at one value and stops at another value. The statements between the For statement and the Next statement are the statements that get repeated in the loop. To see how this works, keep reading.

A For-Next example

The following example uses a For-Next loop to sum the first 1,000 positive numbers. The Total variable starts out as zero. Then the looping occurs. The variable Cnt is the loop counter. It starts out as 1 and is incremented by 1 each time through the loop. The loop ends when Cnt is 1,000.

This example has only one statement inside the loop. This statement adds the value of Cnt to the Total variable. When the loop finishes, a MsgBox displays the sum of the numbers.

```
Sub AddNumbers()
    Dim Total As Double
    Dim Cnt As Long
    Total = 0
    For Cnt = 1 To 1000
        Total = Total + Cnt
    Next Cnt
    MsgBox Total
End Sub
```

Because the loop counter is a normal variable, you can write code to change its value within the block of code between the For and the Next statements. This, however, is a *very bad* practice. Changing the counter within the loop can have unpredictable results. Take special precautions to ensure that your code doesn't change the value of the loop counter.

For-Next examples with a Step

You can use a Step value to skip some counter values in a For-Next loop. Here's the previous example, rewritten to sum only the odd numbers between 1 and 1,000:

```
Sub AddOddNumbers()
    Dim Total As Double
    Dim Cnt As Long
    Total = 0
    For Cnt = 1 To 1000 Step 2
        Total = Total + Cnt
    Next Cnt
    MsgBox Total
End Sub
```

This time, Cnt starts out as 1 and then takes on values of 3, 5, 7, and so on. The Step value determines how the counter is incremented. Notice that the upper loop value (1000) is not actually used because the highest value of Cnt will be 999.

Here's another example that uses a Step value of 3. This procedure works with the active sheet and applies light gray shading to every third row, from row 1 to row 100.

```
Sub ShadeEveryThirdRow()
    Dim i As Long
    For i = 1 To 100 Step 3
        Rows(i).Interior.Color = RGB(200, 200, 200)
    Next i
End Sub
```

Figure 10-2 shows the result of running this macro.

	A	B	C	D	E	F	G
1	403	283	763	531	685	54	39
2	356	382	464	85	424	574	957
3	784	107	121	365	312	802	741
4	903	451	932	411	247	538	261
5	985	506	435	268	141	1	68
6	26	799	615	774	506	967	233
7	881	698	495	667	540	288	817
8	956	152	624	87	435	449	123
9	313	901	337	659	18	246	369
10	973	373	513	112	412	363	148
11	63	382	614	333	950	908	776
12	777	238	453	577	902	127	277
13	991	981	558	720	387	538	116

FIGURE 10-2:
Using a loop to apply background shading to rows.

A For-Next example with an Exit For statement

A For-Next loop can also include one or more Exit For statements within the loop. When VBA encounters this statement, the loop terminates immediately.

The following example, available on the book's website, demonstrates the Exit For statement. This procedure is a Function procedure, intended to be used in a worksheet formula. The function accepts one argument (a variable named Str) and returns the characters to the left of the first numeric digit. For example, if the argument is "KBR98Z," the function returns "KBR."

```
Function TextPart(Str)
    Dim i As Long
    TextPart = ""
    For i = 1 To Len(Str)
        If IsNumeric(Mid(Str, i, 1)) Then
            Exit For
        Else
            TextPart = TextPart & Mid(Str, i, 1)
        End If
    Next i
End Function
```

The For-Next loop starts with 1 and ends with the number that represents the number of characters in the string. The code uses VBA's Mid function to extract a single character within the loop. If a numeric character is found, the Exit For statement is executed, and the loop ends prematurely. If the character is not numeric, it's appended to the returned value (which is the same as the function's name). The only time the loop will examine every character is if the string passed as the argument contains no numeric characters.

Now, you might shout, "Hey, but you said something about always using a single point of exit!" Well, you're right, and obviously, you're getting the hang of this structured programming business. But in some cases, ignoring that rule is a wise decision. In this example, it greatly speeds up your code because there's no reason to continue the loop after the first numeric digit is found.

A nested For-Next example

So far, all this chapter's examples use relatively simple loops. However, you can have any number of statements in the loop and nest For-Next loops inside other For-Next loops.

The following example uses a nested For-Next loop to insert random numbers into a 12-row-by-5-column range of cells, as shown in Figure 10-3. Notice that the procedure executes the *inner loop* (the loop with the Row counter) once for

each iteration of the *outer loop* (the loop with the Col counter). In other words, the procedure executes the Cells(Row, Col) = Rnd statement 60 times.

```
Sub FillRange()
    Dim Col As Long
    Dim Row As Long
    For Col = 1 To 5
        For Row = 1 To 12
            Cells(Row, Col) = Rnd
        Next Row
    Next Col
End Sub
```

	A	B	C	D	E
1	0.102288187	0.886362731	0.239746511	0.971460521	0.258689821
2	0.414246917	0.903576016	0.470133662	0.124356866	0.772190452
3	0.47391516	0.231269658	0.401469767	0.640704453	0.918639243
4	0.74577713	0.547688246	0.177468777	0.604051828	0.855940819
5	0.265091121	0.387433946	0.826949775	0.864339292	0.601592243
6	0.639949441	0.438692451	0.883572698	0.569988132	0.629469514
7	0.904473603	0.760930121	0.886006176	0.181007922	0.938843071
8	0.381103754	0.803677559	0.799299002	0.601549625	0.269206285
9	0.82810539	0.334553897	0.985140741	0.266621292	0.190164983
10	0.793924212	0.702068925	0.587954879	0.428815961	0.62864387
11	0.163496554	0.906591713	0.485994399	0.657502949	0.896642268
12	0.691193104	0.809319735	0.109930038	0.263128996	0.7798419

FIGURE 10-3: These cells were filled using a nested For-Next loop.

The next example uses nested For-Next loops to initialize a three-dimensional array with the value 100. This procedure executes the statement in the middle of all the loops (the assignment statement) 1,000 times (10 * 10 * 10), each time with a different combination of values for i, j, and k:

```
Sub NestedLoops()
    Dim MyArray(10, 10, 10)
    Dim i As Long
    Dim j As Long
    Dim k As Long
    For i = 1 To 10
        For j = 1 To 10
            For k = 1 To 10
                MyArray(i, j, k) = 100
            Next k
        Next j
    Next i
    ' Other statements go here
End Sub
```

Refer to Chapter 7 for information about arrays.

Here's a final example that uses nested For-Next loops, with a Step value. This procedure creates a checkerboard (or chessboard, if you prefer) by changing the background color of alternating cells (see Figure 10-4).

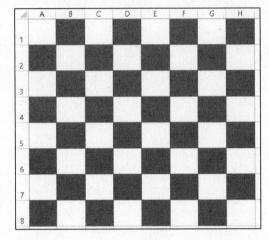

FIGURE 10-4:
Using loops to
create a
checkerboard
pattern.

The Row counter loops from 1 to 8. An If-Then construct determines which nested For-Next structure to use. For odd-numbered rows, the Col counter begins with 2. For even-numbered rows, the Col counter begins with 1. Both loops use a Step value of 2, so alternate cells are affected. Two additional statements make the cells square (just like a real checkerboard).

```
Sub MakeCheckerboard()
    Dim R As Long, C As Long
    For R = 1 To 8
        If WorksheetFunction.IsOdd(R) Then
            For C = 2 To 8 Step 2
                Cells(R, C).Interior.Color = 255
            Next C
        Else
            For C = 1 To 8 Step 2
                Cells(R, C).Interior.Color = 255
            Next C
        End If
    Next R
    Rows("1:8").RowHeight = 35
    Columns("A:H").ColumnWidth = 6.5
End Sub
```

Do-While loop

VBA supports another type of looping structure known as a Do-While loop. Unlike a For-Next loop, a Do-While loop continues until a specified condition is met.

The following example uses a Do-While loop. This procedure uses the active cell as a starting point and then travels down the column, multiplying each cell's value by 2. The loop continues until the procedure encounters an empty cell.

```
Sub DoWhileDemo()
    Do While ActiveCell.Value <> Empty
        ActiveCell.Value = ActiveCell.Value * 2
        ActiveCell.Offset(1, 0).Select
    Loop
End Sub
```

Do-Until loop

The Do-Until loop structure is similar to the Do-While structure. The two structures differ in their handling of the tested condition. A program continues to execute a Do-While loop *while* the condition remains true. In a Do-Until loop, the program executes the loop *until* the condition is true.

The following example is the same one presented for the Do-While loop but recoded to use a Do-Until loop:

```
Sub DoUntilDemo()
    Do Until IsEmpty(ActiveCell.Value)
        ActiveCell.Value = ActiveCell.Value * 2
        ActiveCell.Offset(1, 0).Select
    Loop
End Sub
```

Using For Each-Next Loops with Collections

VBA supports yet another type of looping: looping through each object in a collection of objects. A collection, as you may know, consists of a number of objects of the same type. For example, Excel has a collection of all open workbooks (the Workbooks collection), and each workbook has a collection of worksheets (the Worksheets collection).

The examples in this section are all available at this book's website.

When you need to loop through each object in a collection, use the For Each-Next structure. The following example loops through each worksheet in the active workbook and deletes the worksheet if it's empty:

```
Sub DeleteEmptySheets()
    Dim WkSht As Worksheet
    Application.DisplayAlerts = False
    For Each WkSht In ActiveWorkbook.Worksheets
        If WorksheetFunction.CountA(WkSht.Cells) = 0 Then
            WkSht.Delete
        End If
    Next WkSht
    Application.DisplayAlerts = True
End Sub
```

In this example, the variable WkSht is an object variable that represents each worksheet in the workbook. Nothing is special about the variable name WkSht; you can use any variable name that you like.

The code loops through each worksheet and determines an empty sheet by counting the nonblank cells. If that count is zero, the sheet is empty, and it's deleted. Notice that the DisplayAlerts setting is turned off while the loop is doing its thing. Without that statement, Excel displays a warning every time a sheet is about to be deleted.

If all the worksheets in the workbook are empty, you get an error when Excel attempts to delete the only sheet. Normally, you would write code to handle that situation.

Here's another For Each-Next example. This procedure uses a loop to hide all worksheets in the active workbook except the active sheet.

```
Sub HideSheets()
    Dim Sht As Worksheet
    For Each Sht In ActiveWorkbook.Worksheets
        If Sht.Name <> ActiveSheet.Name Then
            Sht.Visible = xlSheetHidden
        End If
    Next Sht
End Sub
```

The HideSheets procedure checks the sheet name. If it's not the same as the active sheet's name, the sheet is hidden. Notice that the Visible property isn't Boolean. This property can actually take on any of *three* values, and Excel provides three built-in constants. If you're curious about the third possibility (xlVeryHidden), check the Help system.

What gets hidden must eventually get unhidden, so here's a macro that unhides all worksheets in the active workbook:

```
Sub UnhideSheets()
    Dim Sht As Worksheet
    For Each Sht In ActiveWorkbook.Worksheets
        Sht.Visible = xlSheetVisible
    Next Sht
End Sub
```

Not surprisingly, you can create nested For Each–Next loops. The CountBold procedure loops through every cell in the used range on each worksheet in every open workbook and displays a count of the number of cells that are formatted as bold:

```
Sub CountBold()
    Dim WBook As Workbook
    Dim WSheet As Worksheet
    Dim Cell As Range
    Dim Cnt As Long
    For Each WBook In Workbooks
        For Each WSheet In WBook.Worksheets
            For Each Cell In WSheet.UsedRange
                If Cell.Font.Bold = True Then Cnt = Cnt + 1
            Next Cell
        Next WSheet
    Next WBook
    MsgBox Cnt & " bold cells found"
End Sub
```

Chapter **11**

Automatic Procedures and Events

You have a number of ways to execute a VBA Sub procedure. One way is to arrange for the Sub to be executed automatically. In this chapter, you explore the ins and outs of this potentially useful feature, explaining how to set things up so that a macro is executed automatically when a particular event occurs. (No, this chapter is not about capital punishment.)

Preparing for the Big Event

An *event* is basically something that happens Excel. Following are a few examples of the types of events that Excel can recognize:

>> A workbook is opened or closed.

>> A window is activated or deactivated.

>> A worksheet is activated or deactivated.

>> Data is entered into a cell or the cell is edited.

- » A workbook is saved.

- » An object, such as a button, is clicked.

- » A particular key or key combination is pressed.

- » A particular time of day occurs.

- » An error occurs.

Dozens of different types of events are associated with all kinds of Excel objects, such as workbooks, worksheets, pivotTables, and even charts. To simplify things, you can use two other more common types of events: workbook events and worksheet events.

Table 11-1 lists some useful workbook-related events. If, for some reason, you need to see the complete list of workbook-related events, check out the Help system.

TABLE 11-1

Workbook Events

Event	When It's Triggered
Activate	The workbook is activated.
BeforeClose	The command to close the workbook is given.
BeforePrint	The command to print is given.
BeforeSave	The command to save the workbook is given.
Deactivate	The workbook is deactivated.
NewSheet	A new sheet is added to the workbook.
Open	The workbook is opened.
SheetActivate	A sheet in the workbook is activated.
SheetBeforeDoubleClick	A cell in the workbook is double-clicked.
SheetBeforeRightClick	A cell in the workbook is right-clicked.
SheetChange	A change is made to a cell in the workbook.
SheetDeactivate	A sheet in the workbook is deactivated.
SheetSelectionChange	The selection is changed.
WindowActivate	The workbook window is activated.
WindowDeactivate	The workbook window is deactivated.

Table 11-2 lists some useful worksheet-related events.

TABLE 11-2 ## Worksheet Events

Event	When It's Triggered
Activate	The worksheet is activated.
BeforeDoubleClick	A cell in the worksheet is double-clicked.
BeforeRightClick	A cell in the worksheet is right-clicked.
Change	A change is made to a cell in the worksheet.
Deactivate	The worksheet is deactivated.
SelectionChange	The selection is changed.

Are events useful?

At this point, you may be wondering how these events can be useful. Here's a quick example.

Suppose you have a workbook in which you enter values in column A. Your boss, a very compulsive person, tells you that he needs to know exactly when each number was entered. Entering data is an event: a WorksheetChange event. You can write a macro that responds to this event. That macro kicks in whenever the worksheet is changed. If the change was made in column A, the macro puts the date and time in column B, next to the data point that was entered.

In case you're curious, here's what such a macro would look like. Probably a lot simpler than you thought it would be, eh?

```
Private Sub Worksheet_Change(ByVal Target As Range)
    If Target.Column = 1 Then
        Target.Offset(0, 1) = Now
    End If
End Sub
```

By the way, macros that respond to events are very picky about where they are stored. For example, this Worksheet_Change macro *must* be in the Code module for that worksheet. Put it somewhere else, and it won't work. More about this later (see "Where Does the VBA Code Go?").

WARNING

Just because your workbook contains procedures that respond to events doesn't guarantee that those procedures will actually run. As you know, it's possible to open a workbook with macros disabled. In such a case, all macros (even procedures that respond to events) are turned off. Keep this fact in mind when you create workbooks that rely on event-handler procedures.

Programming event-handler procedures

A VBA procedure that executes in response to an event is called an *event-handler procedure*. These are always Sub procedures (as opposed to Function procedures). Writing these event-handlers is relatively straightforward after you understand how the process works.

Creating event-handler procedures boils down to a few steps:

1. **Identify the event you want to trigger the procedure.**

2. **Press Alt+F11 to activate the Visual Basic Editor.**

3. **In the VBE Project window, double-click the appropriate object listed under Microsoft Excel Objects.**

 For workbook-related events, the object is ThisWorkbook. For a worksheet-related event, the object is a Worksheet object (such as Sheet1).

4. **In the Code window for the object, write the event-handler procedure that is executed when the event occurs.**

 This procedure will have a special name that identifies it as an event-handler procedure.

These steps become clearer as you progress through the chapter.

Where Does the VBA Code Go?

It's very important to understand where your event-handler procedures go. They must reside in the Code window of an Object module. They do not go in a standard VBA module. If you put your event-handler procedure in the wrong place, it simply won't work. And you won't see any error messages, either.

Figure 11-1 shows the VBE window with one project displayed in the Project window. (Refer to Chapter 3 for some background on the VBE.) Notice that the VBA project for Book1 is fully expanded and consists of several objects:

>> One object for each worksheet in the workbook (in this case, three Sheet objects)

>> An object labeled ThisWorkbook

>> A VBA module inserted manually (Choose Insert ⇨ Module.)

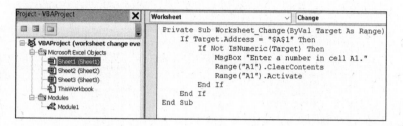

FIGURE 11-1:
The Project window displays items for a single project.

Double-clicking any of these objects displays the code associated with the item, if any.

The event-handler procedures that you write go into the Code window for the ThisWorkbook item (for workbook-related events) or one of the Sheet objects (for worksheet-related events).

In Figure 11-1, the Code window for the Sheet1 object is displayed, and it happens to have a single event-handler procedure defined. Notice the two drop-down controls at the top of the Code module? Keep reading to find out why those are useful.

Writing an Event-Handler Procedure

The VBE helps you out when you're ready to write an event-handler procedure; it displays a list of all events for the selected object.

At the top of each Code window, you find two drop-down lists:

>> The Object drop-down list (the one on the left)

>> The Procedure drop-down list (the one on the right)

By default, the Object drop-down list in the Code window displays General.

If you're writing an event-handler for the ThisWorkbook object, you need to click ThisWorkbook in the Project window and then choose Workbook from the Object drop-down (it's the only other choice).

If you're writing an event-handler for a Sheet object, you need to click the specific Sheet in the Project window and then choose Worksheet from the Object drop-down list (again, the only other choice).

After you've made your choice from the Object drop-down list, you can choose the event from the Procedure drop-down list. Figure 11-2 shows some of the choices for a workbook-related event.

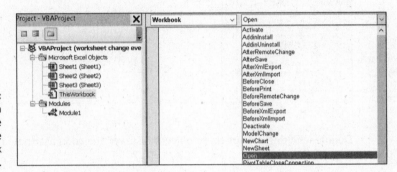

When you select an event from the list, the VBE automatically starts creating an event-handler procedure for you. This is a very useful feature, because it tells you exactly what the proper arguments are.

Here's a little quirk. When you first select Workbook from the Object list, the VBE always assumes that you want to create an event-handler procedure for the Open event and creates it for you. If you're actually creating a Workbook_Open procedure, that's fine. But if you're creating a different event-procedure, you need to delete the empty Workbook_Open Sub that was created.

The VBE's help goes only so far, however. It writes the Sub statement and the End Sub statement. Writing the VBA code that goes between these two statements is your job.

REMEMBER

You don't really have to use those two drop-down lists, but doing so makes your job easier because the name of the event-handler procedure is critically important. If you don't get the name exactly right, the procedure won't work. Also, some event-handler procedures use one or more arguments in the Sub statement. There's no way you can remember what those arguments are. For example, if you select SheetActivate from the event list for a Workbook object, the VBE writes the following Sub statement:

```
Private Sub Workbook_SheetActivate(ByVal Sh As Object)
```

In this case, Sh is the argument passed to the procedure and is a variable that represents the sheet in the activated workbook. Examples in this chapter clarify this point.

Introductory Examples

In this section, you find a few examples so that you can get the hang of this event-handling business.

The Open event for a workbook

One of the most commonly used events is the Workbook Open event. Assume that you have a workbook that you use every day. The Workbook_Open procedure in this example is executed every time the workbook is opened. The procedure checks the day of the week; if it's Friday, the code displays a reminder message for you.

To create the procedure that is executed whenever the Workbook Open event occurs, follow these steps:

1. **Open the workbook.**

 Any workbook will do.

2. **Press Alt+F11 to activate the VBE.**

3. **Locate the workbook in the Project window.**

4. **Double-click the project name to display its items, if necessary.**

5. **Double-click the ThisWorkbook item.**

 The VBE displays an empty Code window for the ThisWorkbook object.

6. **In the Code window, select Workbook from the Object (left) drop-down list.**

 The VBE enters the beginning and ending statements for a Workbook_Open procedure.

7. **Enter the following statements, so the complete event-procedure looks like this:**

```
Private Sub Workbook_Open()
    Dim Msg As String
    If Weekday(Now) = 6 Then
        Msg = "Today is Friday. Don't forget to "
        Msg = Msg & "submit the TPS Report!"
        MsgBox Msg
    End If
End Sub
```

The Code window should look like Figure 11-3.

FIGURE 11-3:
This event-
handler
procedure is
executed when
the workbook
is opened.

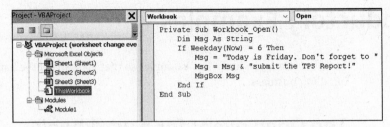

Workbook_Open is executed automatically whenever the workbook is opened. It uses the VBA's WeekDay function to determine the day of the week. If it's Friday (day 6), a message box reminds the user to submit a report. If it's not Friday, nothing happens.

If today isn't Friday, you might have a hard time testing this procedure. You can just change the 6 to correspond to today's actual day number.

And of course, you can modify this procedure any way you like. For example, the following version displays a message every time the workbook is opened. This gets annoying after a while.

```
Private Sub Workbook_Open()
    Msg = "This is Frank's cool workbook!"
    MsgBox Msg
End Sub
```

A Workbook_Open procedure can do almost anything. These event-handlers are often used for the following:

>> Displaying welcome messages (such as in Frank's cool workbook)

>> Opening other workbooks

>> Activating a particular worksheet in the workbook

>> Setting up custom shortcut menus

Here's a final example of a Workbook_Open procedure that uses the GetSetting and SaveSetting functions to keep track of how many times the workbook has been opened. The SaveSetting function writes a value to the Windows registry, and the GetSetting function retrieves that value (see the Help system for details).

The following example retrieves the count from the registry, increments it, and then saves it back to the registry. It also tells the user the value of Cnt that corresponds to the number of times the workbook has been opened (see Figure 11-4).

```
Private Sub Workbook_Open()
    Dim Cnt As Long
    Cnt = GetSetting("MyApp", "Settings", "Open", 0)
    Cnt = Cnt + 1
    SaveSetting "MyApp", "Settings", "Open", Cnt
    MsgBox "This workbook has been opened " & Cnt & " times."
End Sub
```

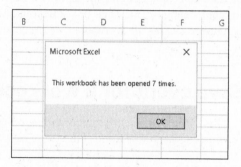

FIGURE 11-4:
Using a
Workbook_Open
event-handler to
keep track of how
many times a
workbook has
been opened.

The BeforeClose event for a workbook

Here's an example of the Workbook_BeforeClose event-handler procedure, which is executed automatically immediately before the workbook is closed. This procedure is located in the Code window for a ThisWorkbook object:

```
Private Sub Workbook_BeforeClose(Cancel As Boolean)
    Dim Msg As String
    Dim Ans As Long
    Dim FName As String
    Msg = "Would you like to make a backup of this file?"
    Ans = MsgBox(Msg, vbYesNo)
    If Ans = vbYes Then
        FName = "F:\BACKUP\" & ThisWorkbook.Name
        ThisWorkbook.SaveCopyAs FName
    End If
End Sub
```

This routine uses a message box to ask the user whether he would like to make a backup copy of the workbook. If the answer is yes, the code uses the SaveCopyAs method to save a backup copy of the file on drive F. If you adapt this procedure for your own use, you need to change the drive and path.

Excel programmers often use a Workbook_BeforeClose procedure to clean up after themselves. For example, if you use a Workbook_Open procedure to change some settings when you open a workbook (hiding the status bar, for example), it's only appropriate that you return the settings to their original state when you close the workbook. You can perform this electronic housekeeping with a Workbook_BeforeClose procedure.

WARNING

When using the Workbook_BeforeClose event, keep this in mind: If you close Excel and any open file has been changed since the last save, Excel shows its usual "Do you want to save your changes" message box. Clicking the Cancel button cancels the entire closing process. But the Workbook_BeforeClose event will have been executed anyway.

The BeforeSave event for a workbook

The BeforeSave event, as its name implies, is triggered before a workbook is saved. This event occurs when you choose File⇨Save or File⇨Save As.

The following procedure, which is placed in the Code window for a ThisWorkbook object, demonstrates the BeforeSave event. The routine updates the value in a cell (cell A1 on Sheet1) every time the workbook is saved. In other words, cell A1 serves as a counter to keep track of the number of times the file was saved.

```
Private Sub Workbook_BeforeSave(ByVal SaveAsUI _
    As Boolean, Cancel As Boolean)
    Dim Counter As Range
    Set Counter = Sheets("Sheet1").Range("A1")
    Counter.Value = Counter.Value + 1
End Sub
```

Notice that the Workbook_BeforeSave procedure has two arguments: SaveAsUI and Cancel. To demonstrate how these arguments work, examine the following macro, which is executed before the workbook is saved. This procedure attempts to prevent the user from saving the workbook with a different name. If the user chooses File⇨Save As, the SaveAsUI argument is True.

When the code executes, it checks the SaveAsUI value. If this variable is True, the procedure displays a message and sets Cancel to True, which cancels the Save operation.

```
Private Sub Workbook_BeforeSave(ByVal SaveAsUI _
    As Boolean, Cancel As Boolean)
    If SaveAsUI Then
        MsgBox "You cannot save a copy of this workbook!"
    Cancel = True
    End If
End Sub
```

Note that this procedure won't really prevent anyone from saving a copy with a different name. If someone really wants to do it, he or she can just open the workbook with macros disabled. When macros are disabled, event-handler procedures are also disabled, which makes sense because they are, after all, macros.

Examples of Activation Events

Another category of events consists of activating and deactivating objects — specifically, sheets and workbooks.

Activate and deactivate events in a sheet

Excel can detect when a particular sheet is activated or deactivated and execute a macro when either of these events occurs. These event-handler procedures go in the Code window for the Sheet object.

TIP

You can quickly access a sheet's Code window by right-clicking the sheet's tab and selecting View Code.

The following example shows a simple procedure that is executed whenever a particular sheet is activated. This code simply pops up an annoying message box that displays the name of the active sheet:

```
Private Sub Worksheet_Activate()
    MsgBox "You just activated " & ActiveSheet.Name
End Sub
```

Here's another example that activates cell A1 whenever the sheet is activated:

```
Private Sub Worksheet_Activate()
    Range("A1").Activate
End Sub
```

Although the code in these two procedures is about as simple as it gets, event-handler procedures can be as complex as you like.

The following procedure (which is stored in the Code window for the Sheet1 object) uses the Deactivate event to prevent a user from activating any other sheet in the workbook. If Sheet1 is deactivated (that is, another sheet is activated), the user gets a message and Sheet1 is activated.

```
Private Sub Worksheet_Deactivate()
    MsgBox "You must stay on Sheet1"
    Sheets("Sheet1").Activate
End Sub
```

By the way, it's not a great idea to use VBA procedures, such as this one, to attempt to take over Excel. These so-called "dictator" applications can be very frustrating and confusing for the user. And of course, they can be defeated easily by disabling macros.

Activate and deactivate events in a workbook

The previous examples use events associated with a specific worksheet. The ThisWorkbook object also handles events that deal with sheet activation and deactivation. The following procedure, which is stored in the Code window for the ThisWorkbook object, is executed when *any* sheet in the workbook is activated. The code displays a message with the name of the activated sheet.

```
Private Sub Workbook_SheetActivate(ByVal Sh As Object)
    MsgBox Sh.Name
End Sub
```

The Workbook_SheetActivate procedure uses the Sh argument. Sh is a variable that represents the active Sheet object. The message box displays the Sheet object's Name property.

The next example is contained in a ThisWorkbook Code window. It consists of two event-handler procedures:

>> **Workbook_SheetDeactivate:** Executed when any sheet in the workbook is deactivated. It stores the sheet that is deactivated in an object variable — but only if the sheet is a worksheet. The Set keyword creates an object variable, which is available to all procedures in the module.

» **Workbook_SheetActivate:** Executed when any sheet in the workbook is activated. It checks the type of sheet that is activated (using the TypeName function). If the sheet is a chart sheet, the user gets a message (see Figure 11-5). When the OK button in the message box is clicked, the *previous* worksheet (which is stored in the OldSheet variable) is reactivated.

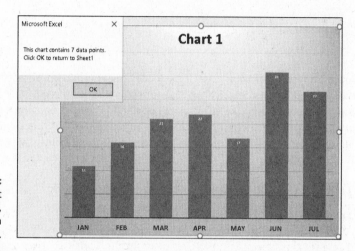

FIGURE 11-5:
When a chart sheet is activated, the user sees a message like this.

TIP

A workbook that contains this code is available at this book's website.

```
Dim OldSheet As Object

Private Sub Workbook_SheetDeactivate(ByVal Sh As Object)
    If TypeName(Sh) = "Worksheet" Then Set OldSheet = Sh
End Sub

Private Sub Workbook_SheetActivate(ByVal Sh As Object)
    Dim Msg As String
    If TypeName(Sh) = "Chart" Then
        Msg = "This chart contains "
        Msg = Msg & ActiveChart.SeriesCollection(1).Points.Count
        Msg = Msg & " data points." & vbNewLine
        Msg = Msg & "Click OK to return to " & OldSheet.Name
        MsgBox Msg
        OldSheet.Activate
    End If
End Sub
```

Workbook activation events

Excel also recognizes the event that occurs when you activate or deactivate a particular workbook. The following code, which is contained in the Code window for the ThisWorkbook object, is executed whenever the workbook is activated. The procedure simply maximizes the workbook's window.

```
Private Sub Workbook_Activate()
    ActiveWindow.WindowState = xlMaximized
End Sub
```

An example of Workbook_Deactivate code appears next. This procedure is executed when a workbook is deactivated. This procedure copies the selected range whenever the workbook is deactivated. It might be useful if you're copying data from lots of areas and pasting them into a different workbook. When this event-procedure is in place, you can select the range to be copied, activate the other workbook, select the destination, and press Ctrl+V (or Enter) to paste the copied data.

```
Private Sub Workbook_Deactivate()
    ThisWorkbook.Windows(1).RangeSelection.Copy
End Sub
```

Other Worksheet-Related Events

The preceding section illustrated examples for worksheet activation and deactivation events. In this section, you find additional events that occur in worksheets: double-clicking a cell, right-clicking a cell, and changing a cell.

The BeforeDoubleClick event

You can set up a VBA procedure to be executed when the user double-clicks a cell. In the following example (which is stored in the Code window for a Sheet object), double-clicking a cell in that sheet makes the cell bold (if it's not bold) or not bold (if it is bold):

```
Private Sub Worksheet_BeforeDoubleClick _
    (ByVal Target As Excel.Range, Cancel As Boolean)
    Target.Font.Bold = Not Target.Font.Bold
    Cancel = True
End Sub
```

The Worksheet_BeforeDoubleClick procedure has two arguments: Target and Cancel. Target represents the cell (a Range object) that was double-clicked. If Cancel is set to True, the default double-click action doesn't occur.

The default action for double-clicking a cell is to put Excel in cell edit mode. In this case, you don't necessarily want to edit the cell when double-clicking the cells, so set Cancel to True.

The BeforeRightClick event

The BeforeRightClick event is similar to the BeforeDoubleClick event except that it consists of right-clicking a cell. The following procedure checks to see whether the cell that was right-clicked contains a numeric value. If so, the code displays the Format Number dialog box and sets the Cancel argument to True (avoiding the normal shortcut menu display). If the cell doesn't contain a numeric value, nothing special happens; the shortcut menu is displayed as usual.

```
Private Sub Worksheet_BeforeRightClick _
    (ByVal Target As Excel.Range, Cancel As Boolean)
    If IsNumeric(Target) And Not IsEmpty(Target) Then
        Application.CommandBars.ExecuteMso ("NumberFormatsDialog")
        Cancel = True
    End If
End Sub
```

TIP

Notice that the code, which is available on this book's website, makes an additional check to see if the cell isn't empty. This is because VBA considers empty cells to be numeric.

The Change event

The Change event occurs whenever any cell in the worksheet is changed. In the following example, the Worksheet_Change procedure effectively prevents a user from entering a nonnumeric value in cell A1. This code is stored in the Code window for a Sheet object.

```
Private Sub Worksheet_Change(ByVal Target As Range)
    If Target.Address = "$A$1" Then
        If Not IsNumeric(Target) Then
            MsgBox "Enter a number in cell A1."
```

```
            Range("A1").ClearContents
            Range("A1").Activate
        End If
    End If
End Sub
```

The single argument for the Worksheet_Change procedure (Target) represents the range that was changed. The first statement checks whether the cell's address is A1. If so, the code uses the IsNumeric function to determine whether the cell contains a numeric value. If not, a message appears, and the cell's value is erased. Cell A1 is then activated — useful if the cell pointer moved to a different cell after the entry was made. If the change occurs in any cell except A1, nothing happens.

Why not use data validation?

You may be familiar with Data ⇨ Data Tools ⇨ Data Validation. This handy feature makes it easy to ensure that only data of the proper type is entered into a particular cell or range. Although Data ⇨ Data Tools ⇨ Data Validation is useful, it's definitely not foolproof.

Try adding data validation to a cell. For example, you can set it up so the cell accepts only a numerical value. It works fine — until you copy another cell and paste it to the data validation cell. Pasting removes the data validation. It's as if it was never there. The severity of this flaw depends on your application.

TECHNICAL STUFF

Pasting wipes out data validation because Excel considers validation to be a format for a cell. Therefore, it's in the same classification as font size, color, or other similar attributes. When you paste a cell, you're replacing the formats in the target cell with those of the source cell. Unfortunately, those formats also include your validation rules.

Preventing data validation from being destroyed

The procedure in this section demonstrates how to prevent users from copying data and wiping out data validation rules. This example assumes that the worksheet has a range named InputArea, and this input area contains data validation rules (set up by choosing Data ⇨ Data Tools ⇨ Data Validation). The range can have any validation rules you want.

TIP

A workbook that contains this code is available at this book's website:

```
Private Sub Worksheet_Change(ByVal Target As Range)
    Dim VT As Long
    'Do all cells in the validation range
    'still have validation?
```

```
    On Error Resume Next
    VT = Range("InputRange").Validation.Type
    If Err.Number <> 0 Then
        Application.Undo
        MsgBox "Your last operation was canceled. " & _
        "It would have deleted data validation rules.", vbCritical
    End If
End Sub
```

The procedure is executed whenever a cell is changed. It checks the validation type of the range (named InputRange) that is *supposed* to contain the data validation rules. If the VT variable contains an error, one or more cells in the InputRange no longer have data validation. (The user probably copied some data over it.) If that's the case, the code executes the Undo method of the Application object and reverses the user's action. Then it displays a message box, as shown in Figure 11-6. See Chapter 12 for more information about using On Error Resume Next.

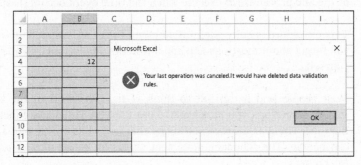

FIGURE 11-6:
Performing data validation with an event procedure.

The net effect? It's impossible to wipe out the validation rules by copying data. When Excel is broken, sometimes you can use VBA to fix it.

Events Not Associated with Objects

The events discussed previously in this chapter are associated with either a workbook object or a worksheet object. This section focuses on two types of events that aren't associated with objects: time and keypresses.

REMEMBER

Because time and keypresses aren't associated with a particular object such as a workbook or a worksheet, you program these events in a normal VBA module (unlike the other events discussed in this chapter).

The OnTime event

The OnTime event occurs when a particular time of day occurs. The following example demonstrates how to get Excel to execute a procedure when the 3 p.m. event occurs. In this case, a robot voice tells you to wake up, accompanied by a message box:

```
Sub SetAlarm()
    Application.OnTime 0.625, "DisplayAlarm"
End Sub
Sub DisplayAlarm()
    Application.Speech.Speak ("Hey, wake up")
    MsgBox " It's time for your afternoon break!"
End Sub
```

In this example, you use the OnTime method of the Application object. This method takes two arguments: the time (0.625, which is 3:00 p.m.) and the name of the Sub procedure to execute when the time event occurs (DisplayAlarm).

This procedure is quite useful if you tend to get so wrapped up in your work that you forget about meetings and appointments. Just set an OnTime event to remind yourself.

TIP

Most people find it difficult to think of time in terms of the Excel numbering system. Therefore, you may want to use the VBA TimeValue function to represent the time. TimeValue converts a string that looks like a time into a value that Excel can handle. The following statement shows an easier way to program an event for 3 p.m.:

```
Application.OnTime TimeValue("3:00:00 pm"), "DisplayAlarm"
```

If you want to schedule an event relative to the current time (for example, 20 minutes from now), you can use a statement like this:

```
Application.OnTime Now + TimeValue("00:20:00"), "DisplayAlarm"
```

You can also use the OnTime method to run a VBA procedure on a particular day. You must make sure that your computer keeps running and that the workbook with the procedure is kept open. The following statement runs the DisplayAlarm procedure at 5 p.m. on December 31, 2019:

```
Application.OnTime DateValue("12/31/2019 5:00 pm"), "DisplayAlarm"
```

This particular code line could come in handy to warn you that you need to go home and get ready for the New Year's Eve festivities.

Here's another example that uses the OnTime event. Executing the UpdateClock procedures writes the time to cell A1 and also programs another event five seconds later. This event reruns the UpdateClock procedure. The net effect is that cell A1 is updated with the current time every five seconds. To stop the events, execute the StopClock procedure (which cancels the event). Note that NextTick is a module-level variable that stores the time for the next event.

```
Dim NextTick As Date

Sub UpdateClock()
'    Updates cell A1 with the current time
     ThisWorkbook.Sheets(1).Range("A1") = Time
'    Set up the next event five seconds from now
     NextTick = Now + TimeValue("00:00:05")
     Application.OnTime NextTick, "UpdateClock"
End Sub

Sub StopClock()
'    Cancels the OnTime event (stops the clock)
     On Error Resume Next
     Application.OnTime NextTick, "UpdateClock", , False
End Sub
```

WARNING

The OnTime event persists even after the workbook is closed. In other words, if you close the workbook without running the StopClock procedure, the workbook reopens itself in five seconds (assuming that Excel is still running). To prevent this, use a Workbook_BeforeClose event procedure that contains the following statement:

```
Call StopClock
```

The OnTime method has two additional arguments. If you plan to use this method, you should refer to the Help system for complete details.

The OnTime method has a ton of utility for all kinds of applications. Figure 11-7 illustrates an analog-clock workbook that uses the OnTime method to tick every second. The clock face is actually a chart, and the chart is updated every second to display the time of day.

Keypress events

While you work, Excel constantly monitors what you type. Because of this, you can set up things so a keystroke or a key combination executes a procedure.

FIGURE 11-7:
An analog-clock
application.

Here's an example that reassigns the PgDn and PgUp keys:

```
Sub Setup_OnKey()
    Application.OnKey "{PgDn}", "PgDn_Sub"
    Application.OnKey "{PgUp}", "PgUp_Sub"
End Sub

Sub PgDn_Sub()
    On Error Resume Next
      ActiveCell.Offset(1, 0).Activate
End Sub

Sub PgUp_Sub()
    On Error Resume Next
      ActiveCell.Offset(-1, 0).Activate
End Sub
```

After setting up the OnKey events by executing the Setup_OnKey procedure, pressing PgDn moves you down one row. Pressing PgUp moves you up one row.

Notice that the key codes are enclosed in braces, not in parentheses. For a complete list of keyboard codes, consult the Help system. Search for *OnKey*.

In this example, On Error Resume Next ignores any errors that are generated. For example, if the active cell is in the first row, trying to move up one row causes an error that can safely be ignored. And if a chart sheet is active, there is no active cell.

By executing the following routine, you cancel the OnKey events:

```
Sub Cancel_OnKey()
    Application.OnKey "{PgDn}"
    Application.OnKey "{PgUp}"
End Sub
```

WARNING

Using an empty string as the second argument for the OnKey method does *not* cancel the OnKey event. Rather, it causes Excel to simply ignore the keystroke. For example, the following statement tells Excel to ignore Alt+F4. The percent sign represents the Alt key:

```
Application.OnKey "%{F4}", ""
```

Although you can use the OnKey method to assign a shortcut key for executing a macro, you should use the Macro Options dialog box for this task. For more details, see Chapter 5.

REMEMBER

If you close the workbook that contains the code and leave Excel open, the OnKey method doesn't reset. As a consequence, pressing the shortcut key causes Excel to automatically open the file with the macro. To prevent this from happening, you should include code in your Workbook_BeforeClose event code (shown earlier in this chapter) to reset the OnKey event.

Chapter **12**

Error-Handling Techniques

To err is human. To anticipate errors is divine. When working with VBA, you should be aware of two broad classes of errors: programming errors and runtime errors. This chapter is all about runtime errors.

A well-written program handles errors the way Fred Astaire danced: gracefully. Fortunately, VBA includes several tools to help you identify errors — and then handle them gracefully.

Types of Errors

If you've tried any of the examples in this book, you have probably encountered one or more error messages. Some of these errors result from bad VBA code. For example, you may spell a keyword incorrectly or type a statement with the wrong syntax. If you make such an error, you won't even be able to execute the procedure until you correct it.

This chapter doesn't deal with those types of errors. Instead, it focuses on runtime errors — the errors that occur while Excel executes your VBA code. More specifically, this chapter covers the following fascinating topics:

>> Identifying errors

>> Doing something about the errors that occur

>> Recovering from errors

>> Creating intentional errors (Yes, sometimes an error can be a good thing.)

The ultimate goal of error handling is to write code that avoids displaying Excel's error messages as much as possible. In other words, you want to anticipate potential errors and deal with them before Excel has a chance to rear its ugly head with a (usually) less-than-informative error message.

An Erroneous Example

To get things started, take a look at the following macro. A macro this simple couldn't produce any errors, right?

Activate the VBE, insert a module, and enter the following code:

```
Sub EnterSquareRoot()
    Dim Num As Double
'   Prompt for a value
    Num = InputBox("Enter a value")
'   Insert the square root
    ActiveCell.Value = Sqr(Num)
End Sub
```

As shown in Figure 12-1, this procedure asks the user for a value. It then performs a magical calculation and enters the square root of that value into the active cell.

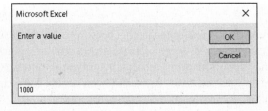

FIGURE 12-1:
The InputBox function displays a dialog box that asks the user for a value.

You can execute this procedure directly from the VBE by pressing F5. Alternatively, you may want to add a button to a worksheet (choose Developer⇨ Controls⇨Insert and select the button in the Form Controls group to do this) and then assign the macro to the button. (Excel prompts you for the macro to assign.) Then you can run the procedure by simply clicking the button.

The macro's not quite perfect

Execute the code a couple of times to try it out. It works pretty well, doesn't it? Now try entering a negative number when you're prompted for a value. Oops. Trying to calculate the square root of a negative number is illegal on this planet.

Excel responds to the request to calculate the square root of a negative number by displaying the runtime error message shown in Figure 12-2. For now, just click the End button. If you click the Debug button, Excel suspends the macro so that you can use the debugging tools to help track down the error. (Debugging tools are covered in Chapter 13.)

FIGURE 12-2:
Excel displays
this error
message when
the procedure
attempts to
calculate the
square root
of a negative
number.

Most folks don't find the Excel error messages (for example, *Invalid procedure call or argument*) particularly helpful. To improve the procedure, you need to anticipate this error and handle it more gracefully. In other words, you need to add some error-handling code.

Here's a modified version of EnterSquareRoot:

```
Sub EnterSquareRoot2()
    Dim Num As Double
'   Prompt for a value
    Num = InputBox("Enter a value")
```

```
'   Make sure the number is nonnegative
    If Num < 0 Then
        MsgBox "You must enter a positive number."
        Exit Sub
    End If

'   Insert the square root
    ActiveCell.Value = Sqr(Num)
End Sub
```

An If-Then structure checks the value contained in the Num variable. If Num is less than 0, the procedure displays a message box containing information that humans can actually understand. Then the procedure ends with the Exit Sub statement, so the runtime error never has a chance to occur.

The macro is still not perfect

So the modified EnterSquareRoot procedure is perfect, right? Not really. Try entering text rather than a value. Or click the Cancel button in the input box. Both of these actions generate an error *(Type mismatch)*. This simple little procedure needs still more error-handling code.

The following modified code uses the IsNumeric function to make sure that Num contains a numeric value. If the user doesn't enter a number, the procedure displays a message and then stops. Also, notice that the Num variable is now declared as a Variant. If it were declared as a Double, the code would generate an unhandled error if the user entered a nonnumeric value into the input box.

```
Sub EnterSquareRoot3()
    Dim Num As Variant
'   Prompt for a value
    Num = InputBox("Enter a value")

'   Make sure Num is a number
    If Not IsNumeric(Num) Then
        MsgBox "You must enter a number."
        Exit Sub
    End If

'   Make sure the number is nonnegative
    If Num < 0 Then
        MsgBox "You must enter a positive number."
        Exit Sub
    End If
```

```
'    Insert the square root
     ActiveCell.Value = Sqr(Num)
End Sub
```

Is the macro perfect yet?

Now this code is absolutely perfect, right? Not quite. Try running the procedure while the active sheet is a chart sheet. Yikes — another runtime error, this time the dreaded Number 91 (see Figure 12-3). This error occurs because there is no active cell when a chart sheet is active or when something other than a range is selected.

FIGURE 12-3:
Running the procedure when a chart is selected generates this error.

The following procedure uses the TypeName function to make sure that the selection is a range. If anything other than a range is selected, this procedure displays a message and then exits:

```
Sub EnterSquareRoot4()
    Dim Num As Variant
'    Make sure a worksheet is active
    If TypeName(Selection) <> "Range" Then
        MsgBox "Select a cell for the result."
        Exit Sub
    End If

'    Prompt for a value
    Num = InputBox("Enter a value")
'    Make sure Num is a number
    If Not IsNumeric(Num) Then
        MsgBox "You must enter a number."
        Exit Sub
    End If
```

```
'    Make sure the number is nonnegative
     If Num < 0 Then
         MsgBox "You must enter a positive number."
         Exit Sub
     End If

'    Insert the square root
     ActiveCell.Value = Sqr(Num)
 End Sub
```

Giving up on perfection

By now, this procedure simply *must* be perfect. Think again, pal.

Protect the worksheet (choose Review ⇨ Changes ⇨ Protect Sheet) and then run the code. Yep, attempting to write to a protected worksheet generates yet another error. And there are probably another half-dozen errors that are impossible to predict. Keep reading for another way to deal with errors — even those you can't anticipate.

Handling Errors Another Way

How can you identify and handle every possible error? Often, you can't. Fortunately, VBA provides another way to deal with errors.

Revisiting the EnterSquareRoot procedure

The following code is a modified version of the procedure from the previous section. Here, an all-purpose On Error statement traps all errors and then checks to see whether the InputBox was canceled.

```
Sub EnterSquareRoot5()
    Dim Num As Variant
    Dim Msg As String

'   Set up error handling
    On Error GoTo BadEntry
'   Prompt for a value
    Num = InputBox("Enter a value")
```

```
'    Exit if cancelled
    If Num = "" Then Exit Sub

'    Insert the square root
    ActiveCell.Value = Sqr(Num)
    Exit Sub

BadEntry:
    Msg = "An error occurred." & vbNewLine & vbNewLine
    Msg = Msg & "Make sure a range is selected, "
    Msg = Msg & "the sheet is not protected, "
    Msg = Msg & "and you enter a nonnegative value."
    MsgBox Msg, vbCritical
End Sub
```

This routine traps *any* type of runtime error. After trapping a runtime error, the revised EnterSquareRoot procedure displays the message box shown in Figure 12-4. This message box describes the most likely causes of the error.

FIGURE 12-4:
A runtime error in the procedure generates this semihelpful error message.

TIP

ON ERROR NOT WORKING?

If an On Error statement isn't working as advertised, you need to change one of your settings:

1. **Activate the VBE.**

2. **Choose Tools ⇨ Options.**

3. **Click the General tab of the Options dialog box.**

4. **Make sure that the Break on All Errors setting is deselected.**

If this setting is selected, Excel essentially ignores any On Error statements. You normally want to keep the Error Trapping options set to Break on Unhandled Errors.

About the On Error statement

Using an On Error statement in your VBA code allows you to bypass Excel's built-in error handling and use your own error-handling code. In the previous example, a runtime error causes macro execution to jump to the statement labeled BadEntry. As a result, you avoid Excel's unfriendly error messages, and you can display your own message to the user.

TIP

Notice that the example uses an Exit Sub statement right before the BadEntry label. This statement is necessary because you don't want to execute the error-handling code if an error does *not* occur.

Handling Errors: The Details

You can use the On Error statement in three ways, as shown in Table 12-1.

TABLE 12-1 **Using the On Error Statement**

Syntax	What It Does
On Error GoTo *label*	After executing this statement, VBA resumes execution at the statement following the specified label. You must include a colon after the label so that VBA recognizes it as a label.
On Error GoTo 0	After executing this statement, VBA resumes its normal error-checking behavior. Use this statement after using one of the other On Error statements or when you want to remove error handling in your procedure.
On Error Resume Next	After executing this statement, VBA simply ignores all errors and resumes execution with the next statement.

Resuming after an error

In some cases, you simply want the routine to end gracefully when an error occurs. For example, you may display a message describing the error and then exit the procedure. (The EnterSquareRoot5 example shown earlier uses this technique.) In other cases, you want to recover from the error, if possible.

To recover from an error, you must use a Resume statement. This clears the error condition and allows you to continue execution at some location. You can use the Resume statement in three ways, as shown in Table 12-2.

TABLE 12-2

Using the Resume Statement

Syntax	What It Does
Resume	Execution resumes with the statement that caused the error. Use this if your error-handling code corrects the problem and it's okay to continue.
Resume Next	Execution resumes with the statement immediately following the statement that caused the error. This essentially ignores the error.
Resume *label*	Execution resumes at the *label* you specify.

The following example uses a Resume statement after an error occurs:

```
Sub EnterSquareRoot6()
    Dim Num As Variant
    Dim Msg As String
    Dim Ans As Integer
TryAgain:
'   Set up error handling
    On Error GoTo BadEntry

'   Prompt for a value
    Num = InputBox("Enter a value")
If Num = "" Then Exit Sub

'   Insert the square root
    ActiveCell.Value = Sqr(Num)

    Exit Sub

BadEntry:
    Msg = Err.Number & ": " & Error(Err.Number)
    Msg = Msg & vbNewLine & vbNewLine
    Msg = Msg & "Make sure a range is selected, "
    Msg = Msg & "the sheet is not protected, "
    Msg = Msg & "and you enter a nonnegative value."
    Msg = Msg & vbNewLine & vbNewLine & "Try again?"
    Ans = MsgBox(Msg, vbYesNo + vbCritical)
    If Ans = vbYes Then Resume TryAgain
End Sub
```

This procedure has another label: TryAgain. If an error occurs, execution continues at the BadEntry label, and the code displays the message shown in Figure 12-5. If the user responds by clicking Yes, the Resume statement kicks in, and execution jumps back to the TryAgain label. If the user clicks No, the procedure ends.

FIGURE 12-5:
If an error occurs,
the user can
decide whether
to try again.

Notice that the error message also includes the error number, along with the "official" error description.

The Resume statement clears the error condition before continuing. To understand what this means, try substituting the following statement for the second-to-last statement in the preceding example:

```
If Ans = vbYes Then GoTo TryAgain
```

The code doesn't work correctly if you use GoTo rather than Resume. To demonstrate, enter a negative number. You get the error prompt. Click Yes to try again and then enter *another* negative number. This second error is not trapped because the original error condition was not cleared.

TIP

This example is available on this book's website.

Error handling in a nutshell

To help you keep all this error-handling business straight, here's a quick-and-dirty summary. A block of error-handling code has the following characteristics:

>> It begins immediately after the label specified in the On Error statement.

>> It should be reached by your macro only if an error occurs. This means that you must use a statement such as Exit Sub or Exit Function immediately before the label.

>> It may require a Resume statement. If you choose not to abort the procedure when an error occurs, you must execute a Resume statement before returning to the main code.

Knowing when to ignore errors

In some cases, it's perfectly okay to ignore errors. That's when the On Error Resume Next statement comes into play.

The following example loops through each cell in the selected range and converts the value to its square root. This procedure generates an error message if any cell in the selection contains a negative number or text:

```
Sub SelectionSqrt()
    Dim cell As Range
    If TypeName(Selection) <> "Range" Then Exit Sub
    For Each cell In Selection
        cell.Value = Sqr(cell.Value)
    Next cell
End Sub
```

In this case, you may want to simply skip any cell that contains a value you can't convert to a square root. You can create all sorts of error-checking capabilities by using If-Then structures, but you can devise a better (and simpler) solution by simply ignoring the errors that occur.

The following routine accomplishes this by using the On Error Resume Next statement:

```
Sub SelectionSqrt()
    Dim cell As Range
    If TypeName(Selection) <> "Range" Then Exit Sub
    On Error Resume Next
    For Each cell In Selection
        cell.Value = Sqr(cell.Value)
    Next cell
End Sub
```

In general, you can use an On Error Resume Next statement if you consider the errors to be harmless or inconsequential to your task.

Identifying specific errors

All errors are not created equal. Some are serious, and some are less serious. Although you may ignore errors you consider to be inconsequential, you must deal with other, more serious errors. In some cases, you need to identify the specific error that occurs.

Every type of error has an official number. When an error occurs, Excel stores the error number in an Error object named Err. This object's Number property contains the error number, and its Description property contains a description of the error. For example, the following statement displays the error number, a colon, and a description of the error:

```
MsgBox Err.Number & ": " & Err.Description
```

Figure 12-5, earlier in this chapter, shows an example. Keep in mind, however, that the Excel error messages are not always very useful — but you already know that.

The following procedure demonstrates how to determine which error occurred. In this case, you can safely ignore errors caused by trying to get the square root of a nonpositive number (that is, error 5) or errors caused by trying to get the square root of a nonnumeric value (error 13). On the other hand, you need to inform the user if the worksheet is protected and the selection contains one or more locked cells. (Otherwise, the user may think the macro worked when it really didn't.) Attempting to write to a locked cell in a protected worksheet causes error 1004.

```
Sub SelectionSqrt()
    Dim cell As Range
    Dim ErrMsg As String
    If TypeName(Selection) <> "Range" Then Exit Sub
    On Error GoTo ErrorHandler
    For Each cell In Selection
        cell.Value = Sqr(cell.Value)
    Next cell
    Exit Sub

ErrorHandler:
    Select Case Err.Number
        Case 5 'Negative number
            Resume Next
        Case 13 'Type mismatch
            Resume Next
        Case 1004 'Locked cell, protected sheet
            MsgBox "Cell is locked. Try again.", vbCritical, cell.Address
            Exit Sub
        Case Else
            ErrMsg = Error(Err.Number)
            MsgBox "ERROR: " & ErrMsg, vbCritical, cell.Address
            Exit Sub
    End Select
End Sub
```

When a runtime error occurs, execution jumps to the code beginning at the ErrorHandler label. The Select Case structure (discussed in Chapter 10) tests for three common error numbers. If the error number is 5 or 13, execution resumes at the next statement. (In other words, the error is ignored.) But if the error number is 1004, the routine advises the user and then ends. The last case, a catch-all for unanticipated errors, traps all other errors and displays the actual error message.

An Intentional Error

Sometimes, you can use an error to your advantage. Suppose that you have a macro that works only if a particular workbook is open. How can you determine whether that workbook is open? One way is to write code that loops through the Workbooks collection, checking to determine whether the workbook you're interested in is in that collection.

Here's an easier way: using a general-purpose function that accepts one argument (a workbook name) and returns True if the workbook is open or False if it's not.

Here's the function:

```
Function WorkbookIsOpen(book As String) As Boolean
    Dim WBName As String
    On Error GoTo NotOpen
    WBName = Workbooks(book).Name
    WorkbookIsOpen = True
    Exit Function
NotOpen:
    WorkbookIsOpen = False
End Function
```

This function takes advantage of the fact that Excel generates an error if you refer to a workbook that isn't open. For example, the following statement generates an error if a workbook named MyBook.xlsx isn't open:

```
WBName = Workbooks("MyBook.xlsx").Name
```

In the WorkbookIsOpen function, the On Error statement tells VBA to continue the macro at the NotOpen statement if an error occurs. Therefore, an error means that the workbook isn't open, and the function returns False. If the workbook *is* open, no error occurs, and the function returns True.

Here's another variation on the WorkbookIsOpen function. This version uses On Error Resume Next to ignore the error. But the code checks Err's Number property. If Err.Number is 0, no error occurred, and the workbook is open. If Err.Number is anything else, it means that an error occurred (and the workbook isn't open).

```
Function WorkbookIsOpen(book) As Boolean
    Dim WBName As String
    On Error Resume Next
    WBName = Workbooks(book).Name
    If Err.Number = 0 Then WorkbookIsOpen = True _
      Else WorkbookIsOpen = False
End Function
```

The following example demonstrates how to use this function in a Sub procedure:

```
Sub UpdatePrices()
    If Not WorkbookIsOpen("Prices.xlsx") Then
        MsgBox "Please open the Prices workbook first!"
        Exit Sub
    End If
'   [Other code goes here]
End Sub
```

The UpdatePrices procedure (which must be in the same workbook as WorkbookIsOpen) calls the WorkbookIsOpen function and passes the workbook name (Prices.xlsx) as an argument. The WorkbookIsOpen function returns either True or False. Therefore, if the workbook is not open, the procedure informs the user of that fact. If the workbook is open, the macro continues.

Error handling can be a tricky proposition. After all, many errors can occur, and you can't anticipate all of them. In general, you should trap errors and correct the situation before Excel intervenes, if possible. Writing effective error-trapping code requires a thorough knowledge of Excel and a clear understanding of how VBA error handling works. Subsequent chapters contain more examples of error handling.

IN THIS CHAPTER

» Defining a bug and knowing why you should squash it

» Recognizing types of program bugs you may encounter

» Using techniques for debugging your code

» Using the VBE's built-in debugging tools

» Presenting a handy list of bug reduction tips

Chapter **13**

Bug Extermination Techniques

I f the word *bugs* conjures up an image of a cartoon rabbit, this chapter can set you straight. Simply put, a bug is an error in your programming. Here, you take a look at the topic of programming bugs — how to identify them and how to wipe them off the face of your module.

Species of Bugs

Welcome to Entomology 101. The term *program bug*, as you probably know, refers to a problem with software. In other words, if software doesn't perform as expected, it has a bug. Fact is, all major software programs have bugs — lots of bugs. Excel itself has hundreds (if not thousands) of bugs. Fortunately, the vast majority of these bugs are relatively obscure and appear in only very specific circumstances.

When you write nontrivial VBA programs, your code probably will have bugs. This is a fact of life and not necessarily a reflection of your programming ability. The bugs may fall into any of the following categories:

>> **Logic flaws in your code:** You can often avoid these bugs by carefully thinking through the problem your program addresses.

>> **Incorrect context bugs:** This type of bug surfaces when you attempt to do something at the wrong time. For example, your code may try to write data to cells in the active sheet when the active sheet is actually a chart sheet (which has no cells).

>> **Extreme-case bugs:** These bugs rear their ugly heads when you encounter data you didn't anticipate, such as very large or very small numbers.

>> **Wrong data-type bugs:** This type of bug occurs when you try to process data of the wrong type, such as attempting to take the square root of a text string.

>> **Wrong version bugs:** This type of bug involves incompatibilities between different Excel versions. For example, you may develop a workbook with Excel 2019 and then find out that the workbook doesn't work with Excel 2003. You can usually avoid such problems by not using version-specific features. Often, the easiest approach is to develop your application by using the lowest version number of Excel that users might have. In all cases, however, you should test your work on all versions you expect it will be used with.

>> **Beyond-your-control bugs:** These are the most frustrating. An example occurs when Microsoft upgrades Excel and makes a minor, undocumented change that causes your macro to bomb. Even security updates have been known to cause problems.

Debugging is the process of identifying and correcting bugs in your program. Developing debugging skills takes time, so don't be discouraged if this process is difficult at first.

REMEMBER

It's important to understand the distinction between *bugs* and *syntax errors*. A syntax error is a language error. For example, you might misspell a keyword, omit the Next statement in a For-Next loop, or have a mismatched parenthesis. Before you can even execute the procedure, you must correct these syntax errors. A program bug is much subtler. You can execute the routine, but it doesn't perform as expected.

Identifying Bugs

Before you can do any debugging, you must determine whether a bug actually exists. You can tell that your macro contains a bug if it doesn't work the way

it should. (Gee, this book is just filled with insight, isn't it?) Usually, but not always, you can easily discern this.

A bug often (but not always) becomes apparent when Excel displays a runtime error message. Figure 13-1 shows an example. Notice that this error message includes a button labeled Debug. More about this later in the "About the Debugger" section.

FIGURE 13-1:
An error message like this often means that your VBA code contains a bug.

A key fact known to all programmers is that bugs often appear when you least expect them. For example, just because your macro works fine with one data set doesn't mean you can assume it works equally as well with all data sets.

The best debugging approach is to start with thorough testing, under a variety of real-life conditions. And because any workbook changes made by your VBA code can't be undone, it's always a good idea to use a backup copy of the workbook that you use for testing.

Debugging Techniques

In this section, you explore the four most common methods for debugging Excel VBA code:

>> Examining the code

>> Inserting MsgBox functions at various locations in your code

>> Inserting Debug.Print statements

>> Using the Excel built-in debugging tools

Examining your code

Perhaps the most straightforward debugging technique is simply taking a close look at your code to see whether you can find the problem. This method, of course, requires knowledge and experience. In other words, you have to know what you're doing. If you're lucky, the error jumps right out, and you slap your forehead and say, "D'oh!" But often times, you discover errors when you have been working on your program for eight hours straight, it's 2 a.m., and you're running on caffeine and willpower. At times like that, you're lucky if you can even see your code, let alone find the bugs. Thus, don't be surprised if simply examining your code isn't enough to make you find and expunge all the bugs it contains.

Using the MsgBox function

A common problem in many programs involves one or more variables not taking on the values you expect. In such cases, monitoring the variable(s) while your code runs is a helpful debugging technique. One way to do this is by inserting temporary MsgBox functions into your routine. For example, if you have a variable named CellCount, you can insert the following statement:

```
MsgBox CellCount
```

When you execute the routine, the MsgBox function displays CellCount's value.

It's often helpful to display the values of two or more variables in the message box. The following statement displays the current value of two variables: LoopIndex (1) and CellCount (72), separated by a space.

```
MsgBox LoopIndex & " " & CellCount
```

Notice that the two variables are combined with the concatenation operator (&) and a space character inserted between them. Otherwise, the message box strings the two values together, making them look like a single value. You can also use the built-in constant, vbNewLine, in place of the space character. vbNewLine inserts a line-feed break, which displays the text on a new line. The following statement displays three variables, each on a separate line (see Figure 13-2):

```
MsgBox LoopIndex & vbNewLine & CellCount & vbNewLine & MyVal
```

This technique isn't limited to monitoring variables. You can use a message box to display all sorts of useful information while your code is running. For example, if your code loops through a series of sheets, the following statement displays the name and type of the active sheet:

```
MsgBox ActiveSheet.Name & " " & TypeName(ActiveSheet)
```

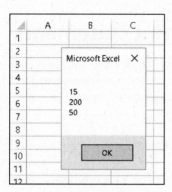

FIGURE 13-2:
Using a message
box to display
the value of
three variables.

If your message box shows something unexpected, press Ctrl+Break, and you see a dialog box that tells you Code execution has been interrupted; as shown in Figure 13-3, you have four choices:

>> Click the Continue button. The code continues executing.

>> Click the End button. Execution stops.

>> Click the Debug button. The VBE goes into Debug mode (explained a bit later in the section "About the Debugger").

>> Click the Help button. A help screen tells you that you pressed Ctrl+Break. In other words, it's not very helpful.

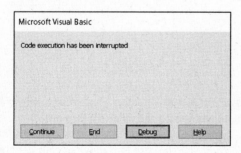

FIGURE 13-3:
Pressing
Ctrl+Break halts
execution of your
code and gives
you some
choices.

TIP

REMEMBER

If your keyboard doesn't have a Break key, try pressing Ctrl+ScrollLock.

Feel free to use MsgBox functions frequently when you debug your code. Just make sure that you remove them after you identify and correct the problem.

Inserting Debug.Print statements

As an alternative to using MsgBox functions in your code, you can insert one or more temporary Debug.Print statements. Use these statements to print the value of one or more variables in the Immediate window. Here's an example that displays the values of three variables:

```
Debug.Print LoopIndex, CellCount, MyVal
```

Notice that the variables are separated with commas. You can display as many variables as you like with a single Debug.Print statement.

REMEMBER

Debug.Print sends output to the Immediate window even if that window is hidden. If VBE's Immediate window is not visible, press Ctrl+G (or choose View ⇨ Immediate Window). Figure 13-4 shows some output in the Immediate window.

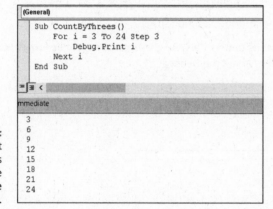

FIGURE 13-4:
A Debug.Print statement sends output to the Immediate window.

Unlike MsgBox, Debug.Print statements don't halt your code. So you need to keep an eye on the Immediate window to see what's going on.

After you've debugged your code, be sure to remove or comment out all the Debug.Print statements. Even big companies like Microsoft occasionally forget to remove their Debug.Print statements. In several previous versions of Excel, every time the Analysis ToolPak add-in was opened, you'd see several strange messages in the Immediate window. That problem was finally fixed in Excel 2007.

Using the VBA debugger

The Excel designers are intimately familiar with the concept of bugs. Consequently, Excel includes a set of debugging tools that can help you correct problems in your VBA code. The VBA debugger is the topic of the next section.

About the Debugger

This section discusses the gory details of using the Excel debugging tools. These tools are much more powerful than the techniques discussed in the previous section. But along with power comes responsibility. Using the debugging tools takes a bit of setup work.

Setting breakpoints in your code

You can use MsgBox functions in your code to monitor the values of certain variables. (See the earlier section, "Using the MsgBox function.") Displaying a message box essentially halts your code in mid-execution, and clicking the OK button resumes execution.

Wouldn't it be nice if you could halt a routine's execution, take a look at the value of *any* of your variables, and then continue execution? Well, that's exactly what you can do by setting a breakpoint. You can set a breakpoint in your VBA code in several ways:

>> Move the cursor to the statement at which you want execution to stop; then press F9.

>> Click the gray margin to the left of the statement at which you want execution to stop.

>> Position the insertion point in the statement at which you want execution to stop. Then choose Debug ⇨ Toggle Breakpoint.

>> Right-click a statement and choose Toggle ⇨ Breakpoint from the shortcut menu.

The results of setting a breakpoint are shown in Figure 13-5. Excel highlights the line to remind you that you set a breakpoint there; it also inserts a large dot in the margin.

When you execute the procedure, Excel goes into *Break mode* before the line with the breakpoint is executed. In Break mode, the word [break] is displayed in the VBE's title bar. To get out of Break mode and continue execution, press F5 or click the Run Sub/UserForm button on the VBE's toolbar. See "Stepping through your code" later in this chapter to find out more.

TIP

To quickly remove a breakpoint, click the large dot in the gray margin or move the cursor to the highlighted line and press F9. To remove all breakpoints in the module, press Ctrl+Shift+F9.

```
(General)

Sub SelectionSqrt()
    Dim cell As Range
    Dim ErrMsg As String
    If TypeName(Selection) <> "Range" Then Exit Sub
    On Error GoTo ErrorHandler
    For Each cell In Selection
        cell.Value = Sqr(cell.Value)
    Next cell
    Exit Sub

ErrorHandler:
    Select Case Err.Number
        Case 5 'Negative number
            Resume Next
        Case 13 'Type mismatch
            Resume Next
        Case 1004 'Locked cell, protected sheet
            MsgBox "Cell is locked. Try again.", vbCritical, cell.
            Exit Sub
        Case Else
            ErrMsg = Error(Err.Number)
            MsgBox "ERROR: " & ErrMsg, vbCritical, cell.Address
            Exit Sub
    End Select
End Sub
```

FIGURE 13-5:
The highlighted statement marks a breakpoint in this procedure.

VBA also has a keyword, which you can insert as a statement, that forces Break mode:

Stop

When your code reaches the Stop keyword, VBA enters Break mode.

What is Break mode? You can think of it as a state of suspended animation. Your VBA code stops running, and the current statement is highlighted in bright yellow. In Break mode, you can

>> Type VBA statements in the Immediate window. (See the next section for details.)

>> Press F8 to step through your code one line at a time to check various things while the program is paused.

>> Move the mouse pointer over a variable to display its value in a small pop-up window.

>> Skip the next statement(s) and continue execution there (or even go back a couple of statements).

>> Edit a statement and then continue.

Figure 13-6 shows some debugging action. A breakpoint is set (notice the big dot), and the F8 key is used to step through the code line by line (notice the arrow that points to the current statement).

TIP

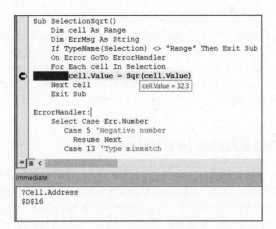

```
Sub SelectionSqrt()
    Dim cell As Range
    Dim ErrMsg As String
    If TypeName(Selection) <> "Range" Then Exit Sub
    On Error GoTo ErrorHandler
    For Each cell In Selection
        cell.Value = Sqr(cell.Value)
    Next cell                    cell.Value = 32.3
    Exit Sub

ErrorHandler:|
    Select Case Err.Number
        Case 5 'Negative number
            Resume Next
        Case 13 'Type mismatch
```

Immediate

```
?Cell.Address
$D$16
```

FIGURE 13-6:
A typical scene in Break mode.

Using the Immediate window

The Immediate window may not be visible in the VBE. You can display the VBE's Immediate window at any time by pressing Ctrl+G.

In Break mode, the Immediate window is particularly useful for finding the current value of any variable in your program. For example, if you want to know the current value of a variable named CellCount, enter the following in the Immediate window and press Enter:

```
Print CellCount
```

You can save a few milliseconds by using a question mark in place of the word `Print`, like this:

```
? CellCount
```

The Immediate window allows you to do other things besides check variable values. For example, you can change the value of a variable, activate a different sheet, or even open a new workbook. Just make sure that the command you enter is a valid VBA statement.

TIP

You can also use the Immediate window when Excel is not in Break mode. The Immediate window makes for a handy place to add small code snippets before incorporating them into your procedures.

Stepping through your code

While in Break mode, you can also step through your code line by line. One statement is executed each time you press F8. Throughout this line-by-line execution of your code, you can activate the Immediate window at any time to check the status of your variables.

TIP

You can use your mouse to change which statement VBA executes next. If you put your mouse pointer in the margin to the left of the currently highlighted statement (which is usually yellow), your pointer changes to a right-pointing arrow. Simply drag your mouse to the statement you want to execute next and watch that statement turn yellow.

Using the Watches window

In some cases, you may want to know whether a certain variable or expression takes on a particular value. Suppose that a procedure loops through 1,000 cells. You notice that a problem occurs during the 900th iteration of the loop. Well, you could insert a breakpoint into the loop, but that would mean responding to 899 prompts before the code finally gets to the iteration you want to see (and that gets boring real fast). A more efficient solution involves setting a *watch expression*.

For example, you can create a watch expression that puts the procedure into Break mode whenever a certain variable takes on a specific value — for example, Counter=900. To create a watch expression, choose Debug ⇨ Add Watch to display the Add Watch dialog box (see Figure 13-7).

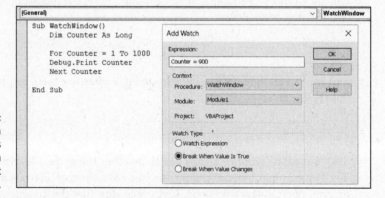

FIGURE 13-7: The Add Watch dialog box lets you specify a condition that causes a break.

The Add Watch dialog box has three parts:

>> **Expression:** Enter a valid VBA expression or a variable here — for example, Counter=900 or just Counter.

>> **Context:** Select the procedure and the module you want to watch. Note that you can select All Procedures and All Modules.

» **Watch Type:** Select the type of watch by clicking an option button. Your choice here depends on the expression you enter. The first choice, Watch Expression, doesn't cause a break; it simply displays the expression's value when a break occurs.

Execute your procedure after setting up your watch expression(s). Things run normally until your watch expression is satisfied (based on the Watch Type you specified). When that happens, Excel enters Break mode (you did set the Watch Type to Break When Value Is True, didn't you?). From there, you can step through the code or use the Immediate window to debug your code.

When you create a watch, the VBE displays the Watches window, shown in Figure 13-8. This window displays the value of all watches that you've defined. In this figure, the value of the Counter variable hit 900, which caused Excel to enter Break mode.

FIGURE 13-8:
The Watches window displays all watches.

To remove a watch, right-click it in the Watches window, and choose Delete Watch from the shortcut menu.

The best way to understand how this Watch business works is to use it and try various options. Before long, you'll probably wonder how you ever got along without it.

Using the Locals window

Another useful debugging aid is the Locals window. You can show this window by choosing View➪ Locals Window in the VBE. When you are in Break mode, this window shows a list of all variables that are local to the current procedure (see Figure 13-9). The nice thing about this window is that you don't have to add a load of watches manually if you want to look at the content of many variables. The VBE has done all the hard work for you.

FIGURE 13-9:
The Locals
window displays
all local variables
and their content.

Locals		
Expression	Value	Type
⊞ Module1		Module1/Module1
Counter	900	Long

Bug Reduction Tips

There is no sure-fire way to completely eliminate bugs in your VBA programs. But here are a few tips to help you keep those bugs to a minimum:

» **Use an Option Explicit statement at the beginning of your modules.** This statement requires you to define the data type for every variable you use. This creates a bit more work for you, but you avoid the common error of misspelling a variable name. And it has a nice side benefit: Your routines run a bit faster.

» **Format your code with indentation.** Using indentations helps delineate different code segments. If your program has several nested For-Next loops, for example, consistent indentation helps you keep track of them all.

» **Be careful with the On Error Resume Next statement.** This statement causes Excel to ignore any errors and continue executing the routine. In some cases, using this statement causes Excel to ignore errors that it shouldn't ignore. Your code may have bugs, and you may not even realize it.

» **Use comments.** Nothing is more frustrating than revisiting code you wrote six months ago and not having a clue as to how it works. By adding a few comments to describe your logic, you can save lots of time down the road.

» **Keep your Sub and Function procedures simple.** By writing your code in small modules, each of which has a single, well-defined purpose, you simplify the debugging process.

» **Use the macro recorder to help identify properties and methods.** When you can't remember the name or the syntax of a property or method, simply record a macro and look at the recorded code.

» **Understand Excel's debugger.** Although it can be a bit daunting at first, the Excel debugger is a useful tool. Invest some time and get to know it.

Chapter **14**

VBA Programming Examples

A good example often communicates a concept much better than a lengthy description of the underlying theory. In that spirit, this chapter presents several examples that demonstrate common VBA techniques.

These examples are organized into the following categories:

» Working with ranges

» Changing Excel settings

» Working with charts

» Speeding up your VBA code

Although you may be able to use some of the examples directly, in most cases you must adapt them to your own needs.

Working with Ranges

Most of your VBA programming probably involves worksheet ranges. (For some background on Range objects, refer to Chapter 8.) When you work with Range objects, keep the following points in mind:

>> Your VBA doesn't need to *select* a range to work with it.

>> If your code does select a range, its worksheet must be active.

>> The macro recorder doesn't always generate the most efficient code. Often, you can create your macro by using the recorder and then edit the code to make it more efficient.

>> It's often a good idea to use named ranges in your VBA code. For example, using Range("Total") is better than using Range("D45"). In the latter case, if you add a row above row 45, you need to modify the macro so that it uses the correct range address (D46). Note that you name a range of cells by choosing Formulas ➪ Defined Names ➪ Define Name.

>> When running a macro that works on the current range selection, the user might select entire columns or rows. In most cases, you don't want to loop through every cell in the selection; that could take a long time. Your macro should create a subset of the selection consisting of only the nonblank cells.

>> Excel allows multiple selections. For example, you can select a range, press Ctrl, and select another range with your mouse. Your code can test for a multiple selection and take appropriate actions.

TIP

The examples in this section, which are available at this book's website, demonstrate these points.

REMEMBER

If you prefer to enter these examples yourself, press Alt+F11 to activate the VBE. Then insert a VBA module and type the code. Make sure that the workbook is set up properly. For example, if the example uses two sheets named Sheet1 and Sheet2, make sure that the workbook has sheets with those names.

Copying a range

Copying a range ranks right up there as one of the favorite Excel activities of all time. When you turn on the macro recorder and copy a range from A1:A5 to B1:B5, you get this VBA macro:

```
Sub CopyRange()
    Range("A1:A5").Select
    Selection.Copy
    Range("B1").Select
    ActiveSheet.Paste
    Application.CutCopyMode = False
End Sub
```

Notice the last statement. This statement was generated by pressing Esc, which cancels the dotted-line outline that appears in the worksheet when you copy a range.

This macro works fine, but you can copy a range more efficiently than this. You can produce the same result with the following one-line macro, which doesn't select any cells (and also doesn't require setting CutCopyMode to False):

```
Sub CopyRange2()
    Range("A1:A5").Copy Range("B1")
End Sub
```

This procedure takes advantage of the fact that the Copy method can use an argument that specifies the destination.

Alternatively, you have the option of including the Destination argument by name to make your code easier to read. For example:

```
Sub CopyRange2()
    Range("A1:A5").Copy Destination:=Range("B1")
End Sub
```

Copying a variable-size range

In many cases, you need to copy a range of cells but don't know the exact row and column dimensions. For example, you might have a workbook that tracks weekly sales. The number of rows changes as you add new data.

Figure 14-1 shows a range in a worksheet. This range consists of several rows, and the number of rows changes from day to day. Because you don't know the exact range address at any given time, you need a way to write code that doesn't use a range address.

◢	A	B	C
1	**Date**	**Calls**	**Orders**
2	4/5/2019	452	89
3	4/6/2019	546	102
4	4/7/2019	587	132
5	4/8/2019	443	65
6	4/9/2019	609	156
7	4/10/2019	592	92
8	4/11/2019	487	95
9	4/12/2019	601	105
10	4/13/2019	515	133
11	4/14/2019	540	122
12			

FIGURE 14-1:
This range can consist of any number of rows.

The following macro demonstrates how to copy this range from Sheet1 to Sheet2 (beginning at cell A1). It uses the CurrentRegion property, which returns a Range object that corresponds to the block of cells around a particular cell. In this case, that cell is A1.

```
Sub CopyCurrentRegion()
    Range("A1").CurrentRegion.Copy
    Sheets("Sheet2").Select
    Range("A1").Select
    ActiveSheet.Paste
    Sheets("Sheet1").Select
    Application.CutCopyMode = False
End Sub
```

Using the CurrentRegion property is equivalent to choosing Home ➪ Editing ➪ Find & Select ➪ GoTo Special (which displays the GoTo Special dialog box) and choosing the Current Region option. To see how this works, record your actions while issuing that command. Generally, the CurrentRegion consists of a rectangular block of cells surrounded by one or more blank rows or columns.

You can make this macro even more efficient by not selecting the destination. The following macro takes advantage of the fact that the Copy method can use an argument for the destination range:

```
Sub CopyCurrentRegion2()
    Range("A1").CurrentRegion.Copy Sheets("Sheet2").Range("A1")
End Sub
```

TIP

It's even a bit easier if the data is in the form of a table (created in Excel; choose Insert ➪ Tables ➪ Table). The table has a name (such as Table1) and expands automatically when new data is added.

```
Sub CopyTable()
    Range("Table1").Copy Sheets("Sheet2").Range("A1")
End Sub
```

If you try this, you'll find that the header row in the table is not copied because the name Table1 doesn't include that row. If you need to include the header row, change the table reference to

```
Range("Table1[#All]")
```

Selecting to the end of a row or column

You're probably in the habit of using key combinations such as Ctrl+Shift+right arrow and Ctrl+Shift+down arrow to select a range that consists of everything from the active cell to the end of a row or a column. Not surprisingly, you can write macros that perform these types of selections.

You can use the CurrentRegion property to select an entire block of cells. But what if you want to select, say, one column from a block of cells? Fortunately, VBA can accommodate this type of action. The following VBA procedure selects the range beginning at the active cell and extending down to the cell just above the first blank cell in the column. After selecting the range, you can do whatever you want with it — copy it, move it, format it, and so on.

```
Sub SelectDown()
    Range(ActiveCell, ActiveCell.End(xlDown)).Select
End Sub
```

You can make this type of selection manually: Select the first cell, hold down the Shift key, press End, and then press the down-arrow key.

This example uses the End method of the ActiveCell object, which returns a Range object. The End method takes one argument, which can be any of the following constants:

>> xlUp

>> xlDown

>> xlToLeft

>> xlToRight

Keep in mind that it's not necessary to select a range before doing something with it. The following macro applies bold formatting to a variable-size (single-column) range without selecting the range:

```
Sub MakeBold()
    Range(ActiveCell, ActiveCell.End(xlDown)).Font.Bold = True
End Sub
```

Selecting a row or column

The following procedure demonstrates how to select the column that contains the active cell. It uses the EntireColumn property, which returns a Range object that consists of a full column:

```
Sub SelectColumn()
    ActiveCell.EntireColumn.Select
End Sub
```

As you may expect, VBA also offers an EntireRow property, which returns a Range object that consists of an entire row.

Moving a range

You move a range by cutting it to the Clipboard and then pasting it in another area. If you record your actions while performing a move operation, the macro recorder generates code like the following:

```
Sub MoveRange()
    Range("A1:C6").Select
    Selection.Cut
    Range("A10").Select
    ActiveSheet.Paste
End Sub
```

As with the copying example earlier in this chapter, this is not the most efficient way to move a range of cells. In fact, you can move a range with a single VBA statement, as follows:

```
Sub MoveRange2()
    Range("A1:C6").Cut Range("A10")
End Sub
```

This macro takes advantage of the fact that the Cut method can use an argument that specifies the destination. Notice also that the range was not selected. The cell pointer remains in its original position.

Looping through a range efficiently

Many macros perform an operation on each cell in a range, or they perform selected actions based on each cell's content. These macros usually include a For-Next loop that processes each cell in the range.

The following example demonstrates how to loop through a range of cells. In this case, the range is the current selection. An object variable named Cell refers to the cell being processed. Within the For Each-Next loop, the single statement evaluates the cell and applies bold formatting if the cell contains a positive value.

```
Sub ProcessCells()
    Dim Cell As Range
    For Each Cell In Selection
        If Cell.Value > 0 Then Cell.Font.Bold = True
    Next Cell
End Sub
```

This example works, but what if the user's selection consists of an entire column or row? This is not uncommon because Excel lets you perform operations on entire columns or rows. In such a case, the macro seems to take forever because it loops through all cells (all 1,048,576 of them) in the column — even the blank cells. To make the macro more efficient, you need a way to process only the nonblank cells.

The following routine does just that by using the SpecialCells method. (Refer to the VBA Help system for specific details about its arguments.) This routine uses the Set keyword to create two new Range objects: the selection's subset that consists of cells with constants and the selection's subset that consists of cells with formulas. The routine processes each of these subsets, with the net effect of skipping all blank cells. Pretty slick, eh?

```
Sub SkipBlanks()
    Dim ConstantCells As Range
    Dim FormulaCells As Range
    Dim cell As Range
'   Ignore errors
    On Error Resume Next
'   Process the constants
    Set ConstantCells = Selection.SpecialCells(xlConstants)
```

```
    For Each cell In ConstantCells
        If cell.Value > 0 Then
            cell.Font.Bold = True
        End If
    Next cell

'   Process the formulas
    Set FormulaCells = Selection.SpecialCells(xlFormulas)
    For Each cell In FormulaCells
        If cell.Value > 0 Then
            cell.Font.Bold = True
        End If
    Next cell
End Sub
```

The SkipBlanks procedure works equally fast, regardless of what you select. For example, you can select the range, all columns in the range, all rows in the range, or even the entire worksheet. It's a vast improvement over the ProcessCells procedure presented earlier in this section.

Notice the use of the following statement in this code:

```
On Error Resume Next
```

This statement tells Excel to ignore any errors that occur and simply process the next statement. (See Chapter 12 for a discussion of error handling.) This statement is necessary because the SpecialCells method produces an error if no cells qualify.

Using the SpecialCells method is equivalent to choosing Home ➪ Editing ➪ Find & Select ➪ GoTo Special and selecting the Constants option or the Formulas option. To get a feel for how this works, record your actions while you issue that command and select various options.

Looping through a range efficiently (Part II)

And now, the sequel. This section demonstrates another way to process cells in an efficient manner. This method takes advantage of the UsedRange property — which returns a Range object that consists only of the used area of the worksheet. It also uses the Intersect method, which returns a Range object that consists of cells that two ranges have in common.

Here's a variation of the SkipBlanks procedure from the previous section:

```vba
Sub SkipBlanks2()
    Dim WorkRange As Range
    Dim cell As Range
    Set WorkRange = Intersect(Selection, ActiveSheet.UsedRange)
    For Each cell In WorkRange
        If cell.Value > 0 Then
            cell.Font.Bold = True
        End If
    Next cell
End Sub
```

The WorkRange object variable consists of cells that are common to the user's selection and the worksheet's used range. Therefore, if an entire column is selected, WorkRange contains only the cells that are in that column and also within the used area of the worksheet. It's fast and efficient, with no time wasted on processing cells that are outside the worksheet's used area.

Prompting for a cell value

As shown in Figure 14-2, you can use VBA's InputBox function to get a value from the user. Then you can insert that value into a cell. The following procedure demonstrates how to ask the user for a value and place the value in cell A1 of the active worksheet, using only one statement:

```vba
Sub GetValue()
    Range("A1").Value = InputBox( _
        "Enter the value for cell A1")
End Sub
```

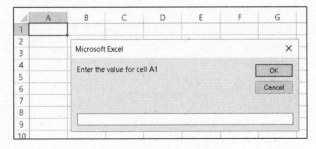

FIGURE 14-2: Use the VBA InputBox function to get a value from the user.

If you try this example, you'll find that clicking the Cancel button in the InputBox erases the current value in cell A1. Erasing the user's data isn't very good programming practice. Clicking Cancel should do nothing at all.

The following macro demonstrates a better approach: using a variable (x) to store the value entered by the user. If the value is not empty (that is, the user didn't click Cancel), the value of x is placed in cell A1. Otherwise, nothing happens.

```
Sub GetValue2()
    Dim x as Variant
    x = InputBox("Enter the value for cell A1")
    If x <> "" Then Range("A1").Value = x
End Sub
```

The variable x is defined as a Variant data type because it could be a number or an empty string (if the user clicks Cancel).

Determining the selection type

If you design your macro to work with a range selection, the macro must be able to determine whether a range is actually selected. If something other than a range is selected (such as a chart or a shape), the macro will probably bomb. The following statement uses the VBA TypeName function to display the type of object that is currently selected:

```
MsgBox TypeName(Selection)
```

If a Range object is selected, the MsgBox displays Range. If your macro works only with ranges, you can use an If statement to ensure that a range is selected. This example displays a message and exits the procedure if the current selection is not a Range object:

```
Sub CheckSelection()
    If TypeName(Selection) <> "Range" Then
        MsgBox "Select a range."
        Exit Sub
    End If
'      ... [Other statements go here]
End Sub
```

Identifying a multiple selection

As you know, Excel allows multiple selections by pressing Ctrl while choosing objects or ranges. This can cause problems with some macros. For example, you can't copy a multiple selection that consists of nonadjacent cells. If you attempt to do so, Excel scolds you with the message shown in Figure 14-3.

FIGURE 14-3:
Excel doesn't like it when you try to copy a multiple selection.

The following macro demonstrates how to determine whether the user made a multiple selection so your macro can take appropriate action:

```
Sub MultipleSelection()
    If Selection.Areas.Count > 1 Then
        MsgBox "Multiple selections not allowed."
        Exit Sub
    End If
'       ... [Other statements go here]
End Sub
```

This example uses the Areas method, which returns a collection of all ranges in the selection. The Count property returns the number of objects in the collection.

Changing Excel Settings

Some of the most useful macros are simple procedures that change one or more of Excel's settings. For example, if you find yourself making frequent trips to the Excel Options dialog box to change a setting, that's a good candidate for a simple time-saving macro.

This section presents two examples that show you how to change settings in Excel. You can apply the general principles demonstrated by these examples to other operations that change settings.

Changing Boolean settings

Like a light switch, a *Boolean* setting is either on or off. For example, you might want to create a macro that turns the worksheet page break display on and off. After you print or preview a worksheet, Excel displays dashed lines to indicate the page breaks. Some people find these dashed lines very annoying. Unfortunately, the only way to get rid of the page break display is to open the Excel Options dialog box, click the Advanced tab, and scroll down until you find the Show Page Breaks check box. If you turn on the macro recorder when you change that option, Excel generates the following code:

```
ActiveSheet.DisplayPageBreaks = False
```

On the other hand, if page breaks aren't visible when you record the macro, Excel generates the following code:

```
ActiveSheet.DisplayPageBreaks = True
```

This may lead you to conclude that you need two macros: one to turn on the page break display and one to turn it off. Not true. The following procedure uses the Not operator, which turns True to False and False to True. Executing the TogglePageBreaks procedure is a simple way to toggle the page break display from True to False and from False to True:

```
Sub TogglePageBreaks()
    On Error Resume Next
    ActiveSheet.DisplayPageBreaks = Not _
      ActiveSheet.DisplayPageBreaks
End Sub
```

The first statement tells Excel to ignore any errors. For example, a chart sheet doesn't display page breaks, so if you execute the macro when a chart sheet is active, you won't see an error message.

You can use this technique to toggle any settings that have Boolean (True or False) values.

Changing non-Boolean settings

You can use a Select Case structure for non-Boolean settings. This example toggles the calculation mode between manual and automatic and displays a message indicating the current mode:

```
Sub ToggleCalcMode()
    Select Case Application.Calculation
        Case xlManual
            Application.Calculation = xlCalculationAutomatic
            MsgBox "Automatic Calculation Mode"
        Case xlAutomatic
            Application.Calculation = xlCalculationManual
            MsgBox "Manual Calculation Mode"
    End Select
End Sub
```

You can adapt this technique for changing other non-Boolean settings.

Working with Charts

Charts are jam-packed with different objects, so manipulating charts with VBA can be a bit of a challenge due to some differences between versions of Excel.

For instance, imagine you were to record a macro in Excel 2019 while you created a basic column chart. While still recording, you decide to delete the chart's gridlines and change the chart's title. Your recorded macro would look similar to this:

```
Sub Macro1()
    ActiveSheet.Shapes.AddChart2(201, xlColumnClustered).Select
    ActiveChart.SetSourceData Source:=Range("Sheet1!$A$1:$A$3")
    ActiveChart.SetElement (msoElementPrimaryValueGridLinesNone)
    ActiveChart.ChartTitle.Select
    ActiveChart.ChartTitle.Text = "This is my chart"
End Sub
```

Note the use of the AddChart2 method (in the first line of code). The AddChart2 method was introduced in Excel 2013.

Now, if you were to record that same macro in Excel 2010, you get this code:

```
Sub Macro1()
    ActiveSheet.Shapes.AddChart.Select
    ActiveChart.ChartType = xlColumnClustered
    ActiveChart.SetSourceData Source:=Range("Sheet1!$A$1:$A$3")
    ActiveChart.Axes(xlValue).MajorGridlines.Select
    Selection.Delete
    ActiveChart.SetElement (msoElementChartTitleAboveChart)
    ActiveChart.ChartTitle.Text = "This is my chart"
End Sub
```

What does it all mean? It means that the macro recorded in Excel 2013 or later versions won't work in Excel 2010. But the macro recorded in Excel 2010 *will* work in Excel 2013 and later. In other words, the Excel 2010 macro exhibits forward compatibility. The Excel 2013 (and later) macro is not backward-compatible.

WARNING

A typical Excel user would probably know nothing about macro compatibility as it relates to chart creation. But if you share your macro with someone who uses an earlier version, you'll find out about it quickly. Bottom line? If you rely on the macro recorder for chart-related macros, make sure that you test the macros with all versions of Excel that will be running the macros.

AddChart versus AddChart2

Here's the official syntax of the AddChart method (which is compatible with Excel 2007 and later):

```
.AddChart(Type, Left, Top, Width, Height)
```

Here's the syntax of the AddChart2 method (which is compatible only with Excel 2013 and later versions):

```
.AddChart2 (Style, XlChartType, Left, Top, Width, Height, NewLayout)
```

As you can see, the AddChart2 method takes several additional arguments — arguments that specify the style, chart type, and layout. The AddChart method, on the other hand, simply creates an empty chart. The specifics for the chart must be provided in additional statements.

Examining the recorded code does reveal a few things that may be helpful in writing your own chart-related macros. If you're curious, here's a handcrafted version of that macro that creates a chart from the selected range:

```
Sub CreateAChart()
    Dim ChartData As Range
    Dim ChartShape As Shape
    Dim NewChart As Chart

'   Create object variables
    Set ChartData = ActiveWindow.RangeSelection
    Set ChartShape = ActiveSheet.Shapes.AddChart
    Set NewChart = ChartShape.Chart
    With NewChart
        .ChartType = xlColumnClustered
        .SetSourceData Source:=Range(ChartData.Address)
        .SetElement (msoElementLegendRight)
        .SetElement (msoElementChartTitleAboveChart)
        .ChartTitle.Text = "This is my chart"
    End With
End Sub
```

The macro is compatible with Excel 2007 and later. The chart that's created is a clustered column chart with a legend and a title. This basic chart-creating macro can be customized easily. One way to do it is to record your actions while you modify the chart and then use the recorded code to guide you.

TIP

By the way, have a look at the With End-With construct later in this chapter. It's a handy way to save some typing and make your code easier to read.

If you need to write VBA macros that manipulate charts, you must understand some terminology. An *embedded chart* on a worksheet is a ChartObject object. You can activate a ChartObject much like you activate a sheet. The following statement activates the ChartObject named Chart 1:

```
ActiveSheet.ChartObjects("Chart 1").Activate
```

After you activate the chart, you can refer to it in your VBA code as the ActiveChart. If the chart is on a separate chart sheet, it becomes the active chart as soon as you activate that chart sheet.

TECHNICAL
STUFF

A ChartObject is also a Shape, which can be a bit confusing. In fact, when your VBA code creates a chart, it starts by adding a new Shape. You can also activate a chart by selecting the Shape object that holds the chart:

```
ActiveSheet.Shapes("Chart 1").Select
```

When you click an embedded chart, Excel actually selects an object *inside* the ChartObject object. You can select the ChartObject itself by pressing Ctrl while clicking the embedded chart.

Modifying the chart type

Here's a confusing statement for you: A ChartObject object acts as a container for a Chart object. Read that a few times, and it might actually make sense.

To modify a chart with VBA, you don't have to activate the chart. Rather, the Chart method can return the chart contained in the ChartObject. Are you thoroughly confused yet? The following two procedures have the same effect: They change the chart named Chart 1 to an area chart. The first procedure activates the chart first and then works with the active chart. The second procedure doesn't activate the chart. Rather, it uses the Chart property to return the Chart object contained in the ChartObject object.

```
Sub ModifyChart1()
    ActiveSheet.ChartObjects("Chart 1").Activate
    ActiveChart.Type = xlArea
End Sub

Sub ModifyChart2()
    ActiveSheet.ChartObjects("Chart 1").Chart.Type = xlArea
End Sub
```

Looping through the ChartObjects collection

This example changes the chart type of every embedded chart in the active sheet. The procedure uses a For Each-Next loop to cycle through each object in the ChartObjects collection, access the Chart object in each, and change its Type property.

```
Sub ChartType()
    Dim cht As ChartObject
    For Each cht In ActiveSheet.ChartObjects
        cht.Chart.Type = xlArea
    Next cht
End Sub
```

The following macro performs the same function but works on all the chart sheets in the active workbook:

```
Sub ChartType2()
    Dim cht As Chart
    For Each cht In ActiveWorkbook.Charts
        cht.Type = xlArea
    Next cht
End Sub
```

Modifying chart properties

The following example changes the Legend font for all charts on the active sheet. It uses a For-Next loop to process all ChartObject objects:

```
Sub LegendMod()
    Dim chtObj As ChartObject
    For Each chtObj In ActiveSheet.ChartObjects
        With chtObj.Chart.Legend.Font
            .Name = "Calibri"
            .FontStyle = "Bold"
            .Size = 12
        End With
    Next cht
End Sub
```

Note that the Font object is contained in the Legend object, which is contained in the Chart object, which is contained in the ChartObjects collection. Now do you understand why it's called an *object hierarchy*?

Applying chart formatting

This example applies several types of formatting to the active chart. Again, you don't have to magically know all the syntax to use. This particular procedure was created by recording a macro, then cleaning the code to remove all the extraneous syntax put in by the macro recorder.

```
Sub ChartMods()
    ActiveChart.Type = xlArea
    ActiveChart.ChartArea.Font.Name = "Calibri"
    ActiveChart.ChartArea.Font.FontStyle = "Regular"
    ActiveChart.ChartArea.Font.Size = 9
```

```
      ActiveChart.PlotArea.Interior.ColorIndex = xlNone
      ActiveChart.Axes(xlValue).TickLabels.Font.Bold = True
      ActiveChart.Axes(xlCategory).TickLabels.Font.Bold = True
      ActiveChart.Legend.Position = xlBottom
   End Sub
```

You must activate a chart before executing the ChartMods macro. Activate an embedded chart by clicking it. To activate a chart in a chart sheet, activate the chart sheet.

To ensure that a chart is selected, you can add a statement to determine whether a chart is active. Here's the modified macro, which displays a message (and ends) if a chart isn't activated:

```
Sub ChartMods2()
    If ActiveChart Is Nothing Then
        MsgBox "Activate a chart."
        Exit Sub
    End If
    ActiveChart.Type = xlArea
    ActiveChart.ChartArea.Font.Name = "Calibri"
    ActiveChart.ChartArea.Font.FontStyle = "Regular"
    ActiveChart.ChartArea.Font.Size = 9
    ActiveChart.PlotArea.Interior.ColorIndex = xlNone
    ActiveChart.Axes(xlValue).TickLabels.Font.Bold = True
    ActiveChart.Axes(xlCategory).TickLabels.Font.Bold = True
    ActiveChart.Legend.Position = xlBottom
End Sub
```

Here's another version that uses the With–End With construct to save some typing and make the code a bit clearer. Flip ahead a few pages to read about the With End–With structure.

```
Sub ChartMods3()
    If ActiveChart Is Nothing Then
        MsgBox "Activate a chart."
        Exit Sub
    End If
    With ActiveChart
        .Type = xlArea
        .ChartArea.Font.Name = "Calibri"
        .ChartArea.Font.FontStyle = "Regular"
        .ChartArea.Font.Size = 9
        .PlotArea.Interior.ColorIndex = xlNone
```

```
        .Axes(xlValue).TickLabels.Font.Bold = True
        .Axes(xlCategory).TickLabels.Font.Bold = True
        .Legend.Position = xlBottom
    End With
End Sub
```

When it comes to using VBA to work with charts, this short section barely scratches the surface. There's a lot more to it, of course, but at least this basic introduction can get you headed in the right direction.

VBA Speed Tips

VBA is fast, but it's not always fast enough. (Computer programs are never fast enough.) This section presents some programming examples you can use to speed up your macros.

Turning off screen updating

When executing a macro, you can sit back and watch all the onscreen action that occurs in the macro. Although doing this can be instructive, after you get the macro working properly, it's often annoying and can slow the performance of your macro considerably. Fortunately, you can disable the screen updating that normally occurs when you execute a macro. To turn off screen updating, use the following statement:

```
Application.ScreenUpdating = False
```

If you want the user to see what's happening at any point during the macro, use the following statement to turn screen updating back on:

```
Application.ScreenUpdating = True
```

To demonstrate the difference in speed, execute this simple macro, which fills a range with numbers:

```
Sub FillRange()
    Dim r as Long, c As Long
    Dim Number as Long
    Number = 0
    For r = 1 To 50
```

```
        For c = 1 To 50
            Number = Number + 1
            Cells(r, c).Select
            Cells(r, c).Value = Number
        Next c
    Next r
End Sub
```

You see each cell being selected and the value being entered in the cells. Now insert the following statement at the beginning of the procedure and execute it again:

```
Application.ScreenUpdating = False
```

The range is filled much faster, and you don't see the result until the macro is finished running and screen updating is (automatically) set to True.

TIP

When you're debugging code, program execution sometimes ends somewhere in the middle without your having turned Screen updating back on. This sometimes causes Excel's application window to become totally unresponsive. The way out of this frozen state is simple: Go back to the VBE, and execute the following statement in the Immediate window:

```
Application.ScreenUpdating = True
```

Turning off automatic calculation

If you have a worksheet with many complex formulas, you may find that you can speed up things considerably by setting the calculation mode to manual while your macro is executing. When the macro finishes, set the calculation mode back to automatic.

The following statement sets the Excel calculation mode to manual:

```
Application.Calculation = xlCalculationManual
```

Execute the next statement to set the calculation mode to automatic:

```
Application.Calculation = xlCalculationAutomatic
```

WARNING

If your code uses cells with formula results, turning off calculation means that the cells aren't recalculated unless you explicitly tell Excel to do so!

Eliminating those pesky alert messages

As you know, a macro can automatically perform a series of actions. In many cases, you can start a macro and then go hang out in the break room while Excel does its thing. Some Excel operations, however, display messages that require a human response. For example, if your macro deletes a nonempty sheet, your code comes to a screeching halt while Excel waits for your response to the message shown in Figure 14-4. These types of messages mean that you can't leave Excel unattended while it executes your macro — unless you know the secret trick.

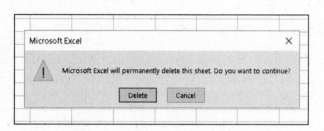

The secret trick to avoiding these alert messages is inserting the following VBA statement into your macro:

```
Application.DisplayAlerts = False
```

Excel executes the default operation for these types of messages. In the case of deleting a sheet, the default operation is Delete (which is just what you want to happen). If you're not sure what the default operation is, perform a test to see what happens.

When the procedure ends, Excel automatically resets the DisplayAlerts property to True (its normal state). If you need to turn the alerts back on before the procedure ends, use this statement:

```
Application.DisplayAlerts = True
```

Simplifying object references

As you probably already know, references to objects can become very lengthy. For example, a fully qualified reference to a Range object may look like this:

```
Workbooks("MyBook.xlsx").Worksheets("Sheet1") _
    .Range("InterestRate")
```

If your macro frequently uses this range, you may want to create an object variable by using the Set command. For example, the following statement assigns this Range object to an object variable named Rate:

```
Set Rate = Workbooks("MyBook.xlsx") _
    .Worksheets("Sheet1").Range("InterestRate")
```

After defining this object variable, you can use the variable Rate rather than the lengthy reference. For example, you can change the value of the cell named InterestRate:

```
Rate.Value = .085
```

This is much easier to type (and understand) than the following statement:

```
Workbooks("MyBook.xlsx").Worksheets("Sheet1"). _
    Range("InterestRate") = .085
```

In addition to simplifying your coding, using object variables speeds up your macros considerably; sometimes twice as fast.

Declaring variable types

You usually don't have to worry about the type of data you assign to a variable. Excel handles all the details for you behind the scenes. For example, if you have a variable named MyVar, you can assign a number of any type to that variable. You can even assign a text string to it later in the procedure.

REMEMBER

If you want your procedures to execute as fast as possible (and avoid some potentially nasty problems), tell Excel what type of data to assigned to each of your variables. This is known as *declaring* a variable's type. (Refer to Chapter 7 for complete details.) Get into the habit of declaring all variables that you use.

In general, you should use the data type that requires the smallest number of bytes yet can still handle all the data assigned to it. When VBA works with data, execution speed depends on the number of bytes VBA has at its disposal. In other words, the fewer bytes data uses, the faster VBA can access and manipulate the data. An exception to this is the Integer data type. If speed is critical, use the Long data type instead.

If you use an object variable (as described in the preceding section), you can declare the variable as a particular object type. Here's an example:

```
Dim Rate as Range
Set Rate = Workbooks("MyBook.xlsx") _
    .Worksheets("Sheet1").Range("InterestRate")
```

Using the With-End With structure

Do you need to set a number of properties for an object? Your code runs faster if you use the With-End With structure. An additional benefit is that your code may be easier to read.

The following code doesn't use With-End With:

```
Selection.HorizontalAlignment = xlCenter
Selection.VerticalAlignment = xlCenter
Selection.WrapText = True
Selection.Orientation = 0
Selection.ShrinkToFit = False
Selection.MergeCells = False
```

Here's the same code, rewritten to use With-End With:

```
With Selection
    .HorizontalAlignment = xlCenter
    .VerticalAlignment = xlCenter
    .WrapText = True
    .Orientation = 0
    .ShrinkToFit = False
    .MergeCells = False
End With
```

As you can see, this code tells tell Excel that the next few statements apply to the Selection object. This is why all the statements inside the With-End With structure begin with a dot. You're simply avoiding the need to reference the same object over and over (in this case, the Selection object). This not only means less typing for you, but it means less processing for Excel.

4

Communicating with Your Users

IN THIS PART . . .

Save time in various ways by using built-in custom dialog box alternatives.

Discover how to develop custom dialog boxes (also known as UserForms).

Work with dialog box controls, such as buttons, list boxes, and check boxes.

Find out lots of useful tips and tricks for creating custom dialog boxes.

Modify Excel's user interface to make running your macros easier.

Chapter 15

Simple Dialog Boxes

You can't use Excel very long without being exposed to dialog boxes. They seem to pop up all the time. Excel — like most Windows programs — uses dialog boxes to obtain information, clarify commands, and display messages. If you develop VBA macros, you can create your own dialog boxes that work just like those built into Excel. Those custom dialog boxes are called UserForms in VBA.

This chapter doesn't tell you anything about creating UserForms. Rather, it describes some very useful techniques you might be able to use in *place* of UserForms. Chapters 16 through 18, however, do cover UserForms.

UserForm Alternatives

Some of the VBA macros you create behave the same every time you execute them. For example, you may develop a macro that enters a list of your employees into a worksheet range. This macro always produces the same result and requires no additional user input.

You might develop other macros, however, that behave differently under various circumstances or that offer the user options. In such cases, the macro may benefit from a custom dialog box. A custom dialog box provides a simple means for getting information from the user. Your macro then uses that information to determine what it should do.

UserForms can be quite useful, but creating them takes time. Before delving into the topic of creating UserForms in the next chapter, you need to know about some potentially timesaving alternatives.

VBA allows you to display several types of dialog boxes that you can sometimes use in place of a handcrafted UserForm. You can customize these built-in dialog boxes in some ways, but they certainly don't offer the options available in a UserForm. In some cases, however, they're just what the doctor ordered.

In this chapter, you read about

>> The MsgBox function

>> The InputBox function

>> The GetOpenFilename method

>> The GetSaveAsFilename method

>> The FileDialog method

Also in this chapter, you discover how to use VBA to display some of the Excel built-in dialog boxes — the dialog boxes that Excel uses to get information from you.

The MsgBox Function

By now, you're probably familiar with the VBA MsgBox function; several of the examples in the preceding chapters make use of the MsgBox function. The MsgBox function, whose main arguments are shown in Table 15-1, is handy for displaying information and getting simple user input. It's able to accept user input because it's a function. A function, as you probably know, returns a value. In the case of the MsgBox function, it uses a dialog box to get the value that it returns. Keep reading to see exactly how it works.

TABLE 15-1

MsgBox Function Arguments

Argument	What It Affects
Prompt	The text Excel displays in the message box
Buttons	A number that specifies which buttons (along with what icon) appear in the message box (optional)
Title	The text that appears in the message box's title bar (optional)

Here's a simplified version of the syntax of the MsgBox function:

```
MsgBox(prompt[, buttons][, title])
```

Displaying a simple message box

You can use the MsgBox function in two ways:

>> **To simply show a message to the user:** In this case, you don't care about the result returned by the function.

>> **To get a response from the user:** In this case, you do care about the result returned by the function. The result depends on the button that the user clicks.

If you use the MsgBox function by itself, don't include parentheses around the arguments. The following example simply displays a message and doesn't return a result. When the message is displayed, the code stops until the user clicks OK.

```
Sub MsgBoxDemo()
    MsgBox "Click OK to begin printing."
    Sheets("Results").PrintOut
End Sub
```

Figure 15-1 shows how this message box looks. In this case, printing commences when the user clicks OK. Do you notice that there is no way to cancel the printing? The next section describes how to fix that.

Getting a response from a message box

If you display a message box that has more than just an OK button, you'll probably want to know which button the user clicks. You're in luck. The MsgBox function returns a value that represents which button is clicked. You can assign the result of the MsgBox function to a variable.

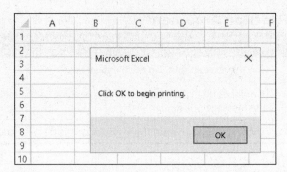

FIGURE 15-1:
A simple
message box.

The following code uses some of the built-in constants (outlined in Table 15-2) that make it easy to work with the values returned by MsgBox:

```
Sub GetAnswer()
    Dim Ans As Long
    Ans = MsgBox("Start printing?", vbYesNo)
    Select Case Ans
        Case vbYes
            ActiveSheet.PrintOut
        Case vbNo
            MsgBox "Printing canceled"
    End Select
End Sub
```

TABLE 15-2

Constants Used in the MsgBox Function

Constant	Value	What It Does
vbOKOnly	0	Displays OK button only.
vbOKCancel	1	Displays OK and Cancel buttons.
vbAbortRetryIgnore	2	Displays Abort, Retry, and Ignore buttons.
vbYesNoCancel	3	Displays Yes, No, and Cancel buttons.
vbYesNo	4	Displays Yes and No buttons.
vbRetryCancel	5	Displays Retry and Cancel buttons.
vbCritical	16	Displays Critical Message icon.
vbQuestion	32	Displays Warning Query icon.
vbExclamation	48	Displays Warning Message icon.
vbInformation	64	Displays Information Message icon.

Constant	Value	What It Does
vbDefaultButton1	0	First button is default.
vbDefaultButton2	256	Second button is default.
vbDefaultButton3	512	Third button is default.
vbDefaultButton4	768	Fourth button is default.

Figure 15-2 shows how it looks. When you execute this procedure, the Ans variable is assigned a value of either vbYes or vbNo, depending on which button the user clicks. The Select Case statement uses the Ans value to determine which action the code should perform.

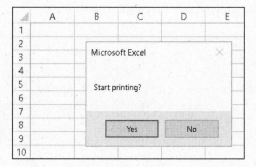

FIGURE 15-2: A simple message box, with two buttons.

You can also use the MsgBox function result without using a variable, as the following example demonstrates:

```
Sub GetAnswer2()
    If MsgBox("Start printing?", vbYesNo) = vbYes Then
'        ...[code if Yes is clicked]...
    Else
'        ...[code if Yes is not clicked]...
    End If
End Sub
```

Customizing message boxes

The flexibility of the buttons argument makes it easy to customize your message boxes. You can choose which buttons to display, determine whether an icon appears, and decide which button is the default (the default button is "clicked" if the user presses Enter).

To use more than one of these constants as an argument, just connect them with a + operator. For example, to display a message box with Yes and No buttons and an exclamation icon, use the following expression as the second MsgBox argument:

```
vbYesNo + vbExclamation
```

Or, if you prefer to make your code less understandable, use a value of 52 (that is, 4 + 48).

The following example uses a combination of constants to display a message box with a Yes button and a No button (vbYesNo) as well as a question-mark icon (vbQuestion). The constant vbDefaultButton2 designates the second button (No) as the default button — that is, the button that is clicked if the user presses Enter. For simplicity, you can assign these constants to the Config variable and then use Config as the second argument in the MsgBox function:

```
Sub GetAnswer3()
    Dim Config As Long
    Dim Ans As Integer
    Config = vbYesNo + vbQuestion + vbDefaultButton2
    Ans = MsgBox("Process the monthly report?", Config)
    If Ans = vbYes Then RunReport
End Sub
```

Figure 15-3 shows the message box Excel displays when you execute the GetAnswer3 procedure. If the user clicks the Yes button, the routine executes the procedure named RunReport (which is not shown). If the user clicks the No button (or presses Enter), the routine ends with no action. Because the procedure omits the title argument in the MsgBox function, Excel uses the default title, Microsoft Excel.

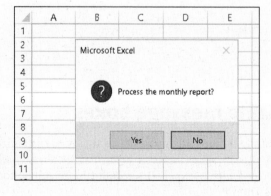

FIGURE 15-3:
The MsgBox function's buttons argument determines what appears in the message box.

The following routine provides another example of using the MsgBox function:

```
Sub GetAnswer4()
    Dim Msg As String, Title As String
    Dim Config As Integer, Ans As Integer
    Msg = "Do you want to process the monthly report?"
    Msg = Msg & vbNewLine & vbNewLine
    Msg = Msg & "Processing the monthly report will "
    Msg = Msg & "take approximately 15 minutes. It "
    Msg = Msg & "will generate a 30-page report for "
    Msg = Msg & "all sales offices for the current "
    Msg = Msg & "month."
    Title = "XYZ Marketing Company"
    Config = vbYesNo + vbQuestion
    Ans = MsgBox(Msg, Config, Title)
    If Ans = vbYes Then RunReport
End Sub
```

This example demonstrates an efficient way to specify a longer message in a message box. Here, the variable (Msg) and the concatenation operator (&) build the message in a series of statements. The vbNewLine constant inserts a line-break character that starts a new line (use it twice to insert a blank line). The Title argument displays a different title in the message box.

Figure 15-4 shows the message box Excel displays when you execute this procedure.

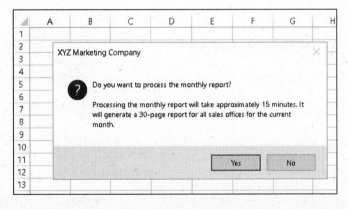

FIGURE 15-4: This dialog box, displayed by the MsgBox function, displays a title, an icon, and two buttons.

Previous examples use constants (such as vbYes and vbNo) for the return value of a MsgBox function. Table 15-3 lists a few other constants.

TABLE 15-3

Constants Used as Return Values for the MsgBox Function

Constant	Value	What It Means
vbOK	1	User clicked OK.
vbCancel	2	User clicked Cancel.
vbAbort	3	User clicked Abort.
vbRetry	4	User clicked Retry.
vbIgnore	5	User clicked Ignore.
vbYes	6	User clicked Yes.
vbNo	7	User clicked No.

And that's pretty much all you need to know about the MsgBox function. Use message boxes with caution, though. There's usually no reason to display message boxes that serve no purpose. For example, people tend to get annoyed when they see a message box every day that reads Good morning. Thanks for loading the Budget Projection workbook.

The InputBox Function

The VBA InputBox function is useful for obtaining a single piece of information typed by the user. That information could be a value, a text string, or even a range address. This is a good alternative to developing a UserForm when you need to get only one value.

InputBox syntax

Here's a simplified version of the syntax of the InputBox function:

```
InputBox(prompt[, title][, default])
```

Table 15-4 shows the key arguments for the InputBox function.

TABLE 15-4

InputBox Function Arguments

Argument	What It Affects
Prompt	The text displayed in the input box
Title	The text displayed in the input box's title bar (optional)
Default	The default value for the user's input (optional)

An InputBox example

Here's a statement that shows how you can use the InputBox function:

```
TheName = InputBox("What is your name?", "Greetings")
```

When you execute this VBA statement, Excel displays the dialog box shown in Figure 15-5. Notice that this example uses only the first two arguments and doesn't supply a default value. When the user enters a value and clicks OK, the code assigns the value to the variable TheName.

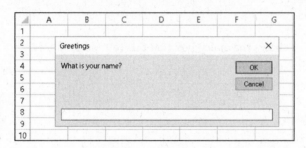

FIGURE 15-5: The InputBox function displays this dialog box.

The following example uses the third argument and provides a default value. The default value is the username stored by Excel (the Application object's UserName property).

```
Sub GetName()
    Dim TheName As String
    TheName = InputBox("What is your name?", _
        "Greetings", Application.UserName)
End Sub
```

The InputBox always displays a Cancel button. If the user clicks Cancel, the InputBox function returns an empty string.

REMEMBER

VBA's InputBox function always returns a string, so if you need to get a value, your code needs to do some additional checking. The following example uses the InputBox function to get a number. It uses the IsNumeric function to check whether the string is a number. If the string does contain a number, all is fine. If the user's entry cannot be interpreted as a number, the code displays a message box.

```
Sub AddSheets()
    Dim Prompt As String
    Dim Caption As String
    Dim DefValue As Long
    Dim NumSheets As String
```

```
        Prompt = "How many sheets do you want to add?"
        Caption = "Tell me..."
        DefValue = 1
        NumSheets = InputBox(Prompt, Caption, DefValue)

        If NumSheets = "" Then Exit Sub ';Canceled
        If IsNumeric(NumSheets) Then
            If NumSheets > 0 Then Sheets.Add Count:=NumSheets
        Else
            MsgBox "Invalid number"
        End If
    End Sub
```

Figure 15-6 shows the dialog box that this routine produces.

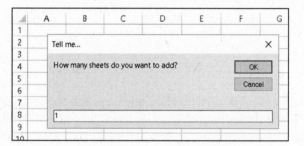

FIGURE 15-6:
Another example
of using the
InputBox
function.

Another type of InputBox

The information presented in this section applies to VBA's InputBox function. Microsoft seems to love confusion, so you also have access to the InputBox *method*, which is a method of the Application object.

One big advantage of using the Application InputBox method is that your code can prompt for a range selection. The user can then select the range in the worksheet by highlighting the cells. Here's a quick example that prompts the user to select a range:

```
Sub GetRange()
    Dim Rng As Range
    On Error Resume Next
    Set Rng = Application.InputBox _
        (prompt:="Specify a range:", Type:=8)
    If Rng Is Nothing Then Exit Sub
    MsgBox "You selected range " & Rng.Address
End Sub
```

Figure 15-7 shows how it looks.

In this simple example, the code tells the user the address of the range that was selected. In real life, your code would actually do something useful with the selected range. A nice thing about this example is that Excel takes care of the error handling. If you enter something that's not a range, Excel tells you about it and lets you try again.

The Application.InputBox method is similar to VBA's InputBox function, but it also has some differences. Check the Help system for complete details.

The GetOpenFilename Method

If your VBA procedure needs to ask the user for a filename, you *could* use the InputBox function and have the user do some typing. An input box usually isn't the best tool for this job, however, because most users find it difficult to remember paths, backslashes, filenames, and file extensions. In other words, it's far too easy to screw up when typing a filename.

For a better solution to this problem, use the GetOpenFilename method of the Application object, which ensures that your code gets its hands on a valid filename, including its complete path. The GetOpenFilename method displays the familiar Open dialog box (a dead ringer for the dialog box Excel displays when you choose File⇨Open⇨Browse).

REMEMBER

The GetOpenFilename method doesn't actually open the specified file. This method simply returns the user-selected filename as a string. Then you can write code to do whatever you want with the filename.

The syntax for the GetOpenFilename method

The official syntax of the GetOpenFilename method is as follows:

```
object.GetOpenFilename ([fileFilter], [filterIndex],
    [title],[buttonText], [multiSelect])
```

GetOpenFilename method takes the optional arguments shown in Table 15-5.

TABLE 15-5

GetOpenFilename Method Arguments

Argument	What It Does
FileFilter	Determines the types of files that appear in the dialog box (for example, *.TXT). You can specify several filters for the user to choose from.
FilterIndex	Determines which of the file filters the dialog box displays by default.
Title	Specifies the caption for the dialog box's title bar.
ButtonText	Ignored (used only for the Macintosh version of Excel).
MultiSelect	If True, the user can select multiple files.

A GetOpenFilename example

The FileFilter argument determines what appears in the dialog box's Files of Type drop-down list. This argument consists of pairs of file filter strings followed by the wildcard file filter specification, with commas separating each part and pair. If omitted, this argument defaults to the following:

```
All Files (*.*), *.*
```

Notice that this string consists of two parts, separated by a comma:

```
All Files (*.*)
```

and

```
*.*
```

The first part of this string is the text displayed in the Files of Type drop-down list. The second part determines which files the dialog box displays. For example, *.* means *all files*.

The code in the following example opens a dialog box that asks the user for a filename. The procedure defines five file filters. Notice that the VBA line-continuation sequencesets up the Filter variable; doing so helps simplify this rather complicated argument.

```
Sub GetImportFileName()
    Dim Finfo As String
    Dim FilterIndex As Long
    Dim Title As String
    Dim FileName As Variant

'   Set up list of file filters
    FInfo = "Text Files (*.txt),*.txt," & _
            "Lotus Files (*.prn),*.prn," & _
            "Comma Separated Files (*.csv),*.csv," & _
            "ASCII Files (*.asc),*.asc," & _
            "All Files (*.*),*.*"

'   Display *.* by default
    FilterIndex = 5

'   Set the dialog box caption
    Title = "Select a File to Import"

'   Get the filename
    FileName = Application.GetOpenFilename (FInfo, _
        FilterIndex, Title)

'   Handle return info from dialog box
    If FileName = False Then
        MsgBox "No file was selected."
    Else
        MsgBox "You selected " & FileName
    End If
End Sub
```

Figure 15-8 shows the dialog box Excel displays when you execute this procedure. The appearance may vary, depending on the version of Windows you use and the display options you've set.

FIGURE 15-8:
The GetOpen
Filename method
displays a
customizable
dialog box and
returns the
selected file's
path and name.
It does not
open the file.

In a real application, you would do something more meaningful with the filename. For example, you might want to open it by using a statement such as this:

```
Workbooks.Open FileName
```

TECHNICAL STUFF

Notice that the FileName variable is declared as a Variant data type. If the user clicks Cancel, that variable contains a Boolean value (False). Otherwise, FileName is a string. Therefore, using a Variant data type handles both possibilities.

The GetSaveAsFilename Method

The Excel GetSaveAsFilename method works just like the GetOpenFilename method, but it displays the Excel Save As dialog box rather than its Open dialog box. The GetSaveAsFilename method gets a path and filename from the user but doesn't do anything with that information. It's up to you to write code that actually saves the file.

The syntax of this method follows:

```
object.GetSaveAsFilename ([InitialFilename], [FileFilter],
    [FilterIndex],[Title], [ButtonText])
```

The GetSaveAsFilename method takes Table 15-6's arguments, all of which are optional.

TABLE 15-6 **GetSaveAsFilename Method Arguments**

Argument	What It Does
InitialFileName	Specifies a default filename that appears in the File Name box.
FileFilter	Determines the types of files Excel displays in the dialog box (for example, *.TXT). You can specify several filters for the user to choose among.
FilterIndex	Determines which of the file filters Excel displays by default.
Title	Defines a caption for the dialog box's title bar.

Getting a Folder Name

Sometimes, you don't need to get a filename; you just need to get a folder name. If that's the case, the FileDialog object is just what the doctor ordered.

The following procedure displays a dialog box that allows the user to select a directory. The selected directory name (or "Canceled") is displayed by the MsgBox function.

```
Sub GetAFolder()
    With Application.FileDialog(msoFileDialogFolderPicker)
        .InitialFileName = Application.DefaultFilePath & "\"
        .Title = "Please select a location for the backup"
        .Show
        If .SelectedItems.Count = 0 Then
            MsgBox "Canceled"
        Else
            MsgBox .SelectedItems(1)
        End If
    End With
End Sub
```

The FileDialog object lets you specify the starting directory by specifying a value for the InitialFileName property. In this case, the code uses Excel's default file path as the starting directory.

Displaying Excel's Built-in Dialog Boxes

One way to look at VBA is that it's a tool that lets you mimic Excel commands. For example, consider this VBA statement:

```
Range("A1:A12").Name = "MonthNames"
```

Executing this VBA statement has the same effect as choosing Formulas ⇨ Defined Names ⇨ Define Name to display the New Name dialog box, typing MonthNames in the Name box and A1:A12 in the Refers to box, and clicking OK.

When you execute the VBA statement, the New Name dialog box doesn't appear. This is almost always what you want to happen; you don't want dialog boxes flashing across the screen while your macro executes.

In some cases, however, you may want your code to display one of Excel's many built-in dialog boxes and let the user make the choices in the dialog box. You can do this by using VBA to execute a Ribbon command. Here's an example that displays the New Name dialog box. The address in the Refers To box represents the range that's selected when the command is executed (see Figure 15-9).

```
Application.CommandBars.ExecuteMso "NameDefine"
```

FIGURE 15-9: Displaying one of Excel's dialog boxes by using VBA.

REMEMBER

Your VBA code can't get any information from the dialog box. For example, if you execute the code to display the New Name dialog box, your code can't get the name entered by the user or the range that's being named.

The ExecuteMso is a method of the CommandBars object and accepts one argument: an idMso parameter that represents a Ribbon control. Unfortunately, these parameters aren't listed in the Help system. And because the Ribbon hasn't

been around forever, code that uses the ExecuteMso method is not compatible with versions before Excel 2007.

Here's another example of using the ExecuteMso method. This statement, when executed, displays the Font tab of the Format Cells dialog box:

```
Application.CommandBars.ExecuteMso "FormatCellsFontDialog"
```

If you try to display a built-in dialog box in an incorrect context, Excel displays an error message. For example, here's a statement that displays the Format Number dialog box:

```
Application.CommandBars.ExecuteMso "NumberFormatsDialog"
```

If you execute this statement when it's not appropriate (for example, a Shape is selected), Excel displays an error message because that dialog box is appropriate only for worksheet cells.

Excel has thousands of commands. How can you find the name of the one you need? One way is to use the Customize Ribbon tab of the Excel Options dialog box. The quick way to get there is to right-click any Ribbon control and choose Customize the Ribbon from the shortcut menu. Virtually every command available in Excel is listed in the left panel. Find the command you need and hover your mouse over it, and you see its secret command name in the tooltip (it's the part in parentheses). Figure 15-10 shows an example.

FIGURE 15-10: Using the Customize Ribbon tab to identify a command name.

Chapter **16**

UserForm Basics

A UserForm is useful if your VBA macro needs to pause and get some information from a user. For example, your macro may have some options that can be specified in a UserForm. If only a few pieces of information are required (for example, a Yes/No answer or a text string), one of the techniques in Chapter 15 may do the job. But if you need to obtain more information, you must create a UserForm. That's what this chapter is all about.

Knowing When to Use a UserForm

This section describes a situation in which a UserForm is useful. The following macro changes the text in each cell in the selection to uppercase letters. It does this by using the VBA built-in UCase function.

```
Sub ChangeCase()
    Dim WorkRange As Range, cell As Range

'   Exit if a range is not selected
    If TypeName(Selection) <> "Range" Then Exit Sub

'   Process only text cells, no formulas
    On Error Resume Next
    Set WorkRange = Selection.SpecialCells _
        (xlCellTypeConstants, xlCellTypeConstants)
```

```
      For Each cell In WorkRange
            cell.Value = UCase(cell.Value)
      Next cell
End Sub
```

You can make this macro even more useful. For example, it would be nice if the macro could also change the text in the cells to either lowercase or proper case (capitalizing the first letter in each word). One approach is to create two additional macros — one for lowercase and one for proper case. Another approach is to modify the macro to handle the other options. If you use the second approach, you need some method of asking the user which type of change to make to the cells.

The solution is to display a dialog box like the one shown in Figure 16-1. You create this dialog box on a UserForm in the VBE and display it by using a VBA macro. The next section offers step-by-step instructions for creating this dialog box.

FIGURE 16-1:
You can get information from the user by displaying a UserForm.

TECHNICAL
STUFF

In VBA, the official name for a dialog box is a UserForm. But a UserForm is really an object that contains what's commonly known as a *dialog box*. This distinction isn't important, so you'll often here these terms used interchangeably.

Creating UserForms: An Overview

When creating a UserForm, you usually take the following general steps:

1. **Determine how the dialog box will be used and at what point it will be displayed in your VBA macro.**

2. **Press Alt+F11 to activate the VBE and insert a new UserForm object.**

 A UserForm object holds a single UserForm.

3. **Add controls to the UserForm.**

 Controls include items such as text boxes, buttons, check boxes, and list boxes.

4. **Use the Properties window to modify the properties for the controls or for the UserForm itself.**

5. **Write event-handler procedures for the controls (for example, a macro that executes when the user clicks a button in the dialog box).**

 These procedures are stored in the Code window for the UserForm object.

6. **Write a procedure (stored in a VBA module) that displays the dialog box to the user.**

Don't worry if some of these steps seem foreign. The following sections provide more details, along with step-by-step instructions for creating a UserForm.

When you're designing a UserForm, you're creating what developers call the Graphical User Interface (GUI) to your application. GUI also stands for Gaming Under the Influence, but that's not relevant here.

Take some time to consider what your form should look like and how your users are likely to want to interact with the elements on the UserForm. Try to guide them through the steps they need to take on the form by carefully considering the arrangement and wording of the controls. Like most things VBA-related, the more you do it, the easier it gets.

Working with UserForms

Each dialog box that you create is stored in its own UserForm object — one dialog box per UserForm. You create and access these UserForms in the Visual Basic Editor.

Inserting a new UserForm

Insert a UserForm object by following these steps:

1. **Activate the VBE by pressing Alt+F11.**

2. **Select the workbook that will hold the UserForm in the Project window.**

3. **Choose Insert ➪ UserForm.**

 The VBE inserts a new UserForm object, which contains an empty dialog box.

Figure 16-2 shows a UserForm — an empty dialog box. Your job, if you choose to accept it, is to add some controls to this UserForm.

FIGURE 16-2:
A new UserForm object.

Adding controls to a UserForm

When you activate a UserForm, the VBE displays the Toolbox in a floating window (refer to Figure 16-2). You use the tools in the Toolbox to add controls to your UserForm. If, for some reason, the Toolbox doesn't appear when you activate your UserForm, choose View ➪ Toolbox.

To add a control, just click the desired control in the Toolbox and drag it into the dialog box to create the control. After you add a control, you can move and resize it by using standard techniques.

Table 16-1 lists the various tools, as well as their capabilities. To determine which tool is which, hover your mouse pointer over the control and read the small pop-up description.

TABLE 16-1　**Toolbox Controls**

Control	What It Does
Label	Shows text
TextBox	Allows the user to enter text
ComboBox	Displays a drop-down list
ListBox	Displays a list of items
CheckBox	Provides options such as on/off or yes/no
OptionButton	Allows the user to select one of several options; used in groups of two or more

Control	What It Does
ToggleButton	Enables the user to switch a button on or off
Frame	Contains other controls
CommandButton	Adds a clickable button
TabStrip	Displays tabs
MultiPage	Creates a tabbed container for other objects
ScrollBar	Enables the user to drag a bar to establish a setting
SpinButton	Enables the user to click a button to change a value
Image	Holds an image
RefEdit	Allows the user to select a range

Changing properties for a UserForm control

Every control you add to a UserForm has properties that determine how the control looks or behaves. In addition, the UserForm itself has its own set of properties. You can change these properties with the aptly named Properties window. Figure 16-3 shows the Properties window when a CommandButton control is selected.

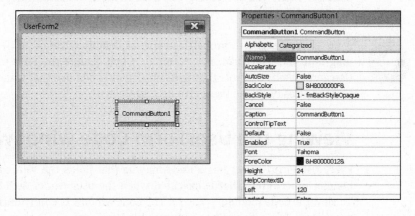

FIGURE 16-3:
Use the Properties windows to change the properties of UserForm controls.

The Properties window appears when you press F4. Alternatively, you can choose View ➪ Properties Window. The properties shown in this window depend on what is selected. If you select a different control, the properties change to those appropriate for that control. To hide the Properties window and get it out of the way, click the Close button in its title bar. Pressing F4 always brings it back when you need it.

Properties for controls include the following:

>> Name

>> Width

>> Height

>> Value

>> Caption

Each control has its own set of properties (although many controls have some common properties). To change a property using the Properties window, follow these steps:

1. Make sure that the correct control is selected in the UserForm.

2. Make sure the Properties window is visible. (Press F4 if it's not.)

3. In the Properties window, click the property that you want to change.

4. Make the change in the right portion of the Properties window.

If you select the UserForm itself (not a control on the UserForm), you can use the Properties window to adjust UserForm properties.

Chapter 17 tells you everything you need to know about working with dialog box controls.

 Some of the UserForm properties serve as default settings for new controls you drag onto the UserForm. For example, if you change the Font property for the UserForm itself, controls that you subsequently add use that same font. Controls that are already on the UserForm aren't affected.

TIP

Viewing the UserForm Code window

Every UserForm object has a Code module that holds the VBA code (the event-handler procedures) that is executed when the user works with the dialog box. To view the Code module, press F7. The Code window is empty until you add some procedures. Press Shift+F7 to return to the UserForm.

Here's another way to switch between the Code window and the UserForm display: Use the View Code and View Object buttons in the Project window's title bar. Or right-click the UserForm and choose View Code. If you're viewing code, double-click the UserForm name in the Project window to return to the UserForm.

Displaying a UserForm

You display a UserForm by using the UserForm's Show method in a VBA procedure.

REMEMBER

The macro that displays the dialog box must be in a VBA module — not in the Code window for the UserForm.

The following procedure displays the dialog box named UserForm1:

```
Sub ShowDialogBox()
    UserForm1.Show
'    Other statements can go here
End Sub
```

When Excel displays the dialog box, the ShowDialogBox macro halts until the user closes the dialog box. Then VBA executes any remaining statements in the procedure. Most of the time, you won't have any more code in the procedure. As you later see, you put your event-handler procedures in the Code window for the UserForm. These procedures kick in when the user works with the controls on the UserForm.

Using information from a UserForm

The VBE provides a name for each control you add to a UserForm. The control's name corresponds to its Name property. Use this name to refer to a particular control in your code. For example, if you add a CheckBox control to a UserForm named UserForm1, the CheckBox control is named CheckBox1 by default. You can use the Properties box to make this control appear with a check mark. Or you can write code to do it:

```
UserForm1.CheckBox1.Value = True
```

Most of the time, you write the code for a UserForm in the UserForm's code module. If that's the case, you can omit the UserForm object qualifier and write the statement like this:

```
CheckBox1.Value = True
```

Your VBA code can also check various properties of the controls and take appropriate actions. The following statement executes a macro named PrintReport if the check box (named CheckBox1) is checked:

```
If CheckBox1.Value = True Then Call PrintReport
```

It's usually a good idea to change the default name the VBE gives to your controls to something more meaningful. You might consider naming the check box something like cbxPrintReport. Note the three-letter prefix (cbx). There is no technical reason for using cbx as the prefix. This is just one example of using a naming convention to differentiate objects in VBA. Using a naming convention like this makes your code easier to read. In the end, the convention you choose is a matter of what you're comfortable with.

A UserForm Example

This section's UserForm example is an enhanced version of the ChangeCase macro from the beginning of the chapter. The original version of this macro changes the text in the selected cells to uppercase. This modified version uses a UserForm to ask the user which type of change to make: uppercase, lowercase, or proper case.

This dialog box needs to obtain one piece of information from the user: the type of change to make to the text. Because the user has three choices, your best bet is a dialog box with three OptionButton controls. The dialog box also needs two more buttons: an OK button and a Cancel button. Clicking the OK button runs the code that does the work. Clicking the Cancel button causes the macro to finish without doing anything.

This workbook is available at the book's website. However, you get more out of this exercise if you follow the steps provided here and create it yourself.

Creating the UserForm

These steps create the UserForm. Start with an empty workbook, and follow these steps:

1. **Press Alt+F11 to activate the VBE.**

2. **If multiple projects are in the Project window, select the project that corresponds to the workbook you're using.**

3. **Choose Insert ⇨ UserForm.**

 The VBE inserts a new UserForm object with an empty dialog box.

4. **Press F4 to display the Properties window.**

5. **In the Properties window, change the dialog box's Caption property to Change Case.**

6. **(Optional) The dialog box is a bit too large, so you may want to click it and use the handles (on the right and bottom sides) to make it smaller.**

 You can do Step 6 after you position all the controls in the dialog box.

Adding the CommandButtons

Ready to add two CommandButtons — OK and Cancel — to the dialog box? Follow along:

1. **Make sure that the Toolbox is displayed; if it isn't, choose View ⇨ Toolbox.**

2. **If the Properties window isn't visible, press F4 to display it.**

3. **In the Toolbox, drag a CommandButton into the dialog box to create a button.**

 As you see in the Properties box, the button has a default name and caption: CommandButton1.

4. **Make sure that the CommandButton is selected; then activate the Properties window and change the following properties:**

Property	Change To
Name	**OKButton**
Caption	**OK**
Default	**True**

5. **Add a second CommandButton object to the UserForm and change the following properties:**

Property	Change To
Name	**CancelButton**
Caption	**Cancel**
Cancel	**True**

6. **Adjust the size and position of the controls so your dialog box looks something like Figure 16-4.**

FIGURE 16-4:
The UserForm
with two
CommandButton
controls.

Adding the OptionButtons

In this section, you add three OptionButtons to the dialog box. Before adding the OptionButtons, you add a Frame object that contains the OptionButtons. The Frame isn't necessary, but it makes the dialog box look a bit more professional so users won't think it was designed by an amateur.

To add the OptionButtons, follow these steps:

1. In the Toolbox, click the Frame tool and drag it into the dialog box.

This step creates a frame to hold the options buttons.

2. Use the Properties window to change the frame's caption to Options.

3. In the Toolbox, click the OptionButton tool and drag it into the dialog box (within the Frame).

Doing this creates an OptionButton control.

4. Select the OptionButton and use the Properties window to change the following properties:

Property	Change To
Name	**OptionUpper**
Caption	**Upper Case**
Accelerator	**U**
Value	**True**

Setting the Value property to True makes this OptionButton the default.

5. **Add another OptionButton and use the Properties window to change the following properties:**

Property	Change To
Name	**OptionLower**
Caption	**Lower Case**
Accelerator	**L**

6. **Add a third OptionButton and use the Properties window to change the following properties:**

Property	Change To
Name	**OptionProper**
Caption	**Proper Case**
Accelerator	**P**

7. **Adjust the size and position of the OptionButtons, Frame, and dialog box.**

Your UserForm should look something like Figure 16-5.

FIGURE 16-5: This is the UserForm after adding three OptionButton controls inside a Frame control.

If you'd like a sneak preview to see what the UserForm looks like when it's displayed, press F5. None of the controls work yet, so you need to click the red X in the title bar to close the dialog box.

The Accelerator property determines which letter in the caption is underlined — and more important, it determines what Alt+key combination selects that control. For example, you can select the Lower Case option by pressing Alt+L because the L is underlined. Accelerator keys are optional, but some users prefer to use the keyboard to navigate dialog boxes.

You may wonder why the OptionButtons have accelerator keys but the CommandButtons lack such a feature. Generally, OK and Cancel buttons never have accelerator keys because they can be accessed from the keyboard. Pressing Enter is equivalent to clicking OK because the control's Default property is True. Pressing Esc is equivalent to clicking Cancel because the control's Cancel property is True.

Adding event-handler procedures

Now it's time to make the UserForm actually do something. Here's how to add an event-handler procedure for the Cancel and OK buttons:

1. **Double-click the Cancel button.**

 The VBE activates the Code window for the UserForm and inserts an empty procedure:

   ```
   Private Sub CancelButton_Click()
   End Sub
   ```

 The procedure named CancelButton_Click is executed when the Cancel button is clicked, but only when the dialog box is displayed. In other words, clicking the Cancel button when you're designing the dialog box won't execute the procedure. Because the Cancel button's Cancel property is set to True, pressing Esc also triggers the CancelButton_Click procedure.

2. **Insert the following statement inside the procedure (before the End Sub statement):**

   ```
   Unload UserForm1
   ```

 This statement closes the UserForm when the Cancel button is clicked.

3. **Press Shift+F7 to return to the UserForm.**

4. **Double-click the OK button.**

 The VBE activates the Code window for the UserForm and inserts an empty Sub procedure called OKButton_Click.

 When the UserForm is displayed, clicking OK executes this procedure. Because this button has its Default property set to True, pressing Enter also executes the OKButton_Click procedure.

5. Enter the following code so the procedure looks like this:

```
Private Sub OKButton_Click()
    Dim WorkRange As Range
    Dim cell As Range

'   Process only text cells, no formulas
    On Error Resume Next
    Set WorkRange = Selection.SpecialCells _
        (xlCellTypeConstants, xlCellTypeConstants)

'   Upper case
    If OptionUpper Then
        For Each cell In WorkRange
            cell.Value = UCase(cell.Value)
        Next cell
    End If

'   Lower case
    If OptionLower Then
        For Each cell In WorkRange
            cell.Value = LCase(cell.Value)
        Next cell
    End If

'   Proper case
    If OptionProper Then
        For Each cell In WorkRange
            cell.Value = Application. _
            WorksheetFunction.Proper(cell.Value)
        Next cell
    End If
    Unload UserForm1
End Sub
```

The preceding code is an enhanced version of the original ChangeCase macro presented at the beginning of the chapter. The macro consists of three separate blocks of code. This code uses three If-Then structures; each one has a For Each-Next loop. Only one block is executed, determined by which OptionButton the user selects. The last statement *unloads* (closes) the dialog box after the work is finished.

Creating a macro to display the dialog box

You're almost finished with this project. The only thing missing is a way to display the dialog box. Follow these steps to create the procedure that makes the dialog box appear:

1. In the VBE window, choose Insert ⇨ Module.

The VBE adds an empty VBA module (named Module1) to the project.

2. Enter the following code:

```
Sub ChangeCase()
    If TypeName(Selection) = "Range" Then
        UserForm1.Show
    Else
        MsgBox "Select a range.", vbCritical
    End If
End Sub
```

This procedure is pretty simple. It checks to make sure that a range is selected. If so, the dialog box is displayed (using the Show method). The user then interacts with the dialog box, and the code stored in the UserForm's Code pane is executed. If a range is not selected, the user sees a MsgBox with the text Select a range.

Making the macro available

At this point, everything should be working properly. But you still need an easy way to execute the macro. Assign a shortcut key (Ctrl+Shift+C) that executes the ChangeCase macro by following these steps:

1. Activate the Excel window by pressing Alt+F11.

2. Choose Developer ⇨ Code ⇨ Macros or press Alt+F8.

3. In the Macros dialog box, select the ChangeCase macro.

4. Click the Options button.

Excel displays its Macro Options dialog box.

5. Enter C for the Shortcut key (see Figure 16-6).

6. Enter a description of the macro in the Description field.

7. Click OK.

8. Click Cancel when you return to the Macro dialog box.

FIGURE 16-6:
Assign a shortcut
key to execute
the ChangeCase
macro.

After you perform this operation, pressing Ctrl+Shift+C executes the ChangeCase macro, which displays the UserForm if a range is selected.

You can also make this macro available from the Quick Access toolbar. Right-click the Quick Access toolbar and choose Customize Quick Access Toolbar. The Excel Options dialog box appears, and the ChangeCase macro is listed below Macros (see Figure 16-7).

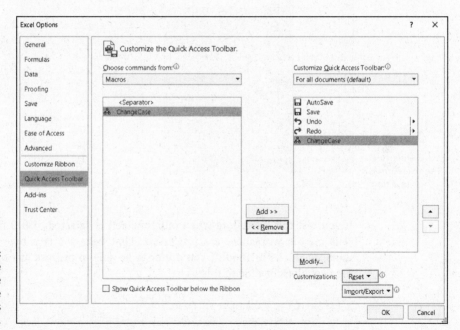

FIGURE 16-7:
Adding the
ChangeChase
macro to the
Quick Access
toolbar.

Testing the macro

Finally, you need to test the macro and dialog box to make sure they work properly, as follows:

1. **Activate a worksheet (any worksheet in any workbook).**

2. **Select some cells that contain text.**

You can even select entire rows or columns.

3. **Press Ctrl+Shift+C.**

The UserForm appears. Figure 16-8 shows how it should look.

4. **Make your choice, and click OK.**

If you did everything correctly, the macro makes the specified change to the text in the selected cells.

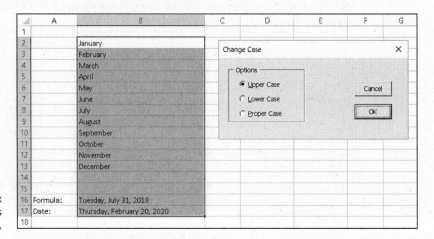

FIGURE 16-8:
The UserForm is in action.

If you test this procedure when only one cell is selected, you'll find that *all* the cells on the worksheet are processed. That behavior is a byproduct of using the SpecialCells method. If you prefer to be able to process just one cell, change the first block of code to this:

```
If Selection.Count = 1 Then
    Set WorkRange = Selection
Else
    Set WorkRange = Selection.SpecialCells _
        (xlCellTypeConstants, xlCellTypeConstants)
End If
```

Figure 16-9 shows the worksheet after converting the text to uppercase. Notice that the formula in cell B16 and the date in cell B17 were not changed. The macro works only with cells that contain text.

	A	B
1		
2		JANUARY
3		FEBRUARY
4		MARCH
5		APRIL
6		MAY
7		JUNE
8		JULY
9		AUGUST
10		SEPTEMBER
11		OCTOBER
12		NOVEMBER
13		DECEMBER
14		
15		
16	Formula:	Tuesday, July 31, 2018
17	Date:	Thursday, February 20, 2020

FIGURE 16-9:
The text has been converted to uppercase.

As long as the workbook is open, you can execute the macro from any other workbook. If you close the workbook that contains your macro, Ctrl+Shift+C no longer has any function.

If the macro doesn't work properly, double-check the preceding steps to locate and correct the error. Don't be alarmed; debugging is a normal part of developing macros. As a last resort, download the completed workbook from this book's website and try to figure out where you went wrong.

Chapter **17**

Using UserForm Controls

A user responds to a custom dialog box (also known as a *UserForm*) by using the various controls (buttons, edit boxes, option buttons, and so on) that the dialog box contains. Your VBA code then makes use of these responses to determine which actions to take. You have quite a few controls at your disposal, and this chapter tells you about them.

If you worked through the hands-on example in Chapter 16, you already have some experience with UserForm controls. This chapter fills in some of the gaps.

Getting Started with Dialog Box Controls

In this section, you explore how to add controls to a UserForm, give them meaningful names, and adjust some of their properties.

REMEMBER

Before you can do any of these things, you must have a UserForm, which you get by choosing Insert ➪ UserForm in the VBE. When you add a UserForm, make sure that the correct project is selected in the Project window (if more than one project is available).

Adding controls

Oddly enough, the VBE doesn't have menu commands that allow you to add controls to a dialog box. You must use the floating Toolbox (described in Chapter 16) to add controls. Normally, the Toolbox pops up automatically when you activate a UserForm in the VBE. If it doesn't, you can display the Toolbox by choosing View ⇨ Toolbox.

Follow along to add a control to the UserForm:

1. **Click the Toolbox tool that corresponds to the control you want to add.**

2. **Click in the UserForm, and drag to size and position the control.**

 Alternatively, you can simply drag a control from the Toolbox to the UserForm to create a control with the default dimensions. Figure 17-1 shows a UserForm that contains a few controls: Two OptionButtons (inside a Frame), a ComboBox, a CheckBox, a ScrollBar, and a CommandButton.

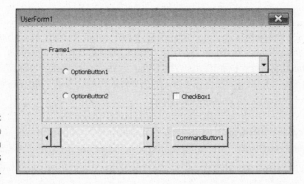

FIGURE 17-1: A UserForm in the VBE, with a few controls added.

TIP

A UserForm may contain vertical and horizontal grid lines, which help align the controls you add. When you add or move a control, it *snaps* to the grid. If you don't like this feature, you can turn off the grids by following these steps:

1. **Choose Tools ⇨ Options in the VBE.**

2. **In the Options dialog box, select the General tab.**

3. **Set your desired options in the Form Grid Settings section.**

Introducing control properties

Every control that you add to a UserForm has properties that determine how the control looks and behaves. You can change a control's properties at the following two times:

>> At design time — when you're designing the UserForm. You do so manually, using the Properties window.

>> At runtime — while your macro is running. You do so by writing VBA code. Changes made at runtime are always temporary; they're made to the copy of the dialog box you're showing, not to the actual UserForm object you designed.

When you add a control to a UserForm, you almost always need to make some design-time adjustments to its properties. You make these changes in the Properties window. (To display the Properties window, press F4.) Figure 17-2 shows the Properties window, which displays properties for the object selected in the UserForm — which happens to be a CheckBox control.

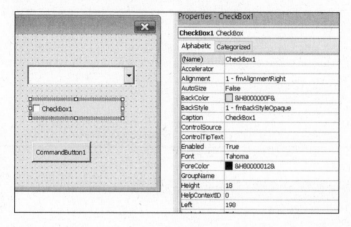

FIGURE 17-2: Use the Properties window to make design-time changes to a control's properties.

REMEMBER

To change a control's properties at runtime, you must write VBA code. For example, you may want to hide a particular control when the user clicks a check box. In such a case, you write code to change the control's Visible property.

Each control has its own set of properties. All controls, however, have some common properties, such as Name, Width, and Height. Table 17-1 lists some of the common properties available for many controls.

When you select a control, that control's properties appear in the Properties window. To change a property, just select it in the Properties window and make the change. Some properties give you some help. For example, if you need to change the TextAlign property, the Properties window displays a drop-down list that contains all valid property values, as shown in Figure 17-3.

TABLE 17-1 ## Common Control Properties

Property	What It Affects
Accelerator	The letter underlined in the control's caption. The user presses this key in conjunction with the Alt key to select the control.
AutoSize	If True, the control resizes itself automatically based on the text in its caption.
BackColor	The control's background color.
BackStyle	The background style (transparent or opaque).
Caption	The text that appears on the control.
Left and Top	Values that determine the control's position.
Name	The control's name. By default, a control's name is based on the control type. You can change the name to any valid name, but each control's name must be unique within the dialog box.
Picture	A graphics image to display. The image can be from a graphics file, or you can select the Picture property and paste an image that you copied to the Clipboard.
Value	The control's value.
Visible	If False, the control is hidden.
Width and Height	Values that determine the control's width and height.

FIGURE 17-3:
Change some
properties by
selecting from
a drop-down
list of valid
property values.

Dialog Box Controls: The Details

The following sections introduce each type of control you can use in custom dialog boxes and discuss some of the most useful properties. Not every property for every control is included because that would require a book that's about four times as thick (and it would be a very boring book).

TIP

The Help system for controls and properties is thorough. To find complete details for a particular property, select the property in the Properties window and press F1.

All the examples in this section are available on this book's website.

CheckBox control

A CheckBox control is useful for getting a binary choice: yes or no, true or false, on or off, and so on. Figure 17-4 shows some examples of CheckBox controls.

FIGURE 17-4:
CheckBox
Controls in a
UserForm.

Following are a CheckBox control's most useful properties:

>> **Accelerator:** A character that lets the user change the value of the control by using the keyboard. For example, if the accelerator is A, pressing Alt+A changes the value of the CheckBox control (from checked to unchecked, or from unchecked to checked). In the example shown in Figure 17-4, numbers are the accelerators (Alt+1, Alt+2, and so on).

>> **ControlSource:** The address of a worksheet cell that's linked to the CheckBox. The cell displays TRUE if the control is checked and FALSE if the control is not checked. This is optional. Most of the time, a CheckBox is not linked to a cell.

>> **Value:** If True, the CheckBox has a check mark. If False, the CheckBox doesn't have a check mark.

WARNING

Don't confuse CheckBox controls with OptionButton controls. They look similar, but they're used for different purposes.

ComboBox control

A ComboBox control is similar to a ListBox control (described later in the "ListBox control" section). A ComboBox, however, is a drop-down control. Another difference is that the user may be allowed to enter a value that doesn't appear in the list of items. Figure 17-5 shows two ComboBox controls. The control on the right (for the year) is being used, so it has dropped down to display its list of options.

FIGURE 17-5:
ComboBox
Controls in a
UserForm.

Following are some useful ComboBox control properties:

>> **ControlSource:** A cell that stores the value selected in the ComboBox.

>> **ListRows:** The number of items to display when the list drops down.

>> **ListStyle:** The appearance of the list items.

>> **RowSource:** A range address that contains the list of items displayed in the ComboBox.

>> **Style:** Determines whether the control acts like a drop-down list or a ComboBox. A drop-down list doesn't allow the user to enter a new value.

>> **Value:** The text of the item selected by the user and displayed in the ComboBox.

TECHNICAL STUFF

If your list of items isn't in a worksheet, you can add items to a ComboBox control by using the AddItem method. More information on this method is in Chapter 18.

CommandButton control

CommandButton is just a common clickable button. It is of no use unless you provide an event-handler procedure to execute when the button is clicked. Figure 17-6 shows a dialog box with nine CommandButtons. Two of these buttons feature clip-art images, which are added by copying the clip art and then pasting it into the Picture field in the Properties window.

FIGURE 17-6:
CommandButton
controls.

When a CommandButton is clicked, it executes an event-handler procedure with a name that consists of the CommandButton's name, an underscore, and the word `Click`. For example, if a CommandButton is named MyButton, clicking it executes the macro named MyButton_Click. This macro is stored in the Code window for the UserForm.

Following are some useful CommandButton control properties:

>> **Cancel:** If True, pressing Esc executes the macro attached to the button. Only one of the form's buttons can have this option set to True.

>> **Default:** If True, pressing Enter executes the macro attached to the button. Again: Just one button can have this option set to True.

Frame control

A Frame control encloses other controls. You use it either for aesthetic purposes or to logically group a set of controls. A frame is particularly useful when the dialog box contains more than one set of OptionButton controls (see "OptionButton control," later in this chapter).

The following list describes some useful Frame control properties:

>> **BorderStyle:** The frame's appearance.

>> **Caption:** The text displayed at the top of the frame. The caption can be an empty string if you don't want the control to display a caption.

Image control

An Image control displays an image. You may want to use an Image control to display your company's logo in a dialog box. Figure 17-7 shows a dialog box with an Image control that displays a photo of a cute little kitten.

FIGURE 17-7:
An Image control
displays a photo.

The following list describes the most useful Image control properties:

>> **Picture:** The graphics image that is displayed.

>> **PictureSizeMode:** How the picture is displayed if the control size doesn't match the image size.

When you click the Picture property, you're prompted for a filename. However, the graphics image (after it's retrieved) is stored in the workbook. That way, if you distribute your workbook to someone else, you don't have to include a copy of the graphics file.

TIP

Rather than retrieve the image from a file, you can copy and paste. To search the web for images, activate Excel and choose Insert➪Illustrations➪Online Pictures, and search for an image to place in your worksheet. Then select the image, and press Ctrl+C to copy it to the Clipboard. Then activate your UserForm, click the Image control, and select the Picture property in the Properties box. Press Ctrl+V to paste the copied image. Then you can delete the image from the worksheet.

WARNING

Some graphics images are very large and can make your workbook size increase dramatically. For best results, use an image that's as small as possible.

Label control

A Label control simply displays text in your dialog box. Figure 17-8 shows a few Label controls. As you can see, you have a great deal of control of the formatting of a Label control.

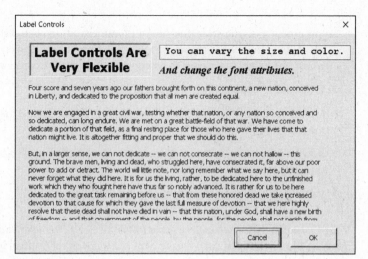

FIGURE 17-8:
Label controls
can take on lots
of different looks.

ListBox control

The ListBox control presents a list of items from which the user can choose one or more. Figure 17-9 shows a dialog box with two ListBox controls.

FIGURE 17-9:
ListBox controls.

ListBox controls are very flexible. For example, you can specify a worksheet range that holds the ListBox items, and the range can consist of multiple columns. Or you can fill the ListBox with items by using VBA code.

If a ListBox isn't tall enough to display all the items in the list, a scroll bar appears so the user can scroll down to see more items.

The following list is a description of the most useful ListBox control properties:

>> **ControlSource:** A cell that stores the value selected in the ListBox.

>> **IntegralHeight:** This is True if the ListBox height adjusts automatically to display full lines of text when the list is scrolled vertically. If False, the ListBox may display partial lines of text when it is scrolled vertically. Note that when

this property is True, the actual height of your ListBox may be slightly different, when your UserForm is shown, from what you had set it originally. In other words, the height may adjust to ensure that the last entry is entirely visible.

>> **ListStyle:** The appearance of the list items.

>> **MultiSelect:** Determines whether the user can select multiple items from the list.

>> **RowSource:** A range address that contains the list of items displayed in the ListBox.

>> **Value:** The text of the selected item in the ListBox.

If the ListBox has its MultiSelect property set to 1 or 2, the user can select multiple items in the ListBox. In such a case, you can't specify a ControlSource; you need to write a macro that determines which items are selected. Chapter 18 demonstrates how to do so.

MultiPage control

A MultiPage control allows you to create tabbed dialog boxes, like the Format Cells dialog box (the one that appears when you press Ctrl+1 in Excel). Figure 17-10 shows an example of a custom dialog box that uses a MultiPage control. This particular control has three pages, or tabs.

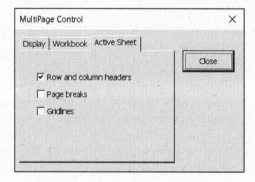

FIGURE 17-10:
Use a MultiPage control to create a tabbed dialog box.

Descriptions of the most useful MultiPage control properties follow:

>> **Style:** Determines the appearance of the control. The tabs can appear normally (on the top), on the left, as buttons, or hidden (no tabs — your VBA code determines which page is displayed).

>> **Value:** Determines which page or tab is displayed. A Value of 0 displays the first page, a Value of 1 displays the second page, and so on.

By default, a MultiPage control has two pages. To add pages, right-click a tab and select New Page from the shortcut menu.

TIP

OptionButton control

OptionButtons are useful when the user needs to choose from a small number of mutually exclusive items. OptionButtons are always used in groups of at least two. Figure 17-11 shows two sets of OptionButtons, and each set is contained in a frame.

FIGURE 17-11: Two sets of OptionButton controls, each contained in a Frame control.

The following is a description of the most useful OptionButton control properties:

>> **Accelerator:** A letter that lets the user select the option by using the keyboard. For example, if the accelerator for an option button is C, pressing Alt+C selects the control.

>> **GroupName:** A name that identifies an option button as being associated with other option buttons with the same GroupName property.

>> **ControlSource:** The worksheet cell that's linked to the option button. The cell displays TRUE if the control is selected or FALSE if the control is not selected.

>> **Value:** If True, the OptionButton is selected. If False, the OptionButton is not selected.

REMEMBER

If your dialog box contains more than one set of OptionButtons, you *must* change the GroupName property for all OptionButtons in a particular set. Otherwise, all OptionButtons become part of the same set. Alternatively, you can enclose each set of OptionButtons in a Frame control, which automatically groups the Option-Buttons in the frame.

RefEdit control

In some cases, you may need the user to select a range of cells in order to pass a valid range to your VBA code. Your procedures can then use the selected range for some specific task. The RefEdit control is used when you need to let the user select a range in a worksheet. Figure 17-12 shows a UserForm with two RefEdit controls. Its Value property holds the address of the selected range (as a text string).

FIGURE 17-12: Two RefEdit controls.

WARNING

The RefEdit control sometimes causes trouble in more complex UserForms. For best results, don't place a RefEdit control inside a Frame or MultiPage control.

ScrollBar control

When you add a ScrollBar control, you can make it horizontal or vertical. The ScrollBar control is similar to a SpinButton control (described later). The difference is that the user can drag the ScrollBar's button to change the control's value in larger increments. Another difference is that when you click the up button on a vertical ScrollBar, the value decreases — which is a bit counterintuitive. So a ScrollBar is not always a good substitute for a SpinButton.

Figure 17-13 shows a ScrollBar control with a horizontal orientation. Its Value property is displayed in a Label control placed below the ScrollBar control.

FIGURE 17-13: A ScrollBar control with a Label control below it.

Following are the most useful properties of a ScrollBar control:

>> **Value:** The control's current value.

>> **Min:** The control's minimum value.

>> **Max:** The control's maximum value.

>> **ControlSource:** The worksheet cell that displays the control's value.

>> **SmallChange:** The amount that the control's value is changed by a click.

>> **LargeChange:** The amount that the control's value is changed by clicking either side of the button.

The ScrollBar control is most useful for specifying a value that extends across a wide range of possible values.

SpinButton control

The SpinButton control lets the user select a value by clicking the control, which has two arrows (one to increase the value and the other to decrease the value). Like a ScrollBar control, a SpinButton can be oriented either horizontally or vertically. Figure 17-14 shows a dialog box that uses two vertically oriented SpinButton controls. Each control is linked to the Label control on the right (by using VBA procedures).

FIGURE 17-14:
SpinButton
controls.

The following descriptions explain the most useful properties of a SpinButton control:

>> **Value:** The control's current value.

>> **Min:** The control's minimum value.

>> **Max:** The control's maximum value.

>> **ControlSource:** The worksheet cell that displays the control's value.

>> **SmallChange:** The amount that the control's value is changed by a click. Usually, this property is set to 1, but you can make it any value.

If you use a ControlSource for a SpinButton, you should understand that the worksheet is recalculated every time the control's value is changed. Therefore, if the user changes the value from 0 to 12, the worksheet is calculated 12 times. If your worksheet takes a long time to calculate, you may want to avoid using a ControlSource to store the value.

TabStrip control

A TabStrip control is designed to navigate different sets of values using a single page with the same set of controls. This control is rarely used, as the MultiPage control provides a much easier way to achieve the same functionality. You can effectively ignore it and use the MultiPage control instead.

TextBox control

A TextBox control lets the user enter text. Figure 17-15 shows a dialog box with two TextBox controls.

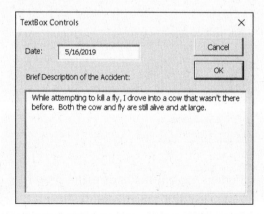

FIGURE 17-15:
TextBox controls.

Following are the most useful TextBox control properties:

>> **AutoSize:** If True, the control adjusts its size automatically, depending on the amount of text.

>> **ControlSource:** The address of a cell that contains the text in the TextBox.

>> **IntegralHeight:** If True, the TextBox height adjusts automatically to display full lines of text when the list is scrolled vertically. If False, the TextBox may display partial lines of text when it is scrolled vertically.

>> **MaxLength:** The maximum number of characters allowed in the TextBox. If 0, the number of characters is unlimited.

>> **MultiLine:** If True, the TextBox can display more than one line of text.

>> **TextAlign:** Determines how the text is aligned in the TextBox.

>> **WordWrap:** Determines whether the control allows word wrap.

>> **ScrollBars:** Determines the type of scroll bars for the control: horizontal, vertical, both, or none.

TIP

When you add a TextBox control, its WordWrap property is set to True, and its MultiLine property is set to False. The net effect? Word wrap doesn't work! So if you want the words to wrap in a TextBox control, make sure that you set the MultiLine property to True.

ToggleButton control

A ToggleButton control has two states: on and off. Clicking the button toggles between these two states, and the button changes its appearance when clicked. Its value is either True (pressed) or False (not pressed). Figure 17-16 shows a dialog box with four ToggleButton controls. The top one is pressed.

FIGURE 17-16:
ToggleButton controls.

Working with Dialog Box Controls

This section offers a few pointers on moving, resizing, and aligning dialog box controls to get your UserForms looking just right.

Moving and resizing controls

After you place a control in a dialog box, you can move it and resize it by using standard mouse techniques. Or for precise control, you can use the Properties window to enter a value for the control's Height, Width, Left, or Top property.

TIP

You can select multiple controls by Ctrl+clicking the controls. Or you can click and drag to "lasso" a group of controls. When multiple controls are selected, the Properties window displays only the properties common to all selected controls. You can change those common properties, and the change is made to all controls you select, which is much quicker than doing them one at a time.

A control can hide another control; in other words, you can stack one control on top of another. Unless you have a good reason for doing so, make sure that you don't overlap controls.

Aligning and spacing controls

The Format menu in the VBE window provides several commands to help you precisely align and space the controls in a dialog box. Before you use these commands, select the controls you want to work with. These commands are fairly self-explanatory.

Figure 17-17 shows a dialog box with several CheckBox controls that are about to be aligned.

FIGURE 17-17:
Choose
Format ⇨ Align
to change
the alignment
of UserForm
controls.

TIP

When you select multiple controls, the last selected control appears with white handles rather than the normal black handles. The control with the white handles is the basis for aligning or resizing the other selected controls when you use the Format menu.

Accommodating keyboard users

Many users prefer to navigate through a dialog box by using the keyboard: Pressing Tab or Shift+Tab cycles through the controls, while pressing a hot key instantly activates a particular control.

To make sure that your dialog box works properly for keyboard users, you must be mindful of two issues:

>> Tab order

>> Accelerator keys

Changing the tab order

The tab order determines the order in which the controls are activated when the user presses Tab or Shift+Tab. It also determines which control has the initial *focus* — that is, which control is the active control when the dialog box first appears. For example, if a user is entering text in a TextBox, the TextBox has the focus. If the user clicks an OptionButton, the OptionButton has the focus. The first control in the tab order has the focus when Excel first displays a dialog box.

To set the control tab order, choose View ⇨ Tab Order. You can also right-click the dialog box and choose Tab Order from the shortcut menu. In either case, Excel displays the Tab Order dialog box, shown in Figure 17-18.

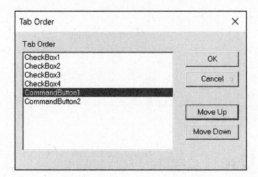

FIGURE 17-18:
The Tab Order dialog box.

The Tab Order dialog box lists all the controls in the UserForm. The tab order in the UserForm corresponds to the order of the items in the list. To change the tab order of a control, select it in the list and then click the Move Up or Move Down button. You can choose more than one control (click while pressing Shift or Ctrl) and move them all at one time.

TIP

Rather than use the Tab Order dialog box, you can set a control's position in the tab order by using the Properties window. The first control in the tab order has a TabIndex property of 0. If you want to remove a control from the tab order, set its TabStop property to False.

REMEMBER

Some controls (such as Frame or MultiPage controls) act as containers for other controls. The controls inside a container control have their own tab order. To set the tab order for a group of OptionButtons inside a Frame control, select the Frame control before you choose the View ⇨ Tab Order command.

Setting hot keys

Normally, you want to assign an accelerator key, or *hot key*, to dialog box controls. You do so by entering a letter for the Accelerator property in the Properties window. If a control doesn't have an Accelerator property (a TextBox, for example), you can still allow direct keyboard access to it by using a Label control. That is, assign an accelerator key to the Label and put the Label directly before the TextBox in the tab order.

Figure 17-19 shows a UserForm with three TextBoxes. The Labels that describe the TextBoxes have accelerator keys, and each Label precedes its corresponding Text-Box in the tab order. Pressing Alt+D, for example, activates the TextBox next to the Department Label.

FIGURE 17-19:
Use Labels to provide direct access to controls that don't have accelerator keys.

Testing a UserForm

The VBE offers three ways to test a UserForm without calling it from a VBA procedure:

>> Choose Run ⇨ Run Sub/UserForm.

>> Press F5.

>> Click the Run Sub/UserForm button on the Standard toolbar.

When a dialog box is displayed in this test mode, you can try the tab order and the accelerator keys.

Dialog Box Aesthetics

Dialog boxes can look good, bad, or somewhere in between. A good-looking dialog box is easy on the eye, has nicely sized and aligned controls, and its function is perfectly clear to the user. Bad-looking dialog boxes confuse the user, have misaligned controls, and give the impression that the developer didn't have a plan (or a clue).

Try to limit the number of controls on your form. If you do need many controls — generally more than ten — consider using a MultiPage control to split the task the user has to do into logical (and smaller) steps.

A good rule to follow is to try to make your dialog boxes look like the Excel built-in dialog boxes. As you gain more experience with dialog box construction, you can duplicate almost all the features of the Excel dialog boxes.

Chapter **18**

UserForm Techniques and Tricks

The previous chapters show you how to insert a UserForm (which contains a custom dialog box), add controls to the UserForm, and adjust some of the control's properties. These skills, however, won't do you much good unless you understand how to make use of UserForms in your VBA code. This chapter provides these missing details and presents some useful techniques and tricks in the process.

Using Dialog Boxes

When you use a custom dialog box in your application, you normally write VBA code that does the following:

>> Initializes the UserForm controls. For example, you may write code that sets the default values for the controls.

>> Displays the dialog box by using the UserForm object's Show method.

>> Responds to the events that occur for the various controls — such as clicking a CommandButton.

>> Validates the information provided by the user (if the user didn't cancel the dialog box). This step is not always necessary.

>> Takes some action with the information provided by the user (if the information is valid).

>> Closes the UserForm by using the Unload method.

A UserForm Example

This example demonstrates the five points described in the preceding section. In this example, you use a dialog box to get two pieces of information: a person's name and sex. The dialog box uses a TextBox control to get the name, and it uses three OptionButtons to get the sex (Male, Female, or Unknown). The information collected in the dialog box is then sent to the next blank row in a worksheet.

Creating the dialog box

Figure 18-1 shows the finished UserForm for this example. For best results, start with a new workbook with only one worksheet in it. Then follow these steps:

1. Press Alt+F11 to activate the VBE.

2. In the Project window, select the empty workbook and choose Insert ⇨ UserForm.

An empty UserForm is added to the project.

3. Change the UserForm's Caption property to Get Name and Sex.

If the Properties window isn't visible, press F4.

FIGURE 18-1:
This dialog box
asks the user to
enter a Name and
choose a Sex.

This dialog box has eight controls with properties that were adjusted:

>> **Label**

Property	Value
Accelerator	N
Caption	Name
TabIndex	0

>> **TextBox**

Property	Value
Name	TextName
TabIndex	1

>> **Frame object**

Property	Value
Caption	Sex
TabIndex	2

>> **OptionButton**

Property	Value
Accelerator	M
Caption	Male
Name	OptionMale
TabIndex	0

>> **Another OptionButton**

Property	Value
Accelerator	F
Caption	Female
Name	OptionFemale
TabIndex	1

>> **Another OptionButton**

Property	Value
Accelerator	U
Caption	Unknown
Name	OptionUnknown
TabIndex	2
Value	True

>> **CommandButton**

Property	Value
Caption	Enter
Default	True
Name	EnterButton
TabIndex	b

>> **CommandButton**

Property	Value
Caption	Close
Cancel	True
Name	CloseButton
TabIndex	4

If you're following along on your computer (and you should be), take a few minutes to create this UserForm by using the preceding information. Make sure to create the Frame object before adding the OptionButtons to it.

In some cases, you may find copying an existing control easier than creating a new one. To copy a control, press Ctrl while you drag the control.

If you prefer to cut to the chase, you can download the example from this book's website.

Writing code to display the dialog box

After you've added the controls to the UserForm, your next step is to develop some VBA code to display this dialog box:

1. In the VBE window, choose Insert ➪ Module to insert a VBA module.

2. Enter the following macro:

```
Sub GetData()
    UserForm1.Show
End Sub
```

This short procedure uses the UserForm object's Show method to display the dialog box.

Making the macro available

The next set of steps gives the user an easy way to execute the procedure:

1. Activate Excel.

2. Choose Developer ➪ Controls ➪ Insert, and click the Button icon in the Form Controls section.

3. Drag in the worksheet to create the button.

The Assign Macro dialog box appears.

4. Assign the GetData macro to the button.

5. Edit the button's caption so that it reads Data Entry.

If you want to get really fancy, you can add an icon to your Quick Access toolbar. Then click the icon to run the GetData macro. To set this up, right-click your Quick Access toolbar and choose Customize Quick Access Toolbar, which displays the Quick Access Toolbar tab of the Excel Options dialog box. From the Choose Commands From drop-down menu, select Macros. Then select the GetData macro and click Add. If you like, you can click the Modify button and change the icon. You can also make the Quick Access Toolbar icon visible only when the appropriate

workbook is activated. Before you add the macro, use the drop-down control at the top-right of the Excel Options dialog box to specify the workbook name, rather than For All Documents (Default).

Trying out your dialog box

Follow these steps to test your dialog box:

1. **Click the Data Entry button on the worksheet, or click the Quick Access toolbar icon if you set one up.**

The dialog box appears, as shown in Figure 18-2.

2. **Enter some text in the edit box.**

3. **Click Enter or Close.**

Nothing happens — which is understandable because you haven't created any procedures yet.

4. **Click the X button on the dialog box's title bar to dismiss the dialog box.**

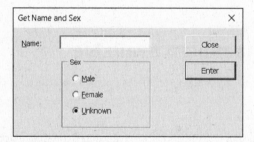

FIGURE 18-2:
Executing the
GetData
procedure
displays the
dialog box.

Adding event-handler procedures

You'ill often want certain procedures to trigger when certain events occur with your dialog boxes. For example, you may want to run a procedure when a dialog box opens. Or maybe you want to force Excel to save the workbook each time the dialog box closes.

This section walks you through an example of writing procedures that handle dialog box events.

Start by following these steps:

1. **Press Alt+F11 to activate the VBE and then make sure that the UserForm is displayed.**

2. **Double-click the Close button on the UserForm.**

The VBE activates the Code window for the UserForm and provides an empty procedure named CloseButton_Click.

3. **Modify the procedure as follows:**

```
Private Sub CloseButton_Click()
    Unload UserForm1
End Sub
```

This procedure, which is executed when the user clicks the Close button, simply unloads the dialog box from memory.

4. **Press Shift+F7 to redisplay UserForm1.**

5. **Double-click the Enter button, and enter the following procedure:**

```
Private Sub EnterButton_Click()
    Dim NextRow As Long

'   Make sure Sheet1 is active
    Sheets("Sheet1").Activate

'   Determine the next empty row
    NextRow = Application.WorksheetFunction. _
      CountA(Range("A:A")) + 1

'   Transfer the name
    Cells(NextRow, 1) = TextName.Text

'   Transfer the sex
    If OptionMale Then Cells(NextRow, 2) = "Male"
    If OptionFemale Then Cells(NextRow, 2) = "Female"
    If OptionUnknown Then Cells(NextRow, 2) = "Unknown"

'   Clear the controls for the next entry
    TextName.Text = ""
    OptionUnknown = True
    TextName.SetFocus
End Sub
```

6. **Activate Excel and run the procedure again by clicking the Data Entry button.**

The dialog box works just fine. Figure 18-3 shows how this looks in action. While the figure shows column headers in row 1, that step is not necessary.

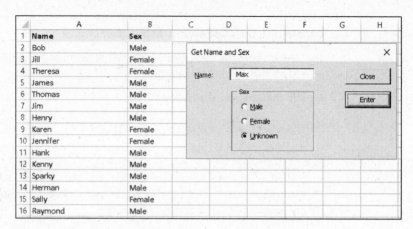

FIGURE 18-3:
Use the custom
dialog box for
data entry.

Here's how the EnterButton_Click procedure works:

1. The code makes sure that the proper worksheet (Sheet1) is active.

2. It then uses the Excel COUNTA function to count the number of entries in column A and to determine the next blank cell in the column.

3. The procedure transfers the text from the TextBox to column A.

4. It uses a series of If statements to determine which OptionButton was selected and writes the appropriate text (Male, Female, or Unknown) to column B.

5. The dialog box is reset to make it ready for the next entry.

Notice that clicking the Enter button doesn't close the dialog box, because the user will probably want to enter more data. To end data entry, click the Close button.

Validating the data

Play around with this routine some more, and you'll find that the macro has a small problem: It doesn't ensure that the user actually enters a name in the Text-Box. The following code — which is inserted into the EnterButton_Click procedure before the text is transferred to the worksheet — ensures that the user enters some text in the TextBox. If the TextBox is empty, a message appears, and the routine stops. The dialog box remains open, however, so the user can correct the problem.

```
'   Make sure a name is entered
    If TextName.Text = "" Then
        MsgBox "You must enter a name."
        Exit Sub
    End If
```

Now the dialog box works

After making these modifications, the dialog box works flawlessly. In real life, you'd probably need to collect more information than just name and sex. However, the same basic principles apply. You just have to deal with more UserForm controls.

One more thing to remember: If the data doesn't begin in row 1 or if the data area contains any blank rows, the counting for the NextRow variable will be wrong. The COUNTA function is counting the number of cells in column A, and the assumption is that there are no blank cells above the last name in the column. Here's another way of determining the next empty row:

```
NextRow = Cells(Rows.Count, 1).End(xlUp).Row + 1
```

The statement simulates activating the last cell in column A, pressing End, pressing the up-arrow key, and then moving down one row. If you do that manually, the cell pointer will be in the next empty cell in column A — even if the data area doesn't begin in row 1 and contains blank rows.

A ListBox Example

ListBoxes are useful controls, but working with them can be a bit tricky. Before displaying a dialog box that uses a ListBox, you need to fill the ListBox with items. Then, when the dialog box is closed, you need to determine which item(s) the user selected.

REMEMBER

When dealing with ListBoxes, you need to know about the following properties and methods:

- **AddItem:** You use this method to add an item to a ListBox.

- **ListCount:** This property returns the number of items in the ListBox.

- **ListIndex:** This property returns the index number of the selected item or sets the item that's selected (single selections only). The first item has a ListIndex of 0 (not 1).

- **MultiSelect:** This property determines whether the user can select more than one item from the ListBox.

- **RemoveAllItems:** Use this method to remove all items from a ListBox.

- **Selected:** This property returns an array indicating selected items (applicable only when multiple selections are allowed).

- **Value:** This property returns the selected item in a ListBox.

TIP

Most of the methods and properties that work with ListBoxes also work with ComboBoxes. So after you've figured out how to handle ListBoxes, you can transfer that knowledge to your work with ComboBoxes.

Filling a ListBox

To keep things simple, start with an empty workbook. The example in this section assumes the following:

>> You've added a UserForm.

>> The UserForm contains a ListBox control named ListBox1.

>> The UserForm has a CommandButton named OKButton.

>> The UserForm has a CommandButton named CancelButton, which has the following event-handler procedure:

```
Private Sub CancelButton_Click()
    Unload UserForm1
End Sub
```

The following procedure is stored in the Initialize procedure for the UserForm. Follow these steps:

1. Select your UserForm, and press F7 to activate its Code window.

The VBE displays the Code window for your form and is ready for you to input the code for the Initialize event.

2. From the Procedure drop-down list at the top of the Code window, choose Initialize.

3. Add the initialization code for the form:

```
Sub UserForm_Initialize()
'    Fill the list box
    With ListBox1
        .AddItem "January"
        .AddItem "February"
        .AddItem "March"
        .AddItem "April"
        .AddItem "May"
        .AddItem "June"
        .AddItem "July"
        .AddItem "August"
```

```
            .AddItem "September"
            .AddItem "October"
            .AddItem "November"
            .AddItem "December"
        End With

'    Select the first list item
        ListBox1.ListIndex = 0
    End Sub
```

This initialization routine runs automatically whenever your UserForm is loaded. So when you use the Show method for the UserForm, the code is executed and your ListBox is populated with 12 items, each added via the AddItem method.

4. **Insert a VBA module, and type this short Sub procedure to display the dialog box:**

```
Sub ShowList()
    UserForm1.Show
End Sub
```

Determining the selected item

The preceding code merely displays a dialog box with a ListBox filled with month names. What's missing is a procedure to determine which item in the ListBox is selected.

Double-click the OKButton, and add the following OKButton_Click procedure:

```
Private Sub OKButton_Click()
    Dim Msg As String
    Msg = "You selected item # "
    Msg = Msg & ListBox1.ListIndex
    Msg = Msg & vbNewLine
    Msg = Msg & ListBox1.Value
    MsgBox Msg
    Unload UserForm1
End Sub
```

This procedure displays a message box with the selected item number and the selected item.

If no item in the ListBox is selected, the ListIndex property returns –1. However, this will never be the case for this particular ListBox, because code in the UserForm_Initialize procedure selected the first item. It's impossible to unselect an item without selecting another item. So there will *always* be a selected item, if the user doesn't actually select a month.

Figure 18-4 shows how this looks.

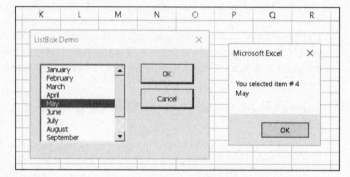

FIGURE 18-4:
Determining which item in a ListBox is selected.

TECHNICAL STUFF

The first item in a ListBox has a ListIndex of 0, not 1 (as you might expect). This is always the case, even if you use an Option Base 1 statement to change the default lower bound for arrays.

This example is available at this book's website.

Determining multiple selections

If your ListBox is set up so that the user can select more than one item, you find that the ListIndex property returns only the *last* item selected. To determine all selected items, you need to use the Selected property, which contains an array.

REMEMBER

To allow multiple selections in a ListBox, set the MultiSelect property to either 1 or 2. You can do so at design time by using the Properties window or at runtime by using a VBA statement such as this:

```
UserForm1.ListBox1.MultiSelect = 1
```

The MultiSelect property has three possible settings. The meaning of each is shown in Table 18-1.

TABLE 18-1

Settings for the MultiSelect Property

Value	VBA Constant	Meaning
0	fmMultiSelectSingle	Only a single item can be selected.
1	fmMultiSelectMulti	Clicking an item or pressing the space bar selects or deselects an item in the list.
2	fmMultiSelectExtended	Items are added to or removed from the selection set by holding down the Shift or Ctrl key as you click items.

The following procedure displays a message box that lists all selected items in a ListBox. Figure 18-5 shows an example.

```vba
Private Sub OKButton_Click()
    Dim Msg As String
    Dim i As Long
    Dim Counter As Long
    Msg = "You selected:" & vbNewLine
    For i = 0 To ListBox1.ListCount - 1
        If ListBox1.Selected(i) Then
            Counter = Counter + 1
            Msg = Msg & ListBox1.List(i) & vbNewLine
        End If
    Next i
    If Counter = 0 Then Msg = Msg & "(nothing)"
    MsgBox Msg
    Unload UserForm1
End Sub
```

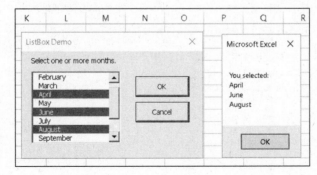

FIGURE 18-5:
Determining the
selected items in
a ListBox that
allows multiple
selections.

This routine uses a For-Next loop to cycle through each item in the ListBox. Notice that the loop starts with item 0 (the first item) and ends with the last item (determined by the value of the ListCount property minus 1). If an item's Selected property is True, it means that the list item was selected. The code also uses a variable (Counter) to keep track of how many items are selected. An If-Then statement modifies the message if nothing is selected.

TIP

This example is available at this book's website.

Selecting a Range

In some cases, you may want the user to select a range while a dialog box is displayed. An example of this type of range selection occurs in the Create Table dialog box, which is displayed when you choose Home ⇨ Insert ⇨ Tables ⇨ Table. The Create Table dialog box has a range selector control that contains Excel's guess regarding the range to be converted — but you can use this control to change the range by selecting cells in the worksheet.

To allow a range selection in your dialog box, add a RefEdit control. The following example displays a dialog box with the current region's range address displayed in a RefEdit control, as shown in Figure 18-6. The current region is the block of nonempty cells that contains the active cell. The user can accept or change this range. When the user clicks OK, the procedure makes the range bold.

	A	B	C	D	E	F	G	H	I	J	K
1	17	8	10	75	11	64					
2	63	8	22	27	11	54					
3	5	45	70	13	6	48					
4	30	22	15	1	3	15					
5	73	56	87	70	24	87					
6	86	93	69	95	49	92					
7	31	37	30	70	26	93					
8	31	68	1	62	63	87					
9	72	97	58	21	42	61					
10	22	28	92	32	76	58					
11	15	90	55	72	22	1					
12	75	14	21	98	18	9					
13	82	79	43	96	50	15					
14	89	38	92	69	32	33					
15	1	38	93	78	58	45					
16	37	42	11	63	0	60					
17	40	59	14	57	2	37					
18	12	1	14	67	74	46					
19	15	10	25	27	70	36					
20	61	41	84	47	29	71					
21	51	78	21	89	16	95					
22	74	5	31	11	7	55					

RefEdit Demo ✕

Range to make bold:

Sheet1!A1:F22

Cancel OK

FIGURE 18-6: This dialog box lets the user select a range.

This example assumes the following:

>> You have a UserForm named UserForm1.

>> The UserForm contains a CommandButton control named OKButton.

>> The UserForm contains a CommandButton control named CancelButton.

>> The UserForm contains a RefEdit control named RefEdit1.

The code is stored in a VBA module and shown here. This code does two things: initializes the dialog box by assigning the current region's address to the RefEdit control and displays the UserForm.

```
Sub BoldCells()
'    Exit if worksheet is not active
    If TypeName(ActiveSheet) <> "Worksheet" Then Exit Sub

'    Select the current region
    ActiveCell.CurrentRegion.Select

'    Initialize RefEdit control
    UserForm1.RefEdit1.Text = Selection.Address

'    Show dialog
    UserForm1.Show
End Sub
```

The following procedure is executed when the OK button is clicked. This procedure does some simple error checking to make sure that the range specified in the RefEdit control is valid.

```
Private Sub OKButton_Click()
    On Error GoTo BadRange
    Range(RefEdit1.Text).Font.Bold = True
    Unload UserForm1
    Exit Sub
BadRange:
    MsgBox "The specified range is not valid."
End Sub
```

If an error occurs (most likely an invalid range specification in the RefEdit control), the code jumps to the BadRange label, and a message box is displayed. The dialog box remains open so the user can select another range.

TIP

If getting a user selected range is the *only* function performed by your UserForm, you can simplify things by using the Application InputBox method (see Chapter 15).

Using Multiple Sets of OptionButtons

Figure 18-7 shows a custom dialog box with three sets of OptionButtons. If your UserForm contains more than one set of OptionButtons, make sure that each set of OptionButtons works as a group. You can do so in either of two ways:

» Enclose each set of OptionButtons in a Frame control. This approach is easier and also makes the dialog box look more organized. It's easier to add the Frame before adding the OptionButtons. You can, however, also drag existing OptionButtons into a Frame.

» Make sure that each set of OptionButtons has a unique GroupName property (which you specify in the Properties box). If the OptionButtons are in a Frame, you don't have to be concerned with the GroupName property.

FIGURE 18-7: This dialog box contains three sets of OptionButton controls.

REMEMBER

Only one OptionButton in a group can have a value of True. To specify a default option for a set of OptionButtons, just set the Value property for the default item to True. You can do this directly in the Properties box or by using VBA code:

```
UserForm1.OptionButton1.Value = True
```

This example is available at this book's website. It also has code that displays the selected options when the user clicks OK.

Using a SpinButton and a TextBox

A SpinButton control lets the user specify a number by clicking arrows. This control consists only of arrows (no text), so you usually want a method to display the selected number. One option is to use a Label control, but this has a disadvantage: The user can't type text in a Label. A better choice is to use a TextBox.

A SpinButton control and TextBox control form a natural pair, and Excel uses them frequently. For example, check out Excel's Page Setup dialog box for a few examples. Ideally, the SpinButton and its TextBox are always in sync: If the user clicks the SpinButton, the SpinButton's value should appear in the TextBox. And if the user enters a value directly into the TextBox, the SpinButton should take on that value. Figure 18-8 shows a custom dialog box with a SpinButton and a TextBox.

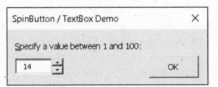

This UserForm contains the following controls:

>> A SpinButton named SpinButton1, with its Min property set to 1 and its Max property set to 100

>> A TextBox named TextBox1, positioned to the left of the SpinButton

>> A CommandButton named OKButton

The event-handler procedure for the SpinButton follows. This procedure handles the Change event, which is triggered whenever the SpinButton value is changed. When the SpinButton's value changes (when it's clicked), this procedure assigns the SpinButton's value to the TextBox. To create this procedure, double-click the SpinButton to activate the Code window for the UserForm. Then enter this code:

```
Private Sub SpinButton1_Change()
    TextBox1.Text = SpinButton1.Value
End Sub
```

The event-handler for the TextBox, which is listed next, is a bit more complicated. To create this procedure, double-click the TextBox to activate the Code window for the UserForm. This procedure is executed whenever the user changes the text in the TextBox.

```
Private Sub TextBox1_Change()
    Dim NewVal As Long

    NewVal = Val(TextBox1.Text)
    If NewVal >= SpinButton1.Min And _
        NewVal <= SpinButton1.Max Then _
        SpinButton1.Value = NewVal
End Sub
```

This procedure uses a variable, which stores the text in the TextBox (converted to a value with the Val function). It then checks to ensure that the value is within the proper range. If so, the SpinButton is set to the value in the TextBox. The net effect is that the SpinButton's value is always equal to the value in the TextBox (assuming that the SpinButton's value is in the proper range).

TECHNICAL
STUFF

If you press F8 to single-step through the code in debugging mode, you'll notice that when the line SpinButton1.Value = NewVal is executed, the change event of the SpinButton immediately fires. In turn, the SpinButton1_Change event sets the value of TextBox1. Luckily, this in turn doesn't fire the TextBox1_Change event, because its value is not actually changed by the SpinButton1_Change event. But you can imagine that this effect can cause surprising results in your UserForm. Confused? Just remember that if your code changes the Value of a control, the Change event of that control will fire.

TIP

This example is available at this book's website. It also has a few other bells and whistles that you may find useful.

Using a UserForm as a Progress Indicator

If you have a macro that takes a long time to run, you might want to display a progress meter so people won't think Excel has crashed. You can use a UserForm to create an attractive progress indicator, as shown in Figure 18-9. Such a use of dialog boxes does, however, require a few tricks.

G	H	I	J	K	L	M	N
744	234	395	958	314	555	597	11
874	857	742	518	89	119	485	95
175	685	307	924	811	377	684	68
736	771	993	287	716	935	442	36
315	150	756	547	540	896	512	55
48	730	936	496	474	999	736	52
397	431	836	39	366	13	872	83
360	57	Progress			×	668	4
919	53	Entering random numbers...				196	74
744	60					426	84
146	15	66%				56	6
282	5					591	69
607	224	693	261	821	782	667	64
575	626	812	173	525	606	635	67
597	341	577	404	506	885	382	92

FIGURE 18-9:
This UserForm functions as a progress indicator for a lengthy macro.

Creating the progress-indicator dialog box

The first step is to create your UserForm. In this example, the dialog box displays the progress while a macro inserts random numbers into 100 columns and 1,000 rows of the active worksheet. To create the dialog box, follow these steps:

1. Activate the VBE, and insert a new UserForm.

2. Change the UserForm's caption to Progress.

3. Add a Frame object, and set the following properties:

Property	Value
Caption	0%
Name	FrameProgress
SpecialEffect	2 — fmSpecialEffectSunken
Width	204
Height	28

4. Add a Label object inside the Frame, and set the following properties:

Property	Value
Name	LabelProgress
BackColor	&H0000C000& (green)
Caption	(no caption)
SpecialEffect	1 — fmSpecialEffectRaised
Width	20

Property	Value
Height	13
Top	5
Left	2

5. **Add another Label above the frame, and change its caption to Entering random numbers. . .**

 The UserForm should resemble Figure 18-10.

FIGURE 18-10: The progress-indicator UserForm.

The procedures

This example uses two procedures and a module-level variable:

» **The module-level variable:** Located in a VBA module, this variable holds the copy of the UserForm:

```
Dim ProgressIndicator as UserForm1
```

» **Ente.rRandomNumbers:** This procedure does all the work and is executed when the UserForm is shown. Notice that it calls the UpdateProgress procedure, which updates the progress indicator in the dialog box:

```
Sub EnterRandomNumbers()
'    Inserts random numbers on the active worksheet
    Dim Counter As Long
    Dim RowMax As Long, ColMax As Long
    Dim r As Long, c As Long
    Dim PctDone As Single
```

314 PART 4 **Communicating with Your Users**

```
'   Create a copy of the form in a variable
    Set ProgressIndicator = New UserForm1

'   Show ProgressIndicator in modeless state
    ProgressIndicator.Show vbModeless
    If TypeName(ActiveSheet) <> "Worksheet" Then
        Unload ProgressIndicator
        Exit Sub
    End If

'   Enter the random numbers
    Cells.Clear
    Counter = 1
    RowMax = 200
    ColMax = 50
    For r = 1 To RowMax
        For c = 1 To ColMax
            Cells(r, c) = Int(Rnd * 1000)
            Counter = Counter + 1
        Next c
        PctDone = Counter / (RowMax * ColMax)
        Call UpdateProgress(PctDone)
    Next r
    Unload ProgressIndicator
    Set ProgressIndicator = Nothing
End Sub
```

>> **UpdateProgress:** This procedure accepts one argument and updates the progress indicator in the dialog box:

```
Sub UpdateProgress(pct)
    With ProgressIndicator
        .FrameProgress.Caption = Format(pct, "0%")
        .LabelProgress.Width = pct * (.FrameProgress _
            .Width - 10)
    End With
'   The DoEvents statement is responsible for the form updating
    DoEvents
End Sub
```

How this example works

When the EnterRandomNumbers procedure is executed, it loads a copy of UserForm1 into the module variable named ProgressIndicator. Then it sets the width of the LabelProgress label to 0 and displays the UserForm in modeless state (so the code will continue to run).

The EnterRandomNumber procedure checks the active sheet. If it's not a worksheet, the UserForm (ProgressIndicator) is closed, and the procedure ends with no action. If the active sheet is a worksheet, the procedure does the following:

1. Erases all cells on the active worksheet.

2. Loops through the rows and columns (specified by the RowMax and ColMax variables) and inserts a random number in each cell.

3. Increments the Counter variable and calculates the percentage completed (which is stored in the PctDone variable).

4. Calls the UpdateProgress procedure, which displays the percentage completed by changing the width of the LabelProgress label and updating the caption of the frame control.

5. Unloads the UserForm.

Using a progress indicator will, of course, make your macro run a bit slower because the code is doing additional work updating the UserForm. If speed is absolutely critical, think twice about using a progress indicator.

REMEMBER

If you adapt this technique for your own use, you need to figure out how to determine the macro's progress, which varies depending on your macro. Then call the UpdateProgress procedure at periodic intervals while your macro is executing.

TIP

This example is available at this book's website.

Creating a Modeless Tabbed Dialog Box

Tabbed dialog boxes are useful because they let you present information in small, organized chunks. Excel's Format Cells dialog box (which is displayed when you right-click a cell and choose Format Cells) is a good example. The dialog box in this example uses three tabs to help organize some of Excel's display options.

Creating your own tabbed dialog boxes is relatively easy, thanks to the MultiPage control. Figure 18-11 shows a custom dialog box that uses a MultiPage control with

three *pages,* or *tabs.* When the user clicks a tab, a new page is activated, and only the controls on that page are displayed.

FIGURE 18-11: The three tabs of a MultiPage control.

Notice that this is a modeless dialog box. In other words, the user can keep it displayed while working. Each of the controls has an immediate effect, so there is no need to have an OK button. Here's the procedure that displays the UserForm so it stays on top:

```
Sub ShowDialog()
    UserForm1.Show vbModeless
End Sub
```

REMEMBER

Keep the following points in mind when using the MultiPage control to create a tabbed dialog box:

» Use only one MultiPage control per dialog box.

» To make some controls (such as OK, Cancel, and Close buttons) visible at all times, place these controls outside the MultiPage control.

» Right-click a tab on the MultiPage control to display a shortcut menu that lets you add, remove, rename, or move a tab.

» At design time, click a tab to activate the page. After it's activated, add other controls to the page by using normal procedures.

>> To select the MultiPage control itself (rather than a page on the control), click the border of the MultiPage control. Keep your eye on the Properties window, which displays the name and type of the selected control. You can also select the MultiPage control by selecting its name from the drop-down list in the Properties window.

>> You can change the look of the MultiPage control by changing the Style and TabOrientation properties.

>> The Value property of a MultiPage control determines which page is displayed. For example, if you write code to set the Value property to 0, the first page of the MultiPage control is displayed.

TIP

This example is available at this book's website.

Displaying a Chart in a UserForm

If you need to display a chart in a UserForm, you find that Excel doesn't provide any direct way to do so. Therefore, you need to get creative. This section describes a technique that allows you to display one or more charts in a UserForm.

Figure 18-12 shows an example that displays three charts. The UserForm has an Image control. The trick is to use VBA code to save the chart as a GIF file and then specify that file as the Image control's Picture property (which loads the image from your disk). The Previous and Next buttons switch the displayed chart.

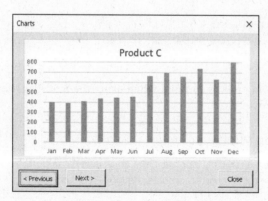

FIGURE 18-12:
Displaying a chart in a UserForm.

TIP

In this example, which is also available on this book's website, the three charts are on a sheet named Charts. The Previous and Next buttons determine which chart to display, and this chart number is stored as a Public variable named ChartNum, which is accessible to all procedures. A procedure named UpdateChart, which is listed here, does the actual work.

```
Private Sub UpdateChart()
    Dim CurrentChart As Chart
    Dim Fname As String

    Set CurrentChart = _
      Sheets("Charts").ChartObjects(ChartNum).Chart
    CurrentChart.Parent.Width = 300
    CurrentChart.Parent.Height = 150

'   Save chart as GIF
    Fname = ThisWorkbook.Path & "\temp.gif"
    CurrentChart.Export FileName:=Fname, FilterName:="GIF"

'   Show the chart
    Image1.Picture = LoadPicture(Fname)
End Sub
```

This procedure determines a name for the saved chart and then uses the Export method to export the GIF file. Finally, it uses the VBA LoadPicture function to specify the Picture property of the Image object.

A Dialog Box Checklist

Remember that a dialog box is essentially your only way to communicate with your end user. After all, dialog boxes are user interfaces.

As you start designing you own user interfaces, run down this checklist to ensure you're building dialog boxes that are both functional and intuitive:

>> Are the controls aligned with one another?

>> Are similar controls the same size?

>> Are the controls evenly spaced?

>> Does the dialog box have an appropriate caption?

>> Is the dialog box overwhelming? If so, you may want to use a series of dialog boxes or divide them over a MultiPage control.

>> Can the user access every control with an accelerator key?

>> Are any accelerator keys duplicated?

>> Are the controls grouped logically, by function?

>> Is the tab order set correctly? The user should be able to tab through the dialog box and access the controls sequentially.

>> If you plan to store the dialog box in an add-in, did you test it thoroughly after creating the add-in?

>> Will your VBA code take appropriate action if the user cancels the dialog box, presses Esc, or uses the Close button?

>> Does the text contain any misspellings? Unfortunately, the Excel spell checker doesn't work with UserForms, so you're on your own when it comes to spelling.

>> Will your dialog box fit on the screen in the lowest resolution to be used (usually, 1024×768 mode)? In other words, if you develop your dialog box by using a high-resolution video mode, your dialog box may be too big to fit on a lower-resolution screen.

>> Do all TextBox controls have the appropriate validation setting?

>> If you intend to use the WordWrap property, is the MultiLine property also set to True?

>> Do all ScrollBars and SpinButtons allow valid values only?

>> Do all ListBoxes have their MultiSelect property set properly?

Start simply and experiment with the controls and their properties. And don't forget about the Help system; it's your best source for details about every control and property.

Chapter **19**

Accessing Your Macros through the User Interface

B efore Office 2007, there was no such thing as a Ribbon. Back then, people used drop-down menus and toolbars. Now the Ribbon is the user interface for Microsoft Office — and Ribbon mania has even spread to other software, including Windows.

You might expect to be able to create custom Ribbon commands using VBA. The bad news is that you can't use VBA to modify the Ribbon. The good news is that you're not completely out of luck. This chapter describes some of the ways to work with Excel's user interface.

Customizing the Ribbon

This section describes ways to customize the Ribbon. You can modify the Ribbon manually, but you can't make changes to the Ribbon by using VBA. Sad, but true. For example, if you write an application and you'd like to add a few new buttons

to the Ribbon, you need to program those changes outside Excel, using something called RibbonX.

Customizing the Ribbon manually

It's very easy to make changes to the Ribbon manually, but you must be using Excel 2010 or later. If you use Excel 2007, you should just skip this section because it doesn't apply to you.

You can customize the Ribbon in these ways:

>> Tabs

- Add a new custom tab.
- Delete custom tabs.
- Add a new group to a tab.
- Change the order of the tabs.
- Change the name of a tab.
- Hide built-in tabs.

>> Groups

- Add new custom groups.
- Add commands to a custom group.
- Remove commands from custom groups.
- Remove groups from a tab.
- Move a group to a different tab.
- Change the order of the groups within a tab.
- Change the name of a group.

That's a fairly comprehensive list of customization options, but there are some actions that you *can't* do (no matter how hard you try):

>> Remove built-in tabs — but you *can* hide them.

>> Remove commands from built-in groups.

>> Change the order of commands in a built-in group.

You make manual changes to the Ribbon in the Customize Ribbon panel of the Excel Options dialog box (see Figure 19-1). The quickest way to display this dialog box is to right-click anywhere in the Ribbon and choose Customize the Ribbon from the shortcut menu.

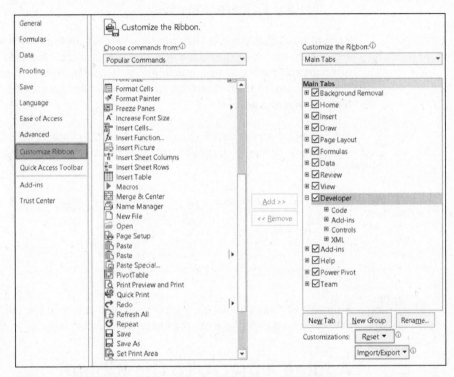

FIGURE 19-1:
The Customize
Ribbon tab of the
Excel Options
dialog box.

The process of customizing the Ribbon is very similar to customizing the Quick Access toolbar, which is described later in this chapter. The only difference is that you need to decide where to put the command within the Ribbon. Follow this general procedure:

1. **Use the drop-down list on the left (labeled Choose Commands From) to display various groups of commands.**

2. **Locate the command in the list box on the left and select it.**

3. **Use the drop-down list on the right (labeled Customize the Ribbon) to choose a group of tabs.**

 Main tabs refer to the tabs that are always visible; Tool tabs refer to the context tabs that appear when a particular object is selected.

4. **In the list box on the right, select the tab and the group where you would like to put the command.**

 You need to click the plus-sign controls to expand the hierarchical lists.

5. **Click the Add button in the middle to add the selected command from the left to the group on the right.**

Keep in mind that you can click the New Tab button to create a new tab and the New Group button to create a new group within a tab. New tabs and groups are given generic names, so you probably want to give them more meaningful names. Use the Rename button to rename the selected tab or group. You can also rename built-in tabs and groups.

Figure 19-2 shows a custom group, named Text To Speech, added to the View tab (to the right of the Zoom group). This new group has four commands.

FIGURE 19-2:
The View tab with a new group named Text To Speech.

REMEMBER

Although you can't remove a built-in tab, you can hide the tab by clearing the check box next to its name on the Customize Ribbon tab.

Adding a macro to the Ribbon

Fortunately, you can also add macros to the Ribbon. Follow the instructions in the previous section, but in Step 1, choose Macros from the drop-down list on the left. All the currently available macros are listed, ready to be added to the Ribbon. You just need to decide on a tab and group for the macro.

If you customize the Ribbon to include a macro, the macro command on the Ribbon is visible even when the workbook that contains the macro is not open. Clicking the command opens the workbook that contains the macro and then executes the macro.

REMEMBER

If you add a button to the Ribbon that executes a macro, that Ribbon modification applies to your copy of Excel only. The Ribbon modifications are not part of the workbook. In other words, if you give your workbook to a colleague, the Ribbon customizations you made won't appear on the colleague's system.

Customizing the Ribbon with XML

In some situations, you may want to modify the Ribbon automatically when a workbook or add-in is opened. Doing so makes it easy for the user to access your macro. It also eliminates the need for the user to modify the Ribbon manually by using the Excel Options dialog box.

You can make automatic changes to the Ribbon with Excel 2007 and later versions, but it's not a simple task. Modifying the Ribbon involves writing XML code in a text editor, copying that XML file into the workbook file, editing a bunch of XML files (which also are stashed away inside the Excel file, which in reality is nothing more than a zipped container of individual files), and then writing VBA procedures to handle the clicking of the controls you put in the XML file.

Fortunately, software is available to assist you with customizing the Ribbon — but you still need to be on familiar terms with XML.

GETTING THE SOFTWARE

If you'd like to follow along with the Ribbon customization example, you need to download a small program called Custom UI Editor for Microsoft Office. This free program greatly simplifies the process of customizing the Ribbon in Microsoft Office applications. Using this software still requires a lot of work, but it's a lot easier than doing it manually.

The download location tends to change, so search the web for *"Custom UI Editor for Microsoft Office"* to find the software. It's a small download, and it's free.

Explaining all the intricate details involved in customizing the Ribbon is well beyond the scope of this book. However, this chapter does walk you through a quick example that demonstrates the steps required to add a new Ribbon group to the Home tab. The new Ribbon group is named Excel VBA For Dummies, and it contains one button, labeled Click Me. Clicking that button runs a VBA macro named ShowMessage.

TIP

You can download a sample file from this book's website, which contains this customization. If you'd like to create it yourself, follow these steps exactly:

1. **Create a new Excel workbook.**

2. **Save the workbook, and name it ribbon modification.xlsm.**

3. **Close the workbook.**

4. **Launch the Custom UI Editor for Microsoft Office.**

 If you don't have this software, you need to find it and install it. Refer to the nearby sidebar "Getting the software."

5. **In the Custom UI Editor, choose File ⇨ Open and find the workbook you saved in Step 2.**

6. **Choose Insert ⇨ Office 2007 Custom UI Part.**

 Choose this command even if you're using a Excel 2010 or a later version.

7. **Type the following code in the code panel (named customUI.xml) displayed in the Custom UI Editor (see Figure 19-3):**

    ```
    <customUI xmlns='http://schemas.microsoft.com/office/2006/01/customui'>
    <ribbon>
    <tabs>
    <tab idMso='TabHome'>
      <group id'Group1' label='Excel VBA For Dummies'>
        <button id='Button1'
            label='Click Me'
            size='large'
            onAction='ShowMessage'
            imageMso='FileStartWorkflow'/>
        </group>
    </tab>
    </tabs>
    </ribbon>
    </customUI>
    ```

8. **Click the Validate button on the toolbar.**

 If the code has any syntax errors, you get a message that describes the problem. If any errors are identified, you must correct them.

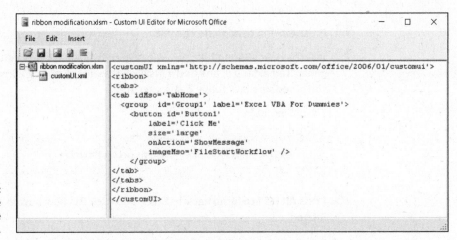

```
ribbon modification.xlsm - Custom UI Editor for Microsoft Office        —   □   ×

File   Edit   Insert

📂 💾 | 🖼 🖼 ≡

⊟ 🗐 ribbon modification.xlsm    <customUI xmlns='http://schemas.microsoft.com/office/2006/01/customui'>
    📄 customUI.xml             <ribbon>
                               <tabs>
                               <tab idMso='TabHome'>
                                 <group  id='Group1' label='Excel VBA For Dummies'>
                                   <button id='Button1'
                                       label='Click Me'
                                       size='large'
                                       onAction='ShowMessage'
                                       imageMso='FileStartWorkflow' />
                                   </group>
                               </tab>
                               </tabs>
                               </ribbon>
                               </customUI>
```

FIGURE 19-3:
RibbonX code
displayed in the
Custom UI Editor.

9. **Click the Generate Callback button.**

The Custom UI Editor creates a VBA Sub procedure that is executed when the
button is clicked (see Figure 19-4). This procedure is not actually inserted into
the workbook, so you need to copy it for later use (or memorize it, if you have
a good memory).

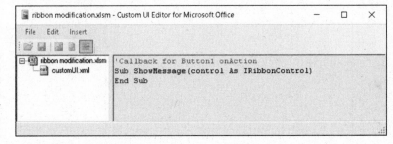

```
ribbon modification.xlsm - Custom UI Editor for Microsoft Office        —   □   ×

File   Edit   Insert

📂 💾 | 🖼 🖼 ≡

⊟ 🗐 ribbon modification.xlsm    'Callback for Button1 onAction
    📄 customUI.xml             Sub ShowMessage(control As IRibbonControl)
                               End Sub
```

FIGURE 19-4:
The VBA callback
procedure that is
executed by
clicking the
Ribbon button.

10. **Go back to the customUI.xml module and choose File ➪ Save (or click the
Save icon on the toolbar).**

11. **Close the file by choosing File ➪ Close.**

12. **Open the workbook in Excel, and click the Home tab.**

You should see the new Ribbon group and Ribbon button. But it doesn't
work yet.

13. Press Alt+F11 to activate the VBE.

14. Insert a new VBA module; paste (or type) the callback procedure that was generated in Step 9; and add a MsgBox statement, so you'll know whether the procedure is actually being executed.

The procedure is

```
Sub ShowMessage(control As IRibbonControl)
    MsgBox "Congrats. You found the new ribbon command."
End Sub
```

15. Press Alt+F11 to jump back to Excel, and click the new button on the Ribbon.

If all goes well, you see the MsgBox shown in Figure 19-5.

FIGURE 19-5:
Proof that adding a new Ribbon command using XML is actually possible.

REMEMBER

In the Custom UI Editor, when you choose Insert ⇨ Office 2007 Custom UI Part, you insert a UI part for Excel 2007. The Custom UI Editor also has an option to insert a UI part for Excel 2010 (this software hasn't been updated for subsequent versions of Office). For maximum compatibility, use the Excel 2007 Custom UI Part.

You probably realize that modifying the Ribbon using XML is not exactly intuitive. Even with a good tool to help (such as the Custom UI Editor), you still need to understand XML. If that sounds appealing to you, search the web or find a book devoted exclusively to customizing the Ribbon interface in Microsoft Office. This book isn't one of them.

ADDING A BUTTON TO THE QUICK ACCESS TOOLBAR

If you create a macro that you use frequently, you may want to add a new button to the Quick Access toolbar. Doing so is easy, but you must do it manually. The Quick Access toolbar is intended to be customized by end users only — not programmers. Here's how to do it:

1. **Right-click the Quick Access toolbar and select Customize Quick Access toolbar from the shortcut menu to display the Quick Access toolbar tab of the Excel Options dialog box.**

2. **From the drop-down list labeled Choose Commands From, select Macros.**

3. **Select your macro from the list.**

4. **Click the Add button to add the macro to the Quick Access toolbar list on the right.**

5. **If you like, click the Modify button to change the icon and (optionally) the display name.**

When you click a macro button on the Quick Access toolbar, the workbook that contains the macro is opened (if it's not already open). And the macro can be executed when any workbook is open.

You'll also find an option to display the Quick Access toolbar button only when a particular workbook is open. Before you add the macro, use the drop-down control at the top-right of the Excel Options dialog box and specify the workbook name rather than For All Documents (Default).

If you have macros that are useful for many workbooks, storing them in your Personal Macro Workbook is a good idea.

Because this XML stuff is way too complex for the beginner VBA programmer, the remainder of this chapter focuses on UI customization that uses the *old* method (VBA only): specifically, how to customize shortcut menus. It's not as slick as the Ribbon, but it's a lot easier, and it still provides quick access to your macros.

Customizing Shortcut Menus

Before Excel 2007, VBA programmers used the CommandBar object for creating custom menus, custom toolbars, and custom shortcut (right-click) menus.

Beginning with Excel 2007, the CommandBar object is in a rather odd position. If you write code to customize a menu or a toolbar, Excel intercepts that code and ignores many of your commands. Instead of displaying your well-thought-out interface enhancement, Excel 2007 (like later versions) simply dumps your customized menus and toolbars into a catch-all Ribbon tab named Add-Ins.

Menu and toolbar customizations end up in the Add-Ins⇨Menu Commands or the Add-Ins⇨Custom Toolbars group. But customizing shortcut menus (which also uses the CommandBar object) still works as it always has — well, sort of. See "What's different since Excel 2007?" later in this chapter.

Bottom line? The CommandBar object is not very useful anymore, but it remains the only way to customize shortcut menus.

Adding a new item to the Cell shortcut menu

This section contains sample code that adds a new item to the shortcut menu that appears when you right-click a cell. Although the technical details are out of the scope for this book, you should be able to adapt these examples to your needs.

Chapter 16 describes the Change Case utility. You can enhance that utility a bit by making it available from the Cell shortcut menu.

TIP

This example is available at this book's website.

The AddToShortcut procedure adds a new menu item to the Cell shortcut menu. You can adapt it to point to your own macros by changing the Caption and OnAction properties of the object named NewControl.

```
Sub AddToShortCut()
    Dim Bar As CommandBar
    Dim NewControl As CommandBarButton
    DeleteFromShortcut
    Set Bar = Application.CommandBars("Cell")
    Set NewControl = Bar.Controls.Add _
        (Type:=msoControlButton, ID:=1, _
        temporary:=True)
    With NewControl
        .Caption = "&Change Case"
        .OnAction = "ChangeCase"
        .Style = msoButtonIconAndCaption
    End With
End Sub
```

REMEMBER

When you modify a shortcut menu, that modification remains in effect until you restart Excel. In other words, modified shortcut menus don't reset themselves when you close the workbook that contains the VBA code. Therefore, if you write code to modify a shortcut menu, you almost always write code to reverse the effect of your modification.

The DeleteFromShortcut procedure removes the new menu item from the Cell shortcut menu:

```
Sub DeleteFromShortcut()
    On Error Resume Next
    Application.CommandBars("Cell").Controls _
        ("&Change Case").Delete
End Sub
```

Figure 19-6 shows the new menu item displayed after you right-click a cell.

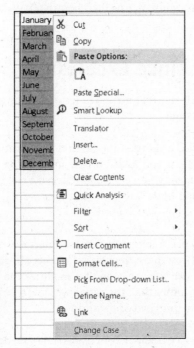

FIGURE 19-6:
The Cell shortcut menu showing a custom menu item: Change Case.

The first actual command after the declaration of a couple of variables calls the DeleteFromShortcut procedure. This statement ensures that only one Change Case menu item appears on the shortcut Cell menu. Try commenting out that line (put an apostrophe at the start of the line) and running the procedure a few times — but don't get carried away! Right-click a cell, and you can see multiple instances of the

Change Case menu item. Get rid of all the entries by running DeleteFromShortcut multiple times (once for each extra menu item).

Finally, you need a way to add the shortcut menu item when the workbook is opened and to delete the menu item when the workbook is closed. Doing this is easy . . . if you've read Chapter 11. Just add these two event procedures to the ThisWorkbook code module:

```
Private Sub Workbook_Open()
    Call AddToShortCut
End Sub

Private Sub Workbook_BeforeClose(Cancel As Boolean)
    Call DeleteFromShortcut
End Sub
```

The Workbook_Open procedure is executed when the workbook is opened, and the Workbook_BeforeClose procedure is executed before the workbook is closed. Just what the doctor ordered.

What's different since Excel 2007?

If you've used VBA to work with shortcut menus in Excel 2007 or earlier, you need to be aware of a significant change.

In the past, if your code modified a shortcut menu, that modification was in effect for all workbooks. For example, if you added a new item to the Cell right-click menu, that new item would appear when you right-clicked a cell in *any* workbook (plus other workbooks that you open later on). In other words, shortcut menu modifications were made at the *application* level.

Excel 2013 and later versions use a single document interface, and that affects shortcut menus. Changes that you make to shortcut menus affect only the active workbook window. When you execute the code that modifies the shortcut menu, the shortcut menu for windows other than the active window aren't changed. This is a radical departure from how things used to work.

Another twist: If the user opens a workbook (or creates a new workbook) when the active window displays the modified shortcut menu, the new workbook also displays the modified shortcut menu. In other words, new windows display the same shortcut menus as the window that was active when the new windows were opened.

Bottom line: In the past, if you opened a workbook or add-in that modified shortcut menus, you could be assured that the modified shortcut menus would be available in all workbooks. You no longer have that assurance.

5 Putting It All Together

IN THIS PART . . .

Find out why you might want to create custom worksheet functions.

Make your custom functions work just like Excel's built-in functions.

Discover Excel add-ins.

Create simple add-ins.

Chapter **20**

Creating Worksheet Functions — and Living to Tell about It

For many macro mavens, VBA's main attraction is the capability to create custom worksheet functions — functions that look, work, and feel just like those that Microsoft built into Excel. A *custom function* offers the added advantage of working exactly how you want it to (because *you* wrote it). Chapter 5 introduces the concept of custom functions. In this chapter, you take a deeper dive with some real-world examples.

Why Create Custom Functions?

You're undoubtedly familiar with Excel's worksheet functions; even Excel novices know how to use common worksheet functions such as SUM, AVERAGE, and IF. Excel contains more than 450 predefined worksheet functions. And if that's not enough, you can create functions by using VBA.

WHAT CUSTOM WORKSHEET FUNCTIONS CAN'T DO

As you develop custom functions for use in your worksheet formulas, it's important that you understand a key point. VBA worksheet Function procedures are essentially *passive*. For example, code within a Function procedure cannot manipulate ranges, change formatting, or do many of the other things that are possible with a Sub procedure. An example may help.

It might be useful to create a function that changes the color of text in a cell based on the cell's value. Try as you might, however, you can't write such a function. It always returns an error value.

Just remember this: A function used in a worksheet formula returns a value. It doesn't perform actions with objects.

That said, this rule has a few exceptions. For example, here's a Function procedure that changes the text in a cell comment:

```
Function ChangeComment(cell, NewText)
    cell.Comment.Text NewText
End Function
```

And here's a formula that uses the function. It works only if cell A1 already has a comment. When the formula is calculated, the comment is changed.

```
=ChangeComment(A1,"I changed the comment!")
```

It's unclear whether this is an oversight or a feature. But it's a rare example of a VBA function that changes something in a worksheet.

With all the functions available in Excel and VBA, you may wonder why you would ever need to create functions. The answer: to simplify your work. With a bit of planning, custom functions are very useful in worksheet formulas and VBA procedures. Often, for example, you can significantly shorten a formula by creating a custom function. After all, shorter formulas are more readable and easier to work with.

Understanding VBA Function Basics

A VBA *function* is a procedure that's stored in a VBA module. You can use these functions in other VBA procedures or in your worksheet formulas. Custom functions can't be created with the macro recorder, although the macro recorder can help you identify relevant properties and methods.

A *module* can contain any number of functions. You can use a custom function in a formula just as though it were a built-in function. If the function is defined in a different workbook, however, you must precede the function name with the workbook name. Suppose that you develop a function called DiscountPrice (which takes one argument) and the function is stored in a workbook named pricing.xlsm.

To use this function in the pricing.xlsm workbook, enter a formula such as this:

```
=DiscountPrice(A1)
```

If you want to use this function in a *different* workbook, enter a formula such as this (and make sure the pricing.xlsm file is open):

```
=pricing.xlsm!discountprice(A1)
```

TIP

If the custom function is stored in an add-in, you don't need to precede the function name with the workbook name. Chapter 21 provides an overview of add-ins.

Custom functions appear in the Insert Function dialog box, in the User Defined category. Pressing Shift+F3 is one way to display the Insert Function dialog box.

Writing Functions

Remember that a function's name acts like a variable. The final value of this variable is the value returned by the function. To demonstrate, examine the following function, which returns the user's first name:

```
Function FirstName()
    Dim FullName As String
    Dim FirstSpace As Long
    FullName = Application.UserName
    FirstSpace = InStr(FullName, " ")
    If FirstSpace = 0 Then
        FirstName = FullName
    Else
        FirstName = Left(FullName, FirstSpace - 1)
    End If
End Function
```

This function starts by assigning the UserName property of the Application object to a variable named FullName. Next, it uses the VBA InStr function to locate the position of the first space in the name. If there is no space, FirstSpace is equal to 0, and FirstName is equal to the entire name. If FullName *does* have a space, the Left function extracts the text to the left of the space and assigns it to FirstName.

Notice that FirstName is the name of the function and is also used as a variable name *in* the function. The final value of FirstName is the value that's returned by the function. Several intermediate calculations may be going on in the function, but the function always returns the last value assigned to the variable that is the same as the function's name.

TIP

All the examples in this chapter are available at this book's website.

Working with Function Arguments

To work with functions, you need to understand how to work with arguments. An argument is not a disagreement between variables. Rather, it's information that is passed to the function and then used by the function to do its thing.

The following points apply to the arguments for Excel worksheet functions and custom VBA functions:

>> *Arguments* can be cell references, variables (including arrays), constants, literal values, or expressions.

>> Some functions have no arguments.

>> Some functions have a fixed number of required arguments.

>> Some functions have a combination of required and optional arguments.

The examples in this section demonstrate how to work with various types of arguments.

A function with no argument

Some functions don't use any arguments. For example, Excel has a few built-in worksheet functions that don't use arguments. These include RAND, TODAY, and NOW.

Here's an example of a custom function with no arguments. The following function returns the UserName property of the Application object. This name appears in the General tab of the Excel Options dialog box. This simple but useful example shows the only way you can get the user's name to appear in a worksheet cell:

```
Function User()
'    Returns the name of the current user
     User = Application.UserName
End Function
```

When you enter the following formula into a worksheet cell, the cell displays the current user's name:

```
=User()
```

As with the Excel built-in functions, you must include a set of empty parentheses when using a function with no arguments. Otherwise, Excel tries to interpret the function as a named range.

A function with one argument

The single-argument function in this section is designed for sales managers who need to calculate the commissions earned by their salespeople. The commission rate depends on the monthly sales volume; those who sell more earn a higher commission rate. The function returns the commission amount based on the monthly sales (which is the function's only argument — a required argument). The calculations in this example are based on Table 20-1.

TABLE 20-1 ## Commission Rates by Sales

Monthly Sales	Commission Rate
$0–$9,999	8.0%
$10,000–$19,999	10.5%
$20,000–$39,999	12.0%
$40,000+	14.0%

You can use several approaches to calculate commissions for sales amounts entered into a worksheet. You *could* write a lengthy worksheet formula such as this:

```
=IF(AND(A1>=0,A1<=9999.99),A1*0.08,IF(AND(A1>=10000,
A1<=19999.99),A1*0.105,IF(AND(A1>=20000,A1<=39999.99),
A1*0.12,IF(A1>=40000,A1*0.14,0))))
```

A couple of reasons make this a bad approach. First, the formula is overly complex. Second, the values are hard-coded into the formula, making the formula difficult to modify if the commission structure changes.

A better approach is to create a table of commission values and use a LOOKUP table function to compute the commissions:

```
=VLOOKUP(A1,Table,2)*A1
```

Another approach, which doesn't require a table of commissions, is to create a custom function:

```
Function Commission(Sales)
'   Calculates sales commissions
    Const Tier1 As Double = 0.08
    Const Tier2 As Double = 0.105
    Const Tier3 As Double = 0.12
    Const Tier4 As Double = 0.14
    Select Case Sales
        Case 0 To 9999.99: Commission = Sales * Tier1
        Case 10000 To 19999.99: Commission = Sales * Tier2
        Case 20000 To 39999.99: Commission = Sales * Tier3
        Case Is >= 40000: Commission = Sales * Tier4
    End Select
    Commission = Round(Commission, 2)
End Function
```

Notice that the four commission rates are declared as constants rather than hard-coded in the statements. This makes it very easy to modify the function if the commission rates change.

After you define this function in a VBA module, you can use it in a worksheet formula. Entering the following formula into a cell produces a result of 3,000. The amount of 25,000 qualifies for a commission rate of 12 percent:

```
=Commission(25000)
```

Figure 20-1 shows a worksheet that uses the Commission function in formulas in column C.

	A	B	C	D
1	Name	Sales	Commission	
2	Adams	$61,983.00	$8,677.62	
3	Baker	$3,506.00	$280.48	
4	Douglas	$38,973.00	$4,676.76	
5	Emmett	$32,092.00	$3,851.04	
6	Franklin	$27,354.00	$3,282.48	
7	Johnson	$17,833.00	$1,872.46	
8	Kent	$41,598.00	$5,823.72	
9	Mays	$32,000.00	$3,840.00	
10	Quincy	$5,000.00	$400.00	
11	Randall	$68,793.00	$9,631.02	
12	Smith	$31,093.00	$3,731.16	
13	Walker	$24,509.00	$2,941.08	
14	Zeller	$41,544.00	$5,816.16	
15				

FIGURE 20-1: Using the Commission function in a worksheet.

A function with two arguments

The next example builds on the preceding one. Imagine that the sales manager implements a new policy to reward long-term employees: The total commission paid increases by 1 percent for every year the salesperson has been with the company.

You can modify the Commission function (defined in the preceding section) so that it takes two arguments, both of which are required arguments. Call this new function Commission2:

```
Function Commission2(Sales, Years)
'    Calculates sales commissions based on years in service
    Const Tier1 As Double = 0.08
    Const Tier2 As Double = 0.105
    Const Tier3 As Double = 0.12
    Const Tier4 As Double = 0.14
```

```
    Select Case Sales
        Case 0 To 9999.99: Commission2 = Sales * Tier1
        Case 10000 To 19999.99: Commission2 = Sales * Tier2
        Case 20000 To 39999.99: Commission2 = Sales * Tier3
        Case Is >= 40000: Commission2 = Sales * Tier4
        End Select
    Commission2 = Commission2 + (Commission2 * Years / 100)
    Commission2 = Round(Commission2, 2)
End Function
```

The procedure simply adds the second argument (Years) to the Function state-
ment and includes an additional computation that adjusts the commission before
exiting the function. This additional computation multiplies the original commis-
sion by the number of years in services, divides by 100, and then adds the result to
the original computation.

Here's an example of how you can write a formula by using this function. (It
assumes that the sales amount is in cell A1; cell B1 specifies the number of years
the salesperson has worked.)

```
=Commission2(A1,B1)
```

Figure 20-2 shows a worksheet that uses the Commission2 function.

	A	B	C	D
18				
19	Name	Sales	Years	Commission2
20	Adams	$61,983.00	4	$9,024.72
21	Baker	$3,506.00	3	$288.89
22	Douglas	$38,973.00	2	$4,770.30
23	Emmett	$32,092.00	1	$3,889.55
24	Franklin	$27,354.00	8	$3,545.08
25	Johnson	$17,833.00	3	$1,928.64
26	Kent	$41,598.00	2	$5,940.19
27	Mays	$32,000.00	1	$3,878.40
28	Quincy	$5,000.00	1	$404.00
29	Randall	$68,793.00	4	$10,016.26
30	Smith	$31,093.00	2	$3,805.78
31	Walker	$24,509.00	2	$2,999.90
32	Zeller	$41,544.00	3	$5,990.64
33				

Cell D23: =Commission2(B23,C23)

FIGURE 20-2:
Using the
Commission2
function, which
takes two
arguments.

A function with a range argument

Using a worksheet range as an argument is not at all tricky; Excel takes care of the
behind-the-scenes details.

Here's a simple but useful function that concatenates the contents of a range. It takes two arguments: InRange (the worksheet range to be concatenated), and Delim (one or more delimiter characters, to be inserted between cells).

```
Function JoinText(InRange, Delim)
    Dim Cell As Range
    For Each Cell In InRange
        JoinText = JoinText & Cell.Value & Delim
    Next Cell
    JoinText = Left(JoinText, Len(JoinText) - Len(Delim))
End Function
```

It uses a For Each–Next construct to loop through each cell in the range. It concatenates the cell contents, followed by the Delim character(s). The last statement removes the final delimiter, which is not needed because there are no more items.

Figure 20-3 shows an example. The second argument is a two-character string (a comma followed by a space).

FIGURE 20-3:
Using the JoinText
function to
concatenate cells.

Here's another example of a function that uses a range argument. Assume that you want to calculate the average of the five largest values in a range named Data. Excel doesn't have a function that can do this, so you would probably write a formula:

```
=(LARGE(Data,1)+LARGE(Data,2)+LARGE(Data,3)+
LARGE(Data,4)+LARGE(Data,5))/5
```

This formula uses Excel's LARGE function, which returns the nth largest value in a range. The formula adds the five largest values in the range named Data and then divides the result by 5. The formula works fine, but it's rather unwieldy. And what if you decide that you need to compute the average of the top six values? You would need to rewrite the formula — and make sure that you update all copies of the formula.

Wouldn't this be easier if Excel had a function named TopAvg? Then you could compute the average by using the following (nonexistent) function:

```
=TopAvg(Data,5)
```

This example shows a case in which a custom function can make things much easier for you. The following custom VBA function, named TopAvg, returns the average of the *N* largest values in a range:

```
Function TopAvg(InRange, N)
'    Returns the average of the highest N values in InRange
    Dim Sum As Double
    Dim i As Long
    Sum = 0
    For i = 1 To N
        Sum = Sum + WorksheetFunction.Large(InRange, i)
    Next i
    TopAvg = Sum / N
End Function
```

This function takes two arguments: InRange (which is a worksheet range) and N (the number of values to average). It starts by initializing the Sum variable to 0. It then uses a For-Next loop to calculate the sum of the *N* largest values in the range. Note the Excel LARGE function within the loop. Finally, TopAvg is assigned the value of the Sum divided by *N*.

TIP

You can use all Excel worksheet functions in your VBA procedures *except* those that have equivalents in VBA. For example, VBA has a Rnd function that returns a random number. Therefore, you can't use the Excel RAND function in a VBA procedure.

A function with an optional argument

Many Excel built-in worksheet functions use optional arguments. An example is the LEFT function, which returns characters from the left side of a string. Its official syntax follows:

```
LEFT(text[,num_chars])
```

The first argument is required, but the second (in square brackets) is optional. If you omit the optional argument, Excel assumes a value of 1. Therefore, the following formulas return the same result:

```
=LEFT(A1,1)
=LEFT(A1)
```

The custom functions you develop in VBA also can have optional arguments. You specify an optional argument by preceding the argument's name with the keyword Optional. The argument's name is then followed by an equal sign and the default value. If the optional argument is missing, the code uses the default value.

REMEMBER

One caveat: If you use optional arguments, they must always come after all required arguments in the argument list.

The following example shows a custom function that uses an optional argument:

```
Function DrawOne(InRange, Optional Recalc = 0)
'    Chooses one cell at random from a range

    Randomize
'    Make function volatile if Recalc is 1
    If Recalc = 1 Then Application.Volatile True

'    Determine a random cell
    DrawOne = InRange(Int((InRange.Count) * Rnd + 1))
End Function
```

DEBUGGING CUSTOM FUNCTIONS

Debugging a Function procedure can be a bit more challenging than debugging a Sub procedure. If you develop a function for use in worksheet formulas, you find that an error in the Function procedure simply results in an error display in the formula cell (usually, #VALUE!). In other words, you don't receive the normal runtime error message that helps you locate the offending statement.

You can choose among three methods for debugging custom functions:

- Place MsgBox functions at strategic locations to monitor the value of specific variables. Fortunately, message boxes in Function procedures pop up when you execute the procedure. Make sure that only one formula in the worksheet uses your function. Otherwise, the message boxes appear for each formula that's evaluated — which could get very annoying.

- Test the procedure by calling it from a Sub procedure. Runtime errors normally appear in a pop-up window, and you can either correct the problem (if you know it) or jump right into the debugger.

- Set a breakpoint in the function and then use the Excel debugger to step through the function. You can then access all the usual debugging tools. Refer to Chapter 13 to find out about the debugger.

This function randomly chooses one cell from an input range. The range passed as an argument is actually an array, and the function selects one item from the array at random. (See Chapter 7 for a refresher on arrays.) If the second argument is 1, the selected value changes whenever the worksheet is recalculated. (The function is made *volatile*.) If the second argument is 0 (or is omitted), the function is not recalculated unless one of the cells in the input range is modified.

The Randomize statement ensures that a different random number "seed" is chosen each time the workbook is opened. Without this statement, the same random numbers are generated each time the workbook is opened.

You can use this function for choosing lottery numbers, selecting a winner from a list of names, and so on.

Introducing Wrapper Functions

This section contains some relatively simple wrapper functions that can be useful in a wide array of tasks.

Wrapper functions consist of code that's wrapped around intrinsic VBA elements. In other words, they allow you to use VBA functions in worksheet formulas.

The earlier section in this chapter, "A function with no argument," shows an example of a wrapper function:

```
Function User()
'    Returns the name of the current user
    User = Application.UserName
End Function
```

This function, in essence, lets your formulas access the UserName property of the Application object.

The remainder of this section contains some additional wrapper functions.

The NumberFormat function

This function simply displays the number format for a cell. It can be useful if you need to ensure that a group of cells all have the same number format.

```
Function NumberFormat(Cell)
'    Returns the cell's number format
     NumberFormat = Cell(1).NumberFormat
End Function
```

Notice the use of `Cell (1)`? If a multicell range is used as an argument, only the first cell is used.

You can easily write similar functions that return a cell's text color, background color, font, and so on.

The ExtractElement function

This wrapper function returns a substring from a text string that contains multiple elements, separated by a separator character. For example, this formula returns cow, which is the third element in a string that uses a space as a separator. The arguments, of course, could be cell references.

```
=ExtractElement("dog horse cow cat", 3, " ")
```

Here's the code, which is a wrapper for VBA's Split function:

```
Function ExtractElement(Txt, n, Sep)
'    Returns the nth element of a text string, where the
'    elements are separated by a specified separator character
     ExtractElement = Split(Application.Trim(Txt), Sep)(n - 1)
End Function
```

Figure 20-4 shows the ExtractElement function used in worksheet formulas. Column A contains the text string, Column B contains the element number to be extracted, and Column C contains the delimiter (cells that appear to be blank contain a space character).

D5		▼ :	✕ ✓ fx	=ExtractElement(A5,B5,C5)	
▲	A	B	C	D	E
1	123-45-78	2	-	45	
2	a b c d e f g	3		c	
3	a b c d	3		c	
4	Jennifer Kelley	1		Jennifer	
5	Jennifer Kelley	2		Kelley	
6	Jennifer Kelley	3		#VALUE!	
7	55/98/44/23	3	/	44	
8	1,2,3,4,5,6,7,8,9,10	5	,	5	
9	98--74--872--9823--23	3	--	872	

FIGURE 20-4: Using the ExtractElement function to return an element from a string.

The SayIt function

This simple function is a wrapper for the Speak method of the Application.Speech object. It uses a synthesized voice to "speak" the argument.

```
Function SayIt(txt)
'    Speaks the argument
     Application.Speech.Speak txt, True
End Function
```

Here's an example:

```
=IF(C10>10000,SayIt("Over budget"),"OK")
```

The formula checks cell C10. If the value is greater than 10,000, the function speaks the text: "Over budget." If the value is less than 10,000, the function displays the text OK (and doesn't say anything).

Use sparingly. If you use this function more than one time, it can be very confusing. Also, remember that this function is evaluated each time the worksheet is calculated, so the voice may get very annoying if you're making many changes. This function is probably more suited for amusement purposes.

The IsLike function

VBA's Like operator is a very flexible way to compare text strings. Check it out in the VBA Help system. This function brings that power to your worksheet formulas:

```
Function IsLike(text, pattern)
'    Returns true if the first argument is like the second
     IsLike = text Like pattern
End Function
```

Working with Functions That Return an Array

Array formulas are one of Excel's most powerful features. If you're familiar with array formulas, you'll be happy to know that you can create VBA functions that return an array.

Returning an array of month names

A simple example of an array is the MonthNames function. It returns a 12-element array of — you guessed it — month names.

```
Function MonthNames()
    MonthNames = Array("January", "February", "March", _
        "April", "May", "June", "July", "August", _
        "September", "October", "November", "December")
End Function
```

To use the MonthNames function in a worksheet, you must enter it as a 12-cell array formula. For example, select range A2:L2 and enter =**MonthNames()**. Then press Ctrl+Shift+Enter to enter the array formula in all 12 selected cells. Figure 20-5 shows the result.

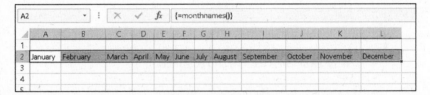

If you want the month names to display in a column, select 12 cells in a column and use this array formula. (Don't forget to enter it by pressing Ctrl+Shift+Enter.)

```
=TRANSPOSE(MonthNames())
```

You can also pick out a single month from the array. Here's a formula (not an array formula) that displays the fourth element of the array: April.

```
=INDEX(MonthNames(),4)
```

Returning a sorted list

Suppose that you have a list of names you want to show in sorted order in another range of cells. Wouldn't it be nice to have a worksheet function do that for you?

The custom function in this section does just that: It takes a single-column range of cells as its argument and then returns an array of those cells sorted. Figure 20-6 shows how it works. Range A2:A13 contains some names. Range C2:C13 contains

this multicell array formula. (Remember that you must enter the formula by pressing Ctrl+Shift+Enter.)

```
=Sorted(A2:A13)
```

FIGURE 20-6:
Using a custom
function to return
a sorted range.

Here's the code for the Sorted function:

```
Function Sorted(Rng As Range)
    Dim SortedData() As Variant
    Dim Cell As Range
    Dim Temp As Variant, i As Long, j As Long
    Dim NonEmpty As Long

'   Transfer data to SortedData
    For Each Cell In Rng
        If Not IsEmpty(Cell) Then
            NonEmpty = NonEmpty + 1
            ReDim Preserve SortedData(1 To NonEmpty)
            SortedData(NonEmpty) = Cell.Value
        End If
    Next Cell
'   Sort the array
    For i = 1 To NonEmpty
        For j = i + 1 To NonEmpty
            If SortedData(i) > SortedData(j) Then
                Temp = SortedData(j)
                SortedData(j) = SortedData(i)
                SortedData(i) = Temp
```

```
        End If
    Next j
  Next i

'   Transpose the array and return it
    Sorted = Application.Transpose(SortedData)
End Function
```

The Sorted function starts by creating an array named SortedData. This array contains all the nonblank values in the argument range. Next, the SortedData array is sorted, using a bubble-sort algorithm. Because the array is a horizontal array, it must be transposed before it's returned by the function.

The Sorted Function works with a range of any size, as long as it's in a single column or row. If the unsorted data is in a row, your formula needs to use Excel's TRANSPOSE function to display the sorted data horizontally. For example:

```
=TRANSPOSE(Sorted(A16:L16))
```

Using the Insert Function Dialog Box

The Excel Insert Function dialog box is a handy tool that allows you to choose a worksheet function from a list and prompts you for the function's arguments. As noted earlier in this chapter, your custom worksheet functions also appear in the Insert Function dialog box. Custom functions appear in the User Defined category.

TIP

Function procedures defined with the Private keyword don't appear in the Insert Function dialog box. Therefore, if you write a Function procedure that's designed to be used only by other VBA procedures (but not in formulas), you should declare the function as Private.

Displaying the function's description

The Insert Function dialog box displays a description of each built-in function. But as shown in Figure 20-7, a custom function displays the following text as its description: No help available.

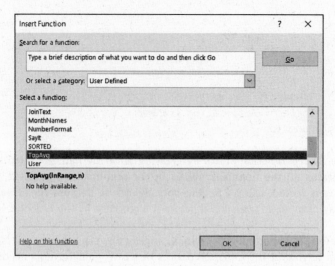

FIGURE 20-7:
By default, the Insert Function dialog box doesn't provide a description for custom functions.

To display a meaningful description of your custom function in the Insert Function dialog box, perform a few additional (nonintuitive) steps:

1. **Activate a worksheet in the workbook that contains the custom function.**

2. **Choose Developer ➪ Code ➪ Macros (or press Alt+F8).**

 The Macro dialog box appears.

3. **In the Macro Name field, type the function's name.**

 Note that the function doesn't appear in the list of macros; you must type the name.

4. **Click the Options button.**

 The Macro Options dialog box appears.

5. **In the Description field, type a description of the function.**

6. **Click OK.**

7. **Click Cancel.**

Now the Insert Function dialog box displays the description of your function (see Figure 20-8).

TIP

Custom functions, by default, are listed in the User Defined category. To add a function to a different category, you need to use VBA. This statement, when executed, adds the TopAvg function to the Math & Trig category (which is category 3):

```
Application.MacroOptions Macro:="TopAvg", Category:=3
```

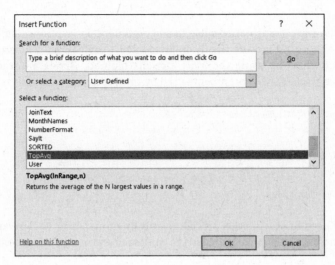

FIGURE 20-8:
The custom function now displays a description.

TopAvg(InRange,n)
Returns the average of the N largest values in a range.

Check the Help system for other category numbers.

REMEMBER

You need to execute this statement only one time. After you execute it (and save the workbook), the category number is permanently assigned to the function.

Adding argument descriptions

When you access a built-in function from the Insert Function dialog box, the Function Arguments dialog box displays descriptions of the arguments (see Figure 20-9).

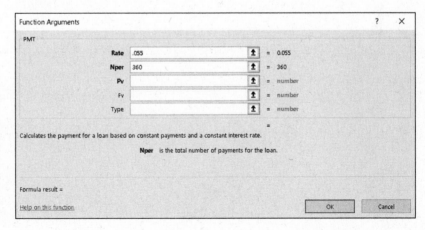

FIGURE 20-9:
By default, the Function Arguments dialog box displays Function argument descriptions for built-in functions only.

In the past, it was not possible to add argument descriptions. But beginning with Excel 2010, Microsoft finally implemented this feature. You provide argument descriptions by using the MacroOptions method. Here's an example that adds descriptions for the arguments used by the TopAvg function:

```
Sub AddArgumentDescriptions()
    Application.MacroOptions Macro:="TopAvg", _
        ArgumentDescriptions:= _
        Array("Range that contains the values", _
        "Number of values to average")
End Sub
```

You need to execute this procedure only one time. After you execute it, the argument descriptions are stored in the workbook and are associated with the function.

Notice that the argument descriptions appear as arguments for the Array function. You must use the Array function even if you're assigning a description for a function that has only one argument.

This chapter provides lots of information about creating custom worksheet functions. Use these examples as models when you create functions for your own work. As usual, the online help provides additional details. Turn to Chapter 21 if you want to find out how to make your custom functions more accessible by storing them in an add-in.

Chapter **21**

Creating Excel Add-Ins

O ne of the slickest features of Excel is the capability to create add-ins. Excel add-ins make it possible for you to package up your VBA procedures, and make them part of your Excel interface. Best of all, you can share these packages with others so that they get the benefit of your VBA prowess.

In this chapter, you explore how to create add-ins by using only the tools built into Excel.

Okay . . . So What's an Add-In?

Glad you asked. An Excel *add-in* is something you add to enhance Excel's functionality. Some add-ins provide new worksheet functions you can use in formulas; other add-ins provide new commands or utilities. If the add-in is designed properly, the new features blend in well with the original interface so they appear to be part of the program.

TIP

Excel ships with several add-ins, including the Analysis ToolPak and Solver. You can also get Excel add-ins from third-party suppliers or as shareware.

Any knowledgeable user can create add-ins, but VBA programming skills are required. An Excel add-in is basically a different form of an XLSM workbook file.

More specifically, an add-in is a normal XLSM workbook with the following differences:

>> The IsAddin property of the Workbook object is True.

>> The workbook window is hidden and can't be unhidden by choosing View ⇨ Window ⇨ Unhide.

>> The workbook isn't a member of the Workbooks collection. Rather, it's in the AddIns collection.

You can convert any workbook file to an add-in, but not all workbooks are good candidates. Because add-ins are always hidden, you can't display worksheets or chart sheets contained in an add-in. However, you can access an add-in's VBA Sub and Function procedures and display dialog boxes contained on UserForms.

REMEMBER

Excel add-ins usually have an XLAM file extension to distinguish them from XLSM worksheet files. Add-ins from pre-2007 versions of Excel have an XLA extension.

Why Create Add-Ins?

You might decide to convert your Excel application to an add-in for any of the following reasons:

>> **Make it more difficult to access your code.** When you distribute an application as an add-in (and you protect its VBA project), casual users can't view the sheets in the workbook. If you use proprietary techniques in your VBA code, you can make it more difficult for others to copy the code. Excel's protection features aren't perfect, though, and password-cracking utilities are available.

>> **Avoid confusion.** If a user loads your application as an add-in, the file is invisible and therefore less likely to confuse novice users or get in the way. Unlike a hidden workbook, the contents of an add-in can't be revealed.

>> **Simplify access to worksheet functions.** Custom worksheet functions that you store in an add-in don't require the workbook name qualifier. For example, if you store a custom function named MOVAVG in a workbook named NEWFUNC.XLSM, you must use syntax like the following to use this function in a different workbook:

```
=NEWFUNC.XLSM!MOVAVG(A1:A50)
```

But if this function is stored in an add-in file that's open, you can use much simpler syntax because you don't need to include the file reference:

```
=MOVAVG(A1:A50)
```

>> **Provide easier access for users.** After you identify the location of your add-in, it appears in the Add-Ins dialog box, with a friendly name and a description of what it does. The user can easily enable or disable your add-in.

>> **Gain better control over loading.** Add-ins can be opened automatically when Excel starts, regardless of the directory in which they're stored.

>> **Avoid displaying prompts when unloading.** When an add-in is closed, the user never sees the dialog box prompt asking whether to save changes in the file.

Working with Add-Ins

You load and unload add-ins by using the Add-Ins dialog box. To display this dialog box, choose File ⇨ Options ⇨ Add-Ins. Then select Excel Add-Ins from the drop-down list at the bottom of this dialog box and click Go. Or take the fast track and choose Developer ⇨ Add-Ins ⇨ Add-Ins. But the easiest method is to just press Alt+TI (the old Excel 2003 keyboard shortcut).

Any of these methods displays the Add-Ins dialog box, shown in Figure 21-1. The list box contains the names of all add-ins that Excel knows about. In this list, check marks identify any currently open add-ins. You can open and close add-ins from the Add-Ins dialog box by selecting or deselecting the check boxes.

To add a new add-in to the list, click Browse and then locate the XLAM file.

WARNING

You can also open most add-in files (as though they were workbook files) by choosing File ⇨ Open ⇨ Browse. An add-in opened in this manner doesn't appear in the Add-Ins dialog box. In addition, if you open the add-in by choosing the Open command, you can't close it by choosing File ⇨ Close. You can remove the add-in only by exiting and restarting Excel or by writing a macro to close the add-in.

When you open an add-in, you may or may not notice anything different. In many cases, however, the Ribbon changes in some way; Excel displays a new tab or one or more new groups on an existing tab. For example, opening the Analysis ToolPak add-in gives you a new item on the Data tab: Analysis ⇨ Data Analysis. If the add-in contains only custom worksheet functions, the new functions appear in the Insert Function dialog box, and you see no change in Excel's user interface.

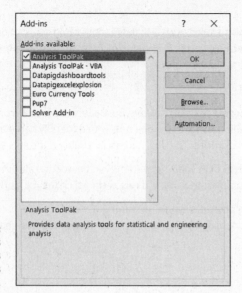

Understanding Add-In Basics

Although you can convert any workbook to an add-in, not all workbooks benefit from this conversion. A workbook with no macros makes a useless add-in. In fact, the only types of workbooks that benefit from being converted to an add-in are those with macros. For example, a workbook that consists of general-purpose macros (Sub and Function procedures) makes an ideal add-in.

Creating an add-in isn't difficult, but it does require a bit of extra work. Follow these steps to create an add-in from a normal workbook file:

1. **Develop your application, and make sure that everything works properly.**

 Don't forget to include a method for executing the macro or macros. You might want to define a shortcut key or customize the user interface in some way (see Chapter 19). If the add-in consists only of functions, there's no need to include a method to execute them because they appear in the Insert Function dialog box.

2. **Test the application by executing it when a *different* workbook is active.**

 Doing so simulates the application's behavior when it's used as an add-in because an add-in is never the active workbook.

3. **Activate the VBE and select the workbook in the Project window; choose Tools ⇨ VBAProject Properties and click the Protection tab; select the Lock Project for Viewing check box and enter a password (twice); then click OK.**

This step is necessary only if you want to prevent others from viewing or modifying your macros or UserForms.

4. **Back in Excel, choose File ⇨ Info, and select Show All Properties at the bottom of the right panel.**

Excel expands the list of properties displayed.

5. **Enter a brief descriptive title in the Title field and a longer description in the Comments field.**

Steps 4 and 5 aren't required but make the add-in easier to use, because the descriptions you enter appear in the Add-Ins dialog box when your add-in is selected.

6. **Still in Backstage, click Save As in the left pane.**

7. **Click Browse on the Save As screen. In the Save As dialog box, select Excel Add-in (*.xlam) from the Save as Type drop-down list.**

8. **Specify the folder that will store the add-in.**

Excel proposes its default add-ins folder (named AddIns), but you can save the file in any folder you like.

9. **Click Save.**

A copy of your workbook is converted to an add-in and saved with an XLAM extension. Your original workbook remains open.

Looking at an Add-In Example

This section discusses the basic steps involved in creating a useful add-in. The example is based on the Change Case text conversion utility described in Chapter 16.

TIP

The XLSM version of this example is available at this book's website. You can create an add-in from this workbook.

Setting up the workbook

The workbook consists of one blank worksheet, a VBA module, and a UserForm. Chapter 19 shows how to implement code that adds a new item to the Cell shortcut menu.

The original version of the utility includes options for uppercase, lowercase, and proper case. The add-in version includes two options to the UserForm so it has the same options as the built-in tool in Microsoft Word:

» **Sentence Case:** Makes the first letter uppercase and all other letters lowercase.

» **Toggle Case:** All uppercase characters are converted to lowercase, and vice versa.

Figure 21-2 shows UserForm1. The five OptionButton controls are inside a Frame control. In addition, the UserForm has a Cancel button (named CancelButton) and an OK button (named OKButton).

FIGURE 21-2:
The UserForm for the Change Case add-in.

The code executed when the Cancel button is clicked is very simple. This procedure unloads the UserForm with no action:

```
Private Sub CancelButton_Click()
    Unload UserForm1
End Sub
```

The code that's executed when the OK button is clicked follows. This code does all the work:

```
Private Sub OKButton_Click()
    Dim TextCells As Range
    Dim cell As Range
    Dim Text As String
    Dim i As Long

    ' Create an object with just text constants
    On Error Resume Next
    Set TextCells = Selection.SpecialCells(xlConstants, xlTextValues)
```

```
' Turn off screen updating
Application.ScreenUpdating = False

'   Loop through the cells
    For Each cell In TextCells
        Text = cell.Value
        Select Case True
        Case OptionLower 'lowercase
            cell.Value = LCase(cell.Value)
        Case OptionUpper 'UPPERCASE
            cell.Value = UCase(cell.Value)
        Case OptionProper 'Proper Case
            cell.Value = WorksheetFunction.Proper(cell.Value)
        Case OptionSentence 'Sentence case
            Text = UCase(Left(cell.Value, 1))
            Text = Text & LCase(Mid(cell.Value, 2, Len(cell.Value)))
            cell.Value = Text
        Case OptionToggle 'tOGGLE CASE
            For i = 1 To Len(Text)
              If Mid(Text, i, 1) Like "[A-Z]" Then
                 Mid(Text, i, 1) = LCase(Mid(Text, i, 1))
              Else
                 Mid(Text, i, 1) = UCase(Mid(Text, i, 1))
              End If
            Next i
            cell.Value = Text
        End Select
    Next

'   Unload the dialog box
    Unload UserForm1
End Sub
```

In addition to the two new options, this version of the Change Case utility differs from the version in Chapter 16 in two other ways:

>> The SpecialCells method creates an object variable that consists of the cells in the selection that contain a text constant (not a formula). This technique makes the routine run a bit faster if the selection contains many formula cells. See Chapter 14 for more information on this technique.

>> Because of the Change Case menu item to the Row and the Column shortcut menus, you can now execute the utility by right-clicking a range selection, a complete row selection, or a complete column selection. Each of these actions displays the Change Case item on the shortcut menu.

Testing the workbook

Test the add-in before converting this workbook. To simulate what happens when the workbook is an add-in, you should test the workbook when a different workbook is active. Because an add-in is never the active sheet or workbook, testing it when a different workbook is open may help you identify some potential errors.

1. **Open a new workbook and enter information in some cells.**

 For testing purposes, enter various types of information, including text, values, and formulas. Or just open an existing workbook and use it for your tests. Remember that any changes to the workbook cannot be undone, so you may want to use a copy.

2. **Select one or more cells (or entire rows and columns).**

3. **Execute the ChangeCase macro by choosing the new Change Case command from your Cell (or Row or Column) shortcut menu.**

REMEMBER

If the Change Case command doesn't appear on your shortcut menu, the most likely reason is that you didn't enable macros when you opened the change case. xlsm workbook. Close the workbook and then reopen it — and make sure that you enable macros.

Adding descriptive information

Although not required, it's considered to be a best practice to enter a description of your add-in. Follow these steps to add a description:

1. **Activate the change case.xlsm workbook.**

2. **Choose File ⇨ Info, and click Show All Properties at the bottom right.**

 Excel expands the Properties list.

3. **Enter a title for the add-in in the Title field.**

 This text appears in the list of add-ins in the Add-Ins dialog box. For this example, enter Change Case.

4. **In the Comments field, enter a description.**

 This information appears at the bottom of the Add-Ins dialog box when the add-in is selected. For this example, enter **Changes the case of text in selected cells.** Access this utility by using the shortcut menu.

Figure 21-3 shows the Properties section with the Title and Comments fields filled out.

FIGURE 21-3:
Use the
Properties
section to enter
descriptive
information
about your
add-in.

Properties ▾	
Size	24.5KB
Title	change case.xlsm
Tags	
Comments	Changes the case of text in selected cells.
Template	
Status	Add text
Categories	Excel VBA Programming For D...
Subject	Example File
Hyperlink Base	Add text
Company	Specify the company

Protecting the VBA code

If you want to add a password to prevent others from viewing the VBA code, follow these steps:

1. **Activate the VBE, and select the change case.xlsm workbook in the Project window.**

2. **Choose Tools ⇨ VBAProject Properties, and click the Protection tab on the dialog box that appears.**

3. **Select the Lock Project for Viewing check box, and enter a password (twice).**

4. **Click OK.**

5. **Save the workbook by choosing File ⇨ Save in the VBE or by going back to the Excel window and choosing File ⇨ Save.**

Creating the add-in

At this point, you've tested the change case.xlsm file, and it's working correctly. The next step is creating the add-in. Follow these steps:

1. **If needed, reactivate Excel.**

2. **Activate the change case.xlsm workbook, and choose File ⇨ Save As ⇨ Browse.**

 Excel displays its Save As dialog box.

3. **From the Save as Type drop-down menu, choose Add-In (*.xlam).**

4. **Specify the location, and click Save.**

 A new add-in file (with an .xlam extension) is created, and the original XLSM version remains open.

Opening the add-in

To avoid confusion, close the XLSM workbook before opening the add-in that you created from that workbook.

Open the add-in by following these steps:

1. **Choose Developer ⇨ Add-Ins ⇨ Add-Ins (or press Alt+TI).**

Excel displays the Add-Ins dialog box.

2. **Click the Browse button.**

3. **Locate and select the add-in you just created.**

4. **Click OK to close the Browse dialog box.**

After you find your new add-in, the Add-Ins dialog box lists the add-in. As shown in Figure 21-4, the Add-Ins dialog box also displays the descriptive information you provided in the Document Properties panel.

5. **Make sure that your new add-in is selected in the Add-Ins dialog box.**

6. **Click OK to close the dialog box.**

Excel opens the add-in. Now you can use it with all your workbooks. As long as it remains selected in the Add-Ins dialog box, the add-in opens every time you start Excel.

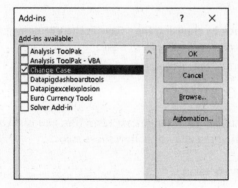

FIGURE 21-4:
The Add-Ins dialog box has the new add-in selected.

Distributing the add-in

If you're in a generous mood, you can distribute this add-in to other Excel users simply by giving them a copy of the XLAM file. (They don't need the XLSM version.) When they open the add-in, the new Change Case command appears on the shortcut menu when they select a range, one or more rows, or one or more

columns. If you lock the VBA project with a password, others cannot view your macro code unless they know the password.

Modifying the add-in

An add-in can be edited just like any other workbook. You can edit the XLAM file directly (you don't need to work with the original XLSM version) by following these steps:

1. **Open your XLAM file, if it's not already open.**

2. **Activate the VBE.**

3. **Double-click the project's name in the Project window.**

 If you protected the code, you're prompted for the password.

4. **Enter your password, and click OK.**

5. **Make your changes to the code.**

6. **Save the file by choosing File ⇨ Save.**

TIP

If you create an add-in that stores information in a worksheet, you must set the workbook's IsAddIn property to False to view the workbook. You do this in the Properties window when the ThisWorkbook object is selected (see Figure 21-5). After you've made your changes to the workbook, make sure that you set the IsAddIn property back to True before you save the file.

FIGURE 21-5:
Making an add-in
not an add-in.

6 The Part of Tens

IN THIS PART . . .

Discover tips on using the VBE.

Expand your knowledge with Excel resources.

Find out what you should and shouldn't do in Excel VBA.

» Copying multiple lines of code at once

» Jumping between modules and procedures

» Teleporting to your functions

» Staying in the right procedure

» Stepping through your code

» Stepping to a specific line in your code

» Stopping your code at a predefined point

» Seeing the beginning and end of variable values

» Turning off auto syntax check

Chapter **22**

Ten Handy Visual Basic Editor Tips

I f you're going to be spending time working the Visual Basic Editor, then why not take advantage of a few of the built-in tools that can make your job easier? Whether you're a fresh-faced analyst new to programming, or a jaded veteran living on Mountain Dew and sunflower seeds, these tips can greatly improve your macro programming experience.

Applying Block Comments

Placing a single apostrophe in front of any statement effectively tells Excel to skip that statement. This is called commenting out code. You can use the single apostrophe to also create comments or notes in your code (see Figure 22-1).

It's sometimes beneficial to comment out multiple lines of code. This way, you can test certain lines of code while telling Excel to ignore the commented lines.

FIGURE 22-1: A single apostrophe in front of any line turns that line into a comment.

```
'Declare your Variables
    Dim ws As Worksheet

'Avoid Error if no formulas are found
    On Error Resume Next

'Start looping through worksheets
    For Each ws In ActiveWorkbook.Worksheets

'Select cells and highlight them
    With ws.Cells.SpecialCells(xlCellTypeFormulas)
    .Interior.ColorIndex = 36
    End With

'Get next worksheet
    Next ws
```

Instead of spending time commenting out one line at a time, you can use the Edit toolbar to comment out whole blocks of code.

You can activate the Edit toolbar by choosing View ⇨ Toolbars ⇨ Edit.

Select the lines of code you want commented out and then click the Comment Block icon on the Edit toolbar (see Figure 22-2).

Apply Comment Remove Comment

FIGURE 22-2: The Edit toolbar allows you to select entire blocks of code, then apply comments to all the lines at once.

TIP

You can ensure the Edit toolbar is always visible by dragging it up to the VBE menu bar. It anchors itself to the location you choose.

Copying Multiple Lines of Code at Once

You can copy entire blocks of code by highlighting the lines you need, and then holding down the Ctrl key on your keyboard while dragging the block where you need it. This is an old Windows trick that works even when you drag across modules.

You know you're dragging a copy when your mouse pointer shows a plus symbol next to it, as shown in Figure 22-3.

FIGURE 22-3: Holding down the Ctrl key while dragging code creates a copy of that code.

```
'Define the target Range.
    Set MyRange = ActiveSheet.UsedRange

'Start reverse looping through the range.
    For iCounter = MyRange.Columns.Count To 1 Step -1

'If entire column is empty then delete it.
        If Application.CountA(Columns(iCounter).EntireColumn) = 0 Then
        Columns(iCounter).Delete
        End If
```

Jumping between Modules and Procedures

After your cache of macro code starts to grow, it can be a pain to quickly move between modules and procedures. You can ease the pain by using a few shortcuts:

>> Press Ctrl+Tab to quickly move between modules.

>> Press Ctrl+Page Up and Ctrl+Page Down to move between procedures within a module.

Teleporting to Your Functions

When reviewing a macro, you may sometimes encounter a variable or function name that's obviously pointing to some other piece of code. Instead of scouring through all the modules to find where that function or variable name comes from, you can simply place your cursor on that function/variable name and press Shift+F2.

As Figure 22-4 shows, you're instantly teleported to the origin of that function or variable name.

Pressing Ctrl+Shift+F2 takes you back to where you started.

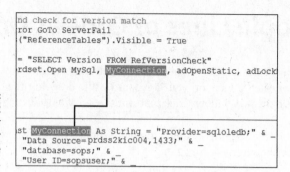

```
nd check for version match
ror GoTo ServerFail
("ReferenceTables").Visible = True

= "SELECT Version FROM RefVersionCheck"
rdset.Open MySql, MyConnection, adOpenStatic, adLock

st MyConnection As String = "Provider=sqloledb;" & _
   "Data Source=prdss2kic004,1433;" & _
   "database=sops;" & _
   "User ID=sopsuser;" &
```

FIGURE 22-4: Pressing Shift+F2 with your cursor on a function or variable name takes you to it.

Staying in the Right Procedure

When your modules contain multiple procedures, it can get difficult to scroll through a particular procedure without inadvertently scrolling into another procedure. You often find yourself scrolling up, then down, trying to get back to the correct piece of code.

To avoid this nonsense, you can click the Procedure View button in the lower-left hand corner of the VBE. (See Figure 22-5.) Clicking this button limits scrolling to only the procedure you're in.

```
Function GetRefTables()
Dim MyRecordset As ADODB.
Dim MySql As String
Dim i As Integer

Set MyRecordset = New ADO

Sheets("ReferenceTables")
```

FIGURE 22-5: Click the Procedure View button to limit scrolling to just the active procedure.

Allows scrolling across all procedures

Limits scrolling to only the active procedure

Stepping Through Your Code

VBA offers several tools to help you "debug" your code. In programming, *debugging* means finding and correcting possible errors in code.

One of the more useful debugging tools is the ability to step through your code one line at a time. When you step through code, you're literally watching as each line executes.

To step through your code, place your cursor anywhere within your macro and press F8. Your macro goes into debug mode.

The first line of code is highlighted and a small arrow appears in the Code window's left margin (see Figure 22-6). Press F8 again to execute the highlighted line of code and move to the next line. You can keep pressing F8 to watch each line be executed until the end of the macro.

As a bonus, while stepping through the code, you can hover over any string or integer variable to see the current value of that variable.

To get out of debug mode, choose Debug ➪ Step Out.

```
'Declare your variables.
    Dim MyRange As Range
    Dim iCounter As Long

'Define the target Range.
    Set MyRange = ActiveSheet.UsedRange

'Start reverse looping through the range.
    For iCounter = MyRange.Columns.Count To 1 Step -1
        iCounter = 12
'If entire column is empty then delete it.
        If Application.CountA(Columns(iCounter).EntireColumn) = 0 Then
        Columns(iCounter).Delete
        End If

'Step 5: Increment the counter down
    Next iCounter
```

Turn to Chapter 13 for a detailed look at the ins and outs of debugging your VBA code.

TIP

Stepping to a Specific Line in Your Code

The last section showed how you can step through your code by placing your cursor anywhere within your macro and pressing F8.

This is great, but what if you want to start stepping through your code at a specific line? Well, you can do just that by simply moving the arrow!

When a line of code is highlighted in debug mode, you can click and drag the arrow in the left margin of the Code window upward or downward, dropping it at whichever line of code you want to execute next. (See Figure 22-7.)

```
'Execute the stored procedure for each row in My
    For Each MyCell In MyRange
        MyCmd.Parameters("@Acctid") = MyAccount
        MyCmd.Parameters("@FType") = MyCell.Offse
        MyCmd.Parameters("@SKey") = MyCell.Offset
        MyCmd.Parameters("@Pd4") = MyCell.Offset
        MyCmd.Parameters("@Pd5") = MyCell.Offset
        MyCmd.Parameters("@Pd6") = MyCell.Offset
```

Stopping Your Code at a Predefined Point

Another useful debugging tool is the ability to set a breakpoint in your code. When you set a breakpoint, your code runs as normal and then halts at the line of code where you defined the breakpoint.

This debugging technique comes in handy when you want to run tests on small blocks of code at a time. For example, if you suspect there is an error in your macro but you know that the majority of the macro runs without any problems, you can set a breakpoint starting at the suspect line of code, and then run the macro. When the macros reaches your breakpoint, execution halts. At this point, you can then press F8 to watch as the macro runs one line at a time.

To set a breakpoint in your code, place your cursor where you want the breakpoint to start, and press F9. As Figure 22-8 shows, VBA clearly marks the breakpoint with a dot in the Code window's left margin, and the code line itself is shaded maroon.

```
'Declare your variables.
    Dim MyRange As Range
    Dim iCounter As Long

'Define the target Range.
    Set MyRange = ActiveSheet.UsedRange

'Start reverse looping through the range.
    For iCounter = MyRange.Columns.Count To 1 Step -1

'If entire column is empty then delete it.
        If Application.CountA(Columns(iCounter).EntireColumn) = 0 Then
        Columns(iCounter).Delete
        End If

'Step 5: Increment the counter down
    Next iCounter
```

When your macro hits a breakpoint, it's effectively in debug mode. To get out of debug mode, choose Debug ⇨ Step Out.

Seeing the Beginning and End of Variable Values

If you hover over a string or integer variable in VBA while in debug mode you can see the value of that variable in a tooltip. You can then see the values that are being passed in and out of variables — very useful.

However, these tooltips can only hold 77 characters (including the variable name). This basically means if the value in your variable is too long, it gets cut off.

To see the last 77 characters, hold down the Ctrl key while you hover.

Figure 22-9 shows what the tooltip looks like when hovering over a variable in debug mode.

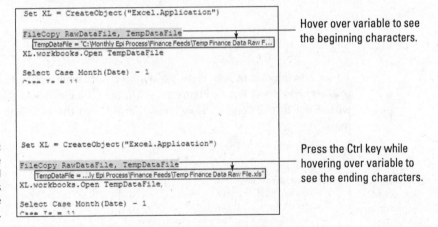

FIGURE 22-9: Showing the beginning and ending characters in a variable tooltip.

Turning Off Auto Syntax Check

Oftentimes, while working on some code, you find that you need to go to another line to copy something. You're not done with the line — you just need to leave it for a second. But the VBE immediately stops you in your tracks with an error message, similar to the one shown in Figure 22-10, warning you about something you already know.

These message boxes force you to stop what you're doing to acknowledge the error by clicking OK. After a half day of these abrupt message boxes, you'll be ready to throw your computer against the wall.

Well, you can save your computer and your sanity by turning off Auto Syntax Check by choosing Tools ⇨ Options.

On the Editor tab of the Options dialog box, uncheck the Auto Syntax Check option to stop these annoying error messages. See Figure 22-11.

FIGURE 22-11:
Uncheck the Auto Syntax Check option to prevent warning messages while coding.

Don't worry about missing a legitimate mistake. Your code still turns red if you make a mistake, providing a visual indication that something is wrong.

Chapter **23**

Resources for VBA Help

No one is going to become a VBA expert in one day. VBA is a journey of time and practice. The good news is that plenty of resources are out there that can help you on your path. In this chapter, you discover ten of the most useful places to turn to when you need an extra push in the right direction.

Letting Excel Write Code for You

One of the best places to get macro help is the macro recorder in Excel. When you record a macro with the macro recorder, Excel writes the underlying VBA for you. After recording, you can review the code, see what the recorder did, and then try to turn the code it creates into something more suited to your needs.

For example, say you need a macro that refreshes all the pivot tables in your workbook and clears all the filters in each pivot table. Writing this macro from a blank canvas would be a daunting task. Instead, you can start the macro recorder and record yourself refreshing all the pivot tables and clearing all the filters. After you stop recording, you can review the macro and make any changes you deem necessary.

TIP

Need a refresher on using the macro recorder? Pop over to Chapter 6, where you can find a detailed overview.

To a new Excel user, the Help system may seem like a clunky add-in that returns a perplexing list of topics that has nothing to do with the original topic being searched. The truth is, however, after you learn how to use the Excel Help system effectively, it's often the fastest and easiest way to get extra help on a topic.

You need to remember two basic tenets of the Excel Help system:

>> **Location matters when asking for help.** Excel actually has two Help systems: one providing help on Excel features and another providing help on VBA programming topics. Instead of doing a global search with your criteria, Excel throws your search criteria only against the Help system that's relevant to your current location. This essentially means that the help you get is determined by the area of Excel in which you're working. So, if you need help on a topic that involves macros and VBA programming, you need to be in the VBE while performing your search. This ensures that your keyword search is performed on the correct Help system.

>> **Online help is better than offline help.** When you search for help on a topic, Excel checks to see if you're connected to the Internet. If you are, Excel returns help results based on online content from Microsoft's website. If you aren't, Excel uses the Help files that are locally stored with Microsoft Office. Online help is generally better because the content is often more detailed and includes updated information, as well as links to other resources not available offline.

Pilfering Code from the Internet

The dirty secret about programming in the Internet-age is that there is no original code anymore. All the macro syntax that will ever be needed has been documented somewhere on the Internet. In many ways, programming has become less about the code you can create from scratch, and more about how to take existing code and apply it creatively to a particular scenario.

If you're stuck trying to create a macro for a particular task, describe the task you're trying to accomplish via your favorite search engine. For the best results, enter "Excel VBA" before your description.

For example, if you're trying to write a macro that deletes all blank rows in a worksheet, search for, "Excel VBA delete blank rows in a worksheet." You can bet two months' salary that someone has tackled the same problem and posted example code that gives you the nugget of information you need to jump start ideas for building your own macro.

Leveraging User Forums

If you find yourself in a bind, post your question in a forum to get customized guidance based on your scenario.

User forums are online communities that revolve around a particular topic. In these forums, you can post questions and have experts offer advise on how to solve particular problems. The folks answering the questions are typically volunteers who have a passion for helping the community solve real-world challenges.

Many forums are dedicated to all things Excel. To find an Excel Forum, type "Excel Forum" in your favorite search engine.

Here are a few tips for getting the most out of user forums:

>> **Always read and follow the forum rules before you get started.** These rules often include advice on posting question and community etiquette guidelines.

>> **Check whether your question has already been asked and answered.** Why not save time by leveraging the forum's archive of questions? Take a moment to search the forum to see whether your question has been asked before.

>> **Use concise and accurate subject titles for your questions.** Don't create forum questions with abstract titles like: Need advice, or Please Help.

>> **Keep the scope of your questions as narrow as possible.** Don't ask questions like: How do I build an invoicing macro in Excel.

>> **Be patient.** Remember the folks answering your questions are volunteers who typically have day jobs. Give the community some time to answer your question.

>> **Check back often.** After posting your question, you may receive requests for more details about your scenario. Do everyone a favor and return to your posting to either review the answers or respond to follow-up questions.

>> **Thank the expert who answered your question.** If you receive an answer that helps you, take a moment to post a thank you to the expert who helped you out.

Visiting Expert Blogs

There are a few dedicated Excel Gurus that share their knowledge through blogs. These blogs are often treasure troves of tips and tricks, offering nuggets that can help build your skills. Best of all, they're free!

Although these blogs won't necessarily speak to your particular needs, they offer articles that advance your knowledge of Excel and can even provide general guidance on how to apply Excel in practical business situations.

Here is a list of a few of the best Excel blogs today:

>> **ExcelGuru:** Ken Puls is a Microsoft Excel MVP who shares knowledge at his blog, `http://www.excelguru.ca/blog`. In addition to his blog, Ken offers several learning resources for advancing your knowledge in Excel.

>> **Chandoo.org:** Purna "Chandoo" Duggirala is a Microsoft Excel MVP out of India, who burst on the scene in 2007. His innovative blog (`http://chandoo.org/`) offers many free templates and article aimed at "making you awesome in Excel."

>> **Contextures:** Debra Dalgleish is a Microsft Excel MVP and the owner of a popular Excel site, `http://www.contextures.com`. With an alphabetized list of over 350 Excel topics, you're sure to find something that will interest you.

- » **DailyDose:** Dick Kusleika is the owner of the longest running Excel blog, `http://www.dailydoseofexcel.com`. He is the king of Excel VBA blogging with over ten years' worth of articles and examples.

- » **MrExcel:** Bill Jelen is the larger-than-life ambassador of Excel. This long-time Excel MVP offers over a thousand free videos and a huge library of training resources on his site, `http://www.mrexcel.com`.

Mining YouTube for Video Training

If you find that you absorb video training better than articles, consider mining YouTube. Dozens of channels are run by amazing folks who have a passion for sharing knowledge. You'll be surprised at how many free high-quality video tutorials you can find.

Go to `www.youtube.com` and search for "Excel VBA."

Attending Live and Online Training Classes

Live and online training events are an awesome way to absorb Excel knowledge from a diverse group of people. Not only is the instructor feeding you techniques, but the lively discussions during the class are a wealth of ideas and new tips you may never even thought of. If you thrive in the energy of live training events, then consider searching for Excel classes.

Here are a few sites that provide excellent instructor-led Excel courses:

- » `http://academy.excelhero.com/excel-hero-academy-tuition`
- » `http://chandoo.org/wp/vba-classes`
- » `https://exceljet.net`

Learning from the Microsoft Office Dev Center

The Microsoft Office Dev Center is dedicated to helping new developers get a quick start in programming Office products. You can get to the Excel portion of this site by going to https://msdn.microsoft.com/en-us/library/office/fp179694.aspx.

Although the site can be a bit difficult to navigate, it's worth a visit to see all the free resources, including sample code, tools, step-by-step instructions, and much more.

Dissecting the Other Excel Files in Your Organization

Like finding gold in your backyard, the existing files in your organization are often a treasure trove for learning. Consider opening Excel files that contain macros, and have a look under the covers. See how others in your organization use macros. Try to go through the macros line-by-line and see if you can spot new techniques.

You could find a few new tricks you never thought of. You may even stumble upon entire chunks of useful code you can copy and implement in your own workbooks.

Asking Your Local Excel Guru

Do you have an Excel genius in your company, department, organization, or community? Make friends with that person today. What you have there is your own personal Excel forum.

Most Excel experts love sharing their knowledge. So don't be afraid to approach your local Excel Guru to ask questions or seek advice on how to tackle certain macro problems.

Chapter **24**

Ten VBA Do's and Don'ts

I f you're reading this final chapter, you've probably read most of the content of this book and are familiar with Excel VBA. Or maybe you just skipped to the end because you wanted to see whether the butler actually did it.

This chapter gives you some advice you should take into account when you start developing your own VBA solutions. Following these guidelines is no panacea to keep you out of (programming) trouble, but following them can help you avoid pitfalls that others have stumbled over.

Do Declare All Variables

How convenient it is: Simply start typing your VBA code without having to go through the tedious chore of declaring each and every variable you want to use. Although Excel allows you to use undeclared variables, doing so is simply asking for trouble.

The first commandment of VBA programming should be this:

Thou shalt declare every variable.

If you lack self-discipline, add an "Option Explicit" statement at the top of your modules. That way, your code won't even run if it includes one or more undeclared variables. Not declaring all variables has only one advantage: You save a few seconds. But using undeclared variables will eventually come back to haunt you. And it will take you more than a few seconds to figure out the problem.

Don't Confuse Passwords with Security

You spent months creating a killer Excel app, with some amazing macros. You're ready to release it to the world, but you don't want others to see your incredible macro programming. Just password-protect the VBA project, and you're safe, right? Wrong.

Using a VBA password can keep most casual users from viewing your code. But if someone *really* wants to check it, he'll figure out how to crack the password.

Bottom line? If you absolutely, positively need to keep your code a secret, Excel isn't the best choice for a development platform.

Do Clean Up Your Code

After your app is working to your satisfaction, you should clean it up. Code housekeeping tasks include the following:

>> Make sure every variable is declared.

>> Make sure all the lines are indented properly so the code structure is apparent.

>> Remove any debugging aids, such as MsgBox statements of Debug.Print statements.

>> Rename any poorly named variables. For example, if you use the variable MyVariable, there's a pretty good chance that you can make the variable name more descriptive. You'll thank yourself later.

>> Your modules probably have a few "test" procedures that you wrote while trying to figure something out. They've served their purpose, so delete them.

>> Add comments so you'll understand how the code works when you revisit it six months from now.

- » Make sure everything is spelled correctly — especially text in UserForms and message boxes.

- » Check for redundant code. If you have two or more procedures that have identical blocks of code, consider creating a new procedure that other procedures can call.

Don't Put Everything in One Procedure

Want to make an unintelligible program? An efficient way to accomplish that is to put all your code inside one nice big procedure. If you ever revisit this program again to make changes, you're bound to make mistakes and introduce some fine-looking bugs.

Do you see the problem? The solution is modular code. Split your program into smaller chunks, with each chunk designed to perform a specific task. After you pick up this habit, you'll find that writing bug-free code is easier than ever.

Do Consider Other Software

Excel is an amazingly versatile program, but it's not suitable for everything. When you're ready to undertake a new project, take some time to consider all your options. To paraphrase an old saying, "When all you know is Excel VBA, everything looks like a VBA macro."

Don't Assume That Everyone Enables Macros

As you know, Excel allows you to open a workbook with its macros disabled. In fact, it's almost as though the designers of recent versions of Excel *want* users to disable macros.

Enabling macros when you open a workbook from an unknown source is not a good idea, of course. So you need to know your users. In some corporate environments, all Microsoft Office macros are disabled, and the user has no choice in the matter.

One thing to consider is adding a digital signature to the workbooks that you distribute to others. That way, the user can be assured that the workbooks actually come from you and that they haven't been altered. Consult the Help system for more information about digital signatures.

Do Get in the Habit of Experimenting

When working on a large-scale Excel project, spend time writing small VBA "experiments." For example, if you're trying to find out about a new object, method, or property, write a simple Sub procedure and play around with it until you're satisfied that you have a thorough understanding of how it works — and the potential problems.

Setting up simple experiments is almost always much more efficient than incorporating a new idea into your existing code without understanding what those experiments bring.

Don't Assume That Your Code Will Work with Other Excel Versions

When you create an Excel app, you have absolutely no guarantee that it will work flawlessly in older versions of Excel (or in future versions for that matter). In some cases, the incompatibilities will be obvious. For example, if your code refers to a new feature introduced in Excel 2019, you know that it won't work in prior versions. But you'll also find that things that should work with an earlier version don't work.

Excel includes a handy compatibility checker (choose File ⇨ Info ⇨ Check For Issues ⇨ Check Compatibility), but it only checks the workbook and ignores the VBA code. The only way to be sure that your application works with versions other than the one you created it with is to test it in those versions.

Do Keep Your Users in Mind

Excel apps fall into two main categories: those that you develop for yourself and those that you develop for others to use. If you develop apps for others, your job is much more difficult because you can't make the same types of assumptions.

For example, you can be more lax with error handling if you're the only user. If an error crops up, you'll have a pretty good idea where to look so you can fix it. If someone else is using your app and the same error appears, he or she will be out of luck. And when you're working with your own application, you can usually get by without instructions.

You need to understand the skill level of those who will be using your workbooks and try to anticipate problems that they might have. Try to picture yourself as a new user of your application, and identify all areas that may cause confusion or problems.

Don't Forget About Backups

Nothing is more discouraging than a hard drive crash without a backup. If you're working on an important project, ask yourself a simple question: "If my computer dies tonight, what will I have lost?" If your answer is more than a few hours of work, you need to take a close look at your data backup procedure. You do have a data backup procedure, right?

Index

C

D

About the Author

Michael Alexander is a Microsoft Certified Application Developer (MCAD) and author of several books on advanced business analysis with Microsoft Access and Microsoft Excel. He has more than 20 years of experience consulting and developing Microsoft Office solutions. Mike has been named a Microsoft MVP for his ongoing contributions to the Excel community. You can find Mike at www.datapig technologies.com.

Publisher's Acknowledgments

Executive Editor: Katie Mohr
Project Editor: Rebecca Senninger
Sr. Editorial Assistant: Cherie Case

Production Editor: Mohammed Zafar Ali
Front Cover Image: ©sankai/iStockphoto

PERSONAL ENRICHMENT

Staying Sharp
9781119187790
USA $26.00
CAN $31.99
UK £19.99

Facebook
9781119179030
USA $21.99
CAN $25.99
UK £16.99

Guitar
9781119293354
USA $24.99
CAN $29.99
UK £17.99

Investing
9781119293347
USA $22.99
CAN $27.99
UK £16.99

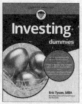

Beekeeping
9781119310068
USA $22.99
CAN $27.99
UK £16.99

Digital Photography
9781119235606
USA $24.99
CAN $29.99
UK £17.99

Meditation
9781119251163
USA $24.99
CAN $29.99
UK £17.99

Pregnancy
9781119235491
USA $26.99
CAN $31.99
UK £19.99

Samsung Galaxy S7
9781119279952
USA $24.99
CAN $29.99
UK £17.99

iPhone
9781119283133
USA $24.99
CAN $29.99
UK £17.99

Crocheting
9781119287117
USA $24.99
CAN $29.99
UK £16.99

Nutrition
9781119130246
USA $22.99
CAN $27.99
UK £16.99

PROFESSIONAL DEVELOPMENT

Windows 10
9781119311041
USA $24.99
CAN $29.99
UK £17.99

AutoCAD
9781119255796
USA $39.99
CAN $47.99
UK £27.99

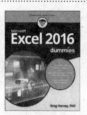

Excel 2016
9781119293439
USA $26.99
CAN $31.99
UK £19.99

QuickBooks 2017
9781119281467
USA $26.99
CAN $31.99
UK £19.99

macOS Sierra
9781119280651
USA $29.99
CAN $35.99
UK £21.99

LinkedIn
9781119251132
USA $24.99
CAN $29.99
UK £17.99

Windows 10
9781119310563
USA $34.00
CAN $41.99
UK £24.99

SharePoint 2016
9781119181705
USA $29.99
CAN $35.99
UK £21.99

Fundamental Analysis
9781119263593
USA $26.99
CAN $31.99
UK £19.99

Networking
9781119257769
USA $29.99
CAN $35.99
UK £21.99

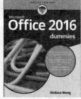

Office 2016
9781119293477
USA $26.99
CAN $31.99
UK £19.99

Office 365
9781119265313
USA $24.99
CAN $29.99
UK £17.99

Salesforce.com
9781119239314
USA $29.99
CAN $35.99
UK £21.99

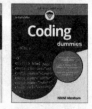

Coding
9781119293323
USA $29.99
CAN $35.99
UK £21.99

dummies.com

dummies
A Wiley Brand